CAMBRIDGE LIBRARY COLLECTION

Books of enduring scholarly value

History

The books reissued in this series include accounts of historical events and movements by eye-witnesses and contemporaries, as well as landmark studies that assembled significant source materials or developed new historiographical methods. The series includes work in social, political and military history on a wide range of periods and regions, giving modern scholars ready access to influential publications of the past.

The Trade Relations of the British Empire

The growth of an 'imperial' outlook in colonial policy at the end of the nineteenth century led to calls for greater imperial integration, prompting studies and scholarly works on the economic relations between Britain and its imperial possessions. This volume, first published in 1903 and written by the economist John William Root (fl. 1900), explores both the internal and external trade relations in the British Empire and its constituent colonies. Focusing on the practical aspects of international trade, Root discusses the customs policies and tariffs, main imports and exports and external influences on trade of the United Kingdom, New Zealand, Australia, the West Indies and Canada. Organised by region, the book also discusses fiscal warfare and the effect of preferential trade tariffs, using Canada as an example. This volume provides a detailed analysis of the system of trade regulations and their impact on imperial trade in the early twentieth century.

Cambridge University Press has long been a pioneer in the reissuing of out-of-print titles from its own backlist, producing digital reprints of books that are still sought after by scholars and students but could not be reprinted economically using traditional technology. The Cambridge Library Collection extends this activity to a wider range of books which are still of importance to researchers and professionals, either for the source material they contain, or as landmarks in the history of their academic discipline.

Drawing from the world-renowned collections in the Cambridge University Library, and guided by the advice of experts in each subject area, Cambridge University Press is using state-of-the-art scanning machines in its own Printing House to capture the content of each book selected for inclusion. The files are processed to give a consistently clear, crisp image, and the books finished to the high quality standard for which the Press is recognised around the world. The latest print-on-demand technology ensures that the books will remain available indefinitely, and that orders for single or multiple copies can quickly be supplied.

The Cambridge Library Collection will bring back to life books of enduring scholarly value (including out-of-copyright works originally issued by other publishers) across a wide range of disciplines in the humanities and social sciences and in science and technology.

The Trade Relations
of the British Empire

JOHN WILLIAM ROOT

CAMBRIDGE
UNIVERSITY PRESS

CAMBRIDGE UNIVERSITY PRESS

Cambridge, New York, Melbourne, Madrid, Cape Town, Singapore,
São Paolo, Delhi, Dubai, Tokyo, Mexico City

Published in the United States of America by Cambridge University Press, New York

www.cambridge.org
Information on this title: www.cambridge.org/9781108024044

© in this compilation Cambridge University Press 2010

This edition first published 1903
This digitally printed version 2010

ISBN 978-1-108-02404-4 Paperback

THE TRADE RELATIONS OF THE
BRITISH EMPIRE

THE

TRADE RELATIONS

OF THE

BRITISH EMPIRE

BY

J. W. ROOT

AUTHOR OF "TARIFF AND TRADE"
"STUDIES IN BRITISH NATIONAL FINANCE" ETC.

LIVERPOOL

J. W. ROOT, COMMERCE CHAMBERS, LORD STREET

1903

Half a Guinea nett.

PRINTED BY
MORRISON AND GIBB LIMITED
EDINBURGH

All Rights Reserved.

PREFACE

RATHER more than five years ago I published the
first edition of *Tariff and Trade*. At that time
the subject of a customs union between the United
Kingdom and the British possessions in all parts of
the world was attracting some amount of attention,
though the ideas and suggestions regarding it were
extremely vague. A single chapter of that book
proved sufficient to exhaust what was then to be
said—the Canadian preferential tariff had just come
into operation, and everybody interested in the
question naturally looked to it for a lead in the
framing of a more far-reaching imperial tariff policy.

Much has happened since, and what has come to
be known as the imperial idea was for a time at
least rampant. With the enormous financial outlays it has involved throughout the British Empire
these pages have nothing to do beyond the trend
given to fiscal policy adopted for the purpose of
meeting them, for although the additions to the tariff

of the United Kingdom have been made to exclude everything in the nature of protection, the hope is not concealed that they may eventually be utilised to that end. The corn tax more especially afforded dangerous facilities in this direction, not only as regards the home grower, but for the possible concession of some preference to the colonial one.

It is no longer possible, therefore, to dismiss the subject in a single chapter of a work dealing with general policy, and nothing short of an entire volume is requisite to handle it in an efficient manner. I have endeavoured in the following pages to deal with it in all its bearings from a practical point of view, as while theory and sentiment are all very well in their proper places, they are dangerous elements to introduce into the business relationships of a great empire, split into many fragments, and very often with little in common beyond political association. It is surprising in how many instances purely foreign connections are essential to economic well-being, and anything that would interfere with them could not be otherwise but injurious.

Events move rapidly, and before the ink is dry on the last sheets, slight additions rather than modifications are called for in the earlier ones. While the work is going through the press news arrives of the provisional adoption of a customs conference in South Africa, but as details are withheld, it is impossible to make any comment on it. Circumstances like these ought to add to, rather than detract from, its value, especially as I have sought carefully to exclude everything that seemed to be of but momentary interest, and to base it on foundations of more permanent policy. Frequent reconsideration of details was never more necessary than at the present time, but there are underlying principles that are not to be departed from without serious risk, if not certain disaster.

J. W. R.

May 1903.

CONTENTS

CHAPTER I

THE BASIS OF CUSTOMS UNION

CHAPTER II

THE WORKING OF THE CANADIAN PREFERENTIAL TARIFF

CHAPTER III

The Foreign Commerce of Australia and New Zealand

CHAPTER IV

South Africa Before and After the War

CHAPTER VII

MISCELLANEOUS POSSESSIONS AND PROTECTORATES

CHAPTER VIII

THE COLONIAL TRADE OF THE UNITED KINGDOM

CHAPTER IX

The Foreign Trade of the United Kingdom

CHAPTER X

General Conclusions

STATISTICAL APPENDIX.

TRADE RELATIONS OF THE BRITISH EMPIRE

———◆———

CHAPTER I

THE BASIS OF CUSTOMS UNION

The Desire for Fiscal Unity—Inapplicability to the British Empire—
Contrast between the British Empire and the United States—
The German Zollverein and the United States Constitution—
How the First came to be Constructed—Want of Elasticity in
the Second—Conflict of Interests in both Countries—Evidence
afforded by Tariff Discussions and Rearrangements—The Case of
Austria-Hungary — Federal Canada and Australia—Modifying
Forces in American Protection—Influence of Railway Connection
—Great Britain and Ireland—What Ireland needs for Industrial
Development — The Essence of Working Partnership — Risks
involved to Minor Possessions.

THE idea of bringing all the countries constituting
the British Empire under the operation of a uniform
federal tariff is of long standing, but has never
crystallised into any practical shape. By some
people, the obstacle is believed to be the want of
a common basis of government in issues that are
imperial, as distinct from those pertaining to what
are merely local, or even state, affairs, and with such,
imperial federation is regarded as the forerunner of

1

any form of customs union. By others, the reverse process is considered the practical one, and efforts are made to construct a fiscal policy from which some common means of imperial defence and government may eventually be evolved.

Assuming that something of the sort were feasible, as well as desirable, it is in the first place necessary to examine the conditions under which it would have to be consummated. The British Empire is a chaos; reduced to some sort of order, it is true, but still anything but symmetrical. The question is, whether its angles and corners and excrescences do not afford the surest means of protection, and whether if these were all nicely rounded off, many additional openings for attack would not be provided a possible enemy, political or commercial. Under existing circumstances, a distinct system of attack is necessary against each unit, as a merchant or manufacturer, to say nothing of a general or an admiral, must either limit the sphere of his activities, or make himself acquainted with a mass of detail such as would not be required in dealing with any other nation in the world. The tactics of Napoleon consisted largely in hurling a mass of troops against an enemy and breaking down its resistance by a single coup. Modern warfare teaches that the art of defence lies in the scattered distribution of the defenders, who, if beaten at one point, are able to present just as bold a front at the next. The world has had recent experience of the

success of such methods, though it may fail, nevertheless, when the next contest comes, to profit by
the lesson.

An apt illustration of this is afforded by the two
great English-speaking nations. In a political sense,
the United States are most likely unconquerable.
Their vast area would simply bewilder a successful
foe, who would not dare to venture very far from his
base of supplies, or imperil his lines of communication. But with a secure footing on American soil,
the country would lie open to him, and though he
might not determine to strike north, south, east, and
west, he would be at liberty to choose in which
direction to operate. In a commercial sense, the
United States are more vulnerable still. They may
be protected by a tariff wall, strong as well as high,
but a breach in it, however minute, once made,
permits the whole country to be flooded through it
until it is repaired. The terror of American protectionists lest a single stone of the coping should
be overthrown, has not only amused and instructed
the world, but fosters the growth of a system of
monopoly under which the entire community groans,
while it prevents the removal of grievances that are
universally admitted to be injurious to the common-
weal.

To conquer and occupy the British Empire in the
limited sense in which this might be accomplished
in the United States, is a virtual impossibility. The
overthrow of Great Britain would not open to the

successful foe Canada, or Australia, or South Africa, to anything like the same extent that Pennsylvania, or Illinois, or California, would be at the mercy of the conquerors of New York or Massachusetts : the conflict would entail the employment of entirely fresh forces, and probably of altogether different tactics and weapons. The work could only be accomplished, temporarily even, by a combination of powers. Russia might undertake the conquest of India and the East, Germany become responsible for South Africa and Australia, France for East and West Africa, the West Indies, and perhaps Canada, while all three might act in concert against Great Britain itself. But this would be equivalent to each part of the Empire waging warfare against a separate foe, and the world would really be witnessing three conflicts, not one. Such an alliance, moreover, is inconceivable, because however much each of the powers named would like the particular countries allotted to it, it would view the acquisitions of its partners as altogether too serious a set off. And further, possibilities of intervention by the United States in their own interests, quite apart from any feeling of frendliness that might be entertained for Great Britain, would have to be entirely ignored.

The difficulties of commercial conquest are equally great. The United States or Germany may capture a market in the United Kingdom and be as far out as ever in Australia or South Africa, whereas, if either gained entrance to a market of the other, it would have the run of the whole territory. Diversity of tariffs and fiscal methods has consequently much in its favour from a strictly British point of view.

It is asserted, on the other hand, that the vaster the area over which a single tariff system prevails, the better it is for the people inhabiting it. The German Zollverein is the favourite instance employed, because it is the creation of modern times, and under it the enormous development of German industry has taken place. It might, in case of need, be dissolved by the forces that created it : the similar bond in the United States must be regarded as nearly indissoluble. It is part and parcel of the constitution of the country, and though the machinery has been provided for effecting necessary changes in that constitution, it is hardly conceivable that it can ever be powerful enough to work one in this particular direction.

The United States have developed still more rapidly, and attained to a higher measure of prosperity than Germany, and as the tariff system of both is much on the same lines — absolute free trade within, and protection from without—it is not altogether surprising that a good deal of the success should be attributed to it, rather than to the peoples, or the natural resources of the countries. In both cases, however, the unit is, or was until quite recently, geographical as well as political, and lines of demarcation would be most difficult to draw. In the case of Germany, it is true, they previously existed, and might presumably, therefore, be resuscitated. But it was only under entirely different political conditions to those that now prevail. Down to the period of the Franco-German War, several of the states now constituting the German Empire were so completely independent, that for a time it was doubtful whether their rulers would cast in their lot with the French or German armies. Neither commerce nor manufacturing industry were taken much account of anywhere on the Continent of Europe outside France, and each state devised its system of taxation almost disregardless of them, and with the main object of filling its coffers in the most efficient manner, often without consideration for the general welfare.

In those days too, both France and the United Kingdom were already commercial units, and any attempt at constructing an entirely new Kingdom or Empire would naturally be based, more or less, on principles long established in what had hitherto been the two greatest and most successful of the European states. Nor were there any serious obstacles to be overcome. In the first enthusiasm for national unity, secondary interests were likely to be surrendered, and commercial interests were certainly regarded as secondary by all but a few of the more far-seeing statesmen, except in one or two instances where they were really paramount. And it is necessary to bear these in mind, because the efficacy of any system that interfered with their independence was so greatly doubted, that they were actually left outside the Zollverein. It is true the Hanse towns which were the centres principally affected, were gradually induced to join, but not always willingly, and the two most important of them, Hamburg and Bremen, held out until 1889 and remained free zones within a tariff Empire. They would probably have continued so down to the present day, had not persuasion, amounting almost to compulsion, brought about their surrender. Hamburg at least has made more progress since than it ever did before, but it would be entirely wrong to attribute it to that cause. The city might have been still more prosperous had it remained a free port.

No part of the United States was ever afforded a choice in the matter; to be subject to the rule of President and Congress, with or without representation in the latter, carried the privilege, or entailed the drawback, whichever point of view might be adopted, of being equally subject to the same tariff and fiscal laws. This rule admits of no exception, and though it was instituted solely in view of the expansion of the United States from the continental boundary lines, which would necessitate no break in continuity of territory, it has had to be extended to oversea possessions. Hawaii and Porto Rico could only be recognised as integral portions of the political union on condition that their trade and tariff regulations were equally assimilated; Cuba

and the Philippines remain outside, partly at anyrate, from objections to grant that condition.

And similar, or even greater, difficulties would
arise, if the United States or Germany had to-day
to construct their customs unions instead of merely
to conserve them.   It would be going too far to
say that such difficulties would prove insurmount-
able, though that is quite possible, in view especially
of recent occurrences. The interests in each country
have become so numerous, as well as so conflicting,
that reconciliation is out of the question, and at
irregular intervals, some sort of compromise or deal
has to be arranged. From the point of view of an
unprejudiced and disinterested outsider, the German
tariff in force during the latter years of the nineteenth century was almost entirely unobjectionable.
Orthodox free traders may not have liked it because
it did involve a certain amount of protection, of
which ultimately in several instances very question-
able use was made. But in hardly any case was
the protection afforded extravagant, and the tariff
answered its purpose as a revenue producer.   It
held the scales as evenly between each section of
the Empire as it is perhaps possible to balance
them.

But one part happened to prosper under it, while
another either did not, or imagined it did not. The
existing scale of duties was quite satisfactory to
nearly everybody engaged in the textile, chemical,
and iron and steel industries, which, with their

numerous offshoots, progressed more rapidly than any others. But the agrarian element in the community became more and more dissatisfied, although the measure of protection afforded it was fully as great, if not greater, than to the others. The particular grievance was not so much a fall in prices as a rise in wages and the cost of production which resulted from the increasing prosperity of the country as a whole. This had either to be checked, or an equivalent given in the form of higher duties on all agricultural products, and the latter was chosen as the less of two evils.

The increased cost of living this was bound to entail was calculated to injure the manufacturing section of the community, which has become the more important one. A conflict thus appeared certain, and would have assumed a still more formidable aspect than it did, had not some sort of acquiescence been purchased by the promise of higher duties, and consequently increased protection, on manufactured goods as well. That would not have settled the difficulty a few years earlier, because such a step would have involved the loss of foreign markets, becoming of such immense importance to German industry. But in the meantime the machinery of what is known as the cartel was brought to a state of nearly absolute perfection, and under the operation of the system it is possible to squeeze the last pfennig of profit permitted by the tariff out of the unfortunate home consumer.

Higher duties, provided they are more than sufficient to cover any increased cost of production, by this means offer a source of additional profit at home which permits foreign markets to be retained without any direct profit at all, and perhaps at possible loss.

The curious spectacle was witnessed of the agrarians, having secured the enactment of higher duties for agricultural products, though not as high as they aimed at, joining forces with the socialist element to prevent increases, and in some instances enforce decreases, of duties from which they would derive no benefit, but would rather enhance the cost of goods they required to purchase. Now it so happens that the states or kingdoms constituting the German Empire have mostly distinct characteristics as regards agriculture and manufacturing industry. Prussia and Bavaria may be classed under the former; Westphalia and Saxony under the latter. Each of course has interests more akin to the others than to itself as a whole, which show themselves in any general assembly of the Empire, but were each state a unit, it is tolerably certain it would adopt the fiscal policy best suited to the majority of its own population, disregardless alike of the minority and of its neighbours.

On the other side of the Atlantic very much the same state of things exists. There never have been national distinctions in the United States, but the economic ones are quite as marked as in the German

Empire. No tariff can ever be framed in the interests
of the Republic as a whole. The Eastern and
Northern States long wielded sufficient political
preponderance to force their policy on the others,
whether it suited them or not, but with the growth
of western and southern influence, this condition of
things has been materially modified, and the western
corn grower and cattleman have now to be allowed
to participate in the deals periodically arranged ;
indeed it is a question whether the so-called " robber
barons " of the Western States, associated more particularly with the meat and mining industries, are
not destined for a time to dictate the fiscal policy
of the union. The interests of New England or
Pennsylvania, and States in the Middle or Far West,
are no more identical than are those of Westphalia
and Prussia, and the same policy applied to both
must either be inimical to one, or so scientifically
adjusted as to victimise a third in the interests of
both. The only policy of strict justice all round
is absolute free trade, external as well as internal,
and that, presumably, is out of the question, for
some time to come at anyrate.

Now if it be to the true interest of Germany to
protect itself against France and Russia, and of the
United States to shut out the competition of Canada
and Mexico, the political boundary lines in each
case being purely imaginary, logic insists that it
must be equally so to carry the divisions farther,
and mark them wherever the interests of com-

munities enter into conflict, as they do in every progressive modern country. Political exigency is the restraining influence, and political exigency is, therefore, the primary basis of customs union.

The experience of other countries, inside as well as outside the British Empire, tends to confirm this. The term Dual Monarchy applied to Austria-Hungary is descriptive in more than the political sense. Though under one King, each country is governed by a separate Ministry and Parliament, and each chafes violently under the system that regulates the finances, and with them the tariff, in the supposed mutual interests of both. It is true, conflict of race has much to do with the difficulties that have arisen in so acute a form, but this would be far more easily allayed were it not for the industrial rivalry that has become so intense. There was quite enough friction when Austria, as a manufacturing, and Hungary, as an agricultural, country, were content to form a Zollverein protecting both against the competition of the outside world, but since Hungary entered the manufacturing arena on an ambitious scale, the strife has tended to become internecine. Contiguity in this case increases, and does not ease, the friction, and if a break up of the Empire should eventually result, as it may do, the seeds of disruption will have been sown by enforced economic, and not political union.

Canada and Australia afford more pleasing pictures, though not entirely free from blotches.

Both the Dominion and the Commonwealth have two distinct conflicting influences at work within them, though they are not quite the same, and in neither is there any complication arising from racial distinctions, to the limited extent even that is found in Germany and the United States. Canada is partly French, but that element of the population is scarcely heard in economic disputes ; Australia is almost too British.

The Dominion, however, contains an active and aggressive manufacturing element stimulated by the success it has seen achieved on the other side of the boundary. The interests of the country are essentially agricultural, and prosperity must, for a long time to come, be bound up with that important industry. Everything that tends to check it, therefore, must be detrimental to the progress of the Dominion, and foremost is the excessive cost of living certain to result from high protection.

Australia has not gone so far in this direction as Canada, and tries to regulate its tariff more with a view to the maintenance of high wages than of big profits. These, it is supposed, can best be assured when there is a multiplicity of industries, and Australian protection aims at this rather than the encouragement of one or two big ones. New South Wales, and more particularly Sydney, largely owe their premier position on the island continent to that freedom from fiscal restriction which enabled them to become the mart of the southern and eastern seas, a position that may be sacrificed by federation, which means that fiscal policy can no longer be regulated in the exclusive interests of one state.

It is quite certain that in every instance named customs union entails serious disadvantages on some portions of the population affected by it. That is no argument for abolition, because a tariff war is infinitely worse than a fight over a tariff. Austria-Hungary, in the position in which it is situated, is likely to be better off in the second than in the first state, but were the two countries separated by an ocean, or even by a Mediterranean Sea, there would be no hesitation about recommending at least a fiscal and economic dissolution of partnership.

Where these drawbacks do not actually exist it appears senseless to create them. The British Empire bound together by a common fiscal system would still have more diversified interests, and consequently be liable to more frequent conflicts, than either Germany or the United States. The latter country has a far wider range of production than the former, but in this respect cannot touch the British Empire, taken as a whole, which yields to a greater or less extent every conceivable human want, and were the American principle adopted of making dutiable every commodity produced, or capable of being produced, within the federated area, the British tariff would have no free list whatever. There is this initial difference, that whereas the United States yield all they want for their own use, and a considerable surplus beyond, of most of the actual necessaries of life and of many of the principal raw materials of manufacture, that is far from being the case of the British Empire; the important commodities so situated might be numbered on the fingers of both hands, if not of one. The American people have consequently not hitherto suffered severely from the theoretical disadvantages usually associated with a high tariff, inasmuch as the superabundance of food and raw material has kept the first at as low a level of price as in any other similarly situated country, and has exercised a modifying influence on the cost of the manufactures produced from the second. Had there been, instead of a surplus, a deficiency requiring to be made good by foreign import, price conditions might, and probably would, have been entirely different, and all enterprise seriously hampered.

The United States enjoy the further distinct advantage of unbroken lines of communication. Given any two points touched by a railway system, however remote from one another, it is nearly always possible to transfer goods from one to the other without breaking bulk. That may not by any means always be actually done, because traffic moves in well-defined grooves, and anything outside them requires to be specially handled, but facilities are at hand for making a new groove whenever the need for it arises. This cannot be the case where seas and oceans intervene. Ocean may be cheaper than land carriage in theory, but when it comes to practice, the cost of transport over long distances may be less by the second than the first, if the goods require to be handled less frequently.

Nor is cost the only element to be considered; convenience counts for a great deal. Direct and unbroken means of communication between England and Scotland, and between England and Wales, have resulted in all three countries sharing whatever industrial prosperity is going, whereas the greater part of Ireland is excluded from it, except to the extent that there may be a slightly better demand for its agricultural produce. Ireland is at the disadvantage of being without minerals; at least none have yet been discovered under sufficiently favourable conditions to invite extensive development. Yet that has not prevented Belfast becoming one of the most active industrial centres of the United Kingdom. It is the custom to attribute this to the special characteristics of the people inhabiting the district; the real reason is to be found in its favourable location, which permits of the conveyance of material from the principal sources of supply at as cheap, or nearly as cheap a rate, as in any other part of the United Kingdom. It is this that has attracted the people, and not the people whose particular ability has made the place.

Ireland generally offers every inducement for similar expansion, did the circumstances warrant it. The population is suitable whatever may be said to

the contrary, because Irishmen are often found to be
the most active, and sometimes the most skilled,
labourers in British workshops. Nor is it the
climate or surroundings in the island itself which
are the chief enervating influences. Put Ireland
into as easy and direct communication with England
as either Scotland or Wales, and development will
be equally rapid. There would be a commingling of
races, each supplying what the others lacked, and the
whirr of the spindle and the thud of the steam
hammer would be as common a sound throughout
Ireland as Great Britain. Nature has refused the
opportunity; possibly to some extent this can be
remedied by man, and were a tunnel constructed
under the channel sufficiently commodious to ensure
an exchange of traffic as free, and on as reasonable
terms, as between the three countries constituting
Great Britain, a marvellous change might speedily
be brought about. A serious obstacle to this exists
in the difference of railway gauge.

Something of the kind may, or may not, prove
practicable in the future. Meanwhile, Ireland,
possessed of distinct physical characteristics, suffers
from the tremendous disadvantage of being bound
by a customs union to a country having totally
different ones. It is sometimes asserted that such
Irish industries as at one time existed were wilfully
destroyed by rival British manufacturers. That was
not necessary, because they could not in any case
long have survived the superior advantages enjoyed

2

on the other side of the channel. Either the countries must be made physically one, or Ireland, when it is conceded a much larger measure of self-government than it now enjoys, which is bound to happen sooner or later, must be granted at the same time considerable freedom in the regulation of its fiscal policy. Not fiscal, any more than political, independence, but with sufficient guarantee furnished against mere spiteful legislation levied at British industry, a wide latitude in the manipulation of its financial system, which, provided each item becomes a legitimate, and not too burdensome, source of revenue, need not be regulated too strictly on the arbitrary lines of free trade or protection.

Canada, Australasia, South Africa, and India, are vastly superior, both in extent of territory and natural resources to Ireland, and so widely separated from one another and from the central seat of Empire, as to make direct connection, present or future, an absolute impossibility. Each varies, too, so considerably in its special productions and characteristics as to leave not a great deal in common. That might be used as an argument for rendering each more dependent on the others, but there is just sufficient in common to incur the risk of creating similar friction as already exists between Great Britain and Ireland if anything like similar connections were established. In such a partnership one element must be predominant. It may work amicably for generations, but that is only likely where, in case of difference of opinion among the members, there is one in whose justice and integrity all the others impose implicit confidence, and whose decision they will accept as final. That may, and often does, occur in a limited partnership of individuals; it can hardly happen in one of peoples. To the rest of the Empire, Great Britain may stand, sentimentally, for everything that is upright and disinterested. But Great Britain is actually constituted of farmers and traders and manufacturers, each with their own special interests to serve, and neither better nor worse than the corresponding classes in every other part of the Empire, and these constitute the motive governing force. Whatever deference, therefore, is shown the mother country, must be more apparent than real.

On the other hand, one partner may ride roughshod over the others, as Great Britain does over Ireland, which must bear whatever burden is imposed on it, and is consulted about neither its exact shape nor weight. Needless to say such relationship would be utterly impossible with any self-governing portion of the British Empire, and would be equally impossible with Ireland were it situated a thousand miles from the shores of Britain. There is a third alternative, the subservience of the senior to the junior members of the combination, and that is what might happen at first in a British Zollverein. But it could not last, and Great Britain, unlike Ireland, would have the strength to cast off the yoke as soon as it became intolerable.

Some portions of the Empire would remain in any event without adequate protection against possible injustice. Not all are self-governing, though very few are without some form of local legislature. But in the latter case it is invariably representative of a small minority of the population, and for that reason edicts and recommendations are carefully scrutinised before being confirmed by the central authority at home. It nevertheless happens that measures bearing with great hardship on considerable majorities do at times secure confirmation. There is nearly always an independent and unbiassed British public opinion to appeal to in such cases, though it often happens that it is too indifferent to listen, and only now and again does it bestir itself to right a manifest wrong. Such instances would become still rarer if any considerable section of that public were interested parties, as they must be if fiscal control passes into their hands. The persistent refusal of justice to the West Indies is a case in point, and though it is frequently used as an argument in favour of customs union, those who employ it fail to recognise that the complication of self interests that would arise would enormously increase in number the precisely same class of difficulty. If Great Britain, possessed of the necessary legislative powers, refuses to make use of them because it benefits substantially from existing conditions, what reason is there to suppose that any other part of the Empire, armed with equal or similar powers, would use them more generously where its own individual interests were at stake ? In this case, no doubt, the principle of free trade has, rightly or wrongly, been appealed to, but what injustice is ever perpetrated or persisted in, in the cause of which some great or sacred principle is not invoked ?

On broad grounds then, the policy of fiscal union stands condemned. Were the entire British Empire located on a single continent, the question would assume an altogether different aspect, supposing, even, that it stretched from the poles to the equator and embraced within it the same variety of characteristics and resources as it does now. Zones of production and of interest shade off into each other so gradually that no dividing line can ever be equitably drawn. In the United States, north and south are historical entities, but where does one end and the other begin ? Some people would say at the Mason and Dixon line. Or again, the great staple of production in the south being cotton, the test of where that is grown might be established. But from the centres where hardly anything else is seen, and where cotton is indubitably king, to the circumference where there are a few scattered fields, there is taking place an almost imperceptible change of interests which it might be difficult to reconcile unless they were governed by one single system.

There is no need to go to America for illustra-
tions; here at home they abound. Lancashire is
the greatest hive of industry the world has ever
seen, yet within a few miles of some of its busiest
centres are to be found secluded hamlets that would
appear more in keeping with Norfolk or Devonshire.
Nothing beyond minor local distinctions can ever
be asked for, or expected, in such cases. Every
country, large or small, must include innumerable
similar instances of apparently conflicting interests,
though they are not necessarily so. But nature has
furnished the British Empire with broad bands of
separation between its greatest zones, and has thus
helped to solve for the British people one of the
most difficult problems confronting mankind.

All this however is arguing in generalities,
and the broadest and most widely accepted of
principles, unless established on a moral foundation,
require at times to be departed from. There might
be special circumstances of the hour or the situation
demanding that in the interests of political integrity,
these interstices should be filled up, or at least
bridged over. The best way of arriving at whether
this is the case or not, is to consider each component
part in detail, and that will be the work of the
succeeding chapters.

CHAPTER II

THE WORKING OF THE CANADIAN PREFERENTIAL TARIFF

Natural Affinities of Canada and the United States—Causes of Fiscal Warfare between them—The Dingley Tariff and Canadian Sentiment—Policy of Canadian Liberals—Objects and Nature of the Preferential Tariff—Trade History of the Dominion with the United States—Politics and Commerce—Extent of Reduction in Duties—Development of Canadian Trade since 1896—The Share of the United States—Participation of the United Kingdom—Trade with British Possessions—With Foreign Countries—The Iron and Steel Industry—Threatened Revolution—Cotton Imports and Manufacture—The Woollen Industry—Movements in Miscellaneous Imports—The True Canadian Policy.

A MORE suitable country could hardly have been selected for a real test of the policy of a preferential oversea tariff than the Dominion of Canada. Its commercial and industrial interests are bound up with one continent, its political sympathies with another, and the latter, for the time being at any-rate, having come uppermost, a determined effort has been made to utilise them for extending the material connection. Canada is a part, indeed it is the half, of the North American Continent, though so geographically situated that it can never hope to attain the wide diversity of production which is so marked a feature of the more favoured United

States. But the boundary line of the two runs continuously for nearly three thousand miles, and, except for the comparatively short distance where the northern and southern shores of the great lakes constitute the dividing mark, there is nothing physically or otherwise to denote it. The inhabitants spring from the same stock, speak the same language, profess the same religious beliefs, and, as far as such a thing is possible, think the same thoughts, and nothing would be more natural than that business and social intercourse should be free and unrestricted.

But fate has decreed otherwise, and hardly anywhere else in the world has more bitter fiscal warfare been waged than between Canada and the United States. It must be recognised that the stronger power has generally been the aggressor, the weaker adopting retaliation as a means of defence. Not a very chivalrous situation, and the explanation must be sought in something beyond mere commercial rivalry. Political ambition is undoubtedly at the bottom of it. Join us, say the United States, and you shall participate to the full in our vast schemes of development, with all the opportunities for wealth and material prosperity they afford; remain outside our Union and we will make things as hard for you as possible. We mean sooner or later to control the Western hemisphere, and your intimate association with the greatest of the Old World States seriously interferes with our plans, and while you insist on retaining your independence of us you must expect no countenance or favour from us. But Canada has preferred that independence before anything else, and who shall blame her for it? An integral part of the British Empire, she enjoys as complete a form of self-government as any nation in the world ever experienced, and if her advance under it has until recently been slow, she has breathed the air of freedom which is the most life - sustaining and invigorating in the world.

It can readily be understood then, why it is that successive United States tariffs bear on the face of them such unvarying animosity to the sister State. There have been no exceptions, though it is in those promoted and passed by the disciples of high protection that the greatest outrages on common sense have been perpetrated. There has never been the slightest probability that the agricultural producers of either country would trespass seriously on the home preserves of the other. The New England States would undoubtedly benefit could they feed themselves on the produce of Ontario and Quebec instead of the Middle and Far West, but New England has always been the most clamorous for protection and must take the husks with the kernel. It is significant, however, that the inhabitants of this part of the United States who are groaning under the exactions of the Trusts and have never yet succeeded in taking revenge by forming combinations of their

own particular industries, are now the most eager
for closer trade relationship with Canada which the
Dominion no longer seems so anxious to establish.

There are one or two other interests, notably
those associated with the lumber and fishery industries, that have come into sharp competition, and
whenever the protectionist sentiment has been
rampant in the United States it has been an easy
matter to turn it in these particular directions.
Once let loose, it is apt to run wild, and never
has it gone to such extravagant lengths as under the
existing tariff associated with the name of Dingley,
which forbids a man gathering blackberries on one
side of an imaginary line and eating them on the
other without first obtaining consent and paying toll
to the Government.

The Dingley tariff was the direct outcome of the
Presidential Election of 1896. The late President
M'Kinley become the supreme head of the United
States on the 4th March 1897, and one of his first
acts was the summoning of a special session of
Congress, which would not in the ordinary course
have met until the following December, for the
express purpose of passing the most stringent
measure of protection that even the United States
had ever before been subjected to. Canada, as
usual, was specially singled out, but Canada
had also been moving politically, though in an·
opposite direction, and was no longer willing to
take the slaps administered by its big neighbour

without at least making an attempt to retaliate. While there had always been a party willing to lend an attentive ear to the blandishments of the United States, and to advocate political incorporation with them, the one so many years in a majority and holding office was strongly opposed to anything of the sort, and not merely stood up for the British connection, but strongly advocated some system of preferential trade with the mother country. It too, however, was strongly protectionist, and would listen to nothing in the nature of what it was pleased to call a one-sided preference. It wanted Canada to have the nut and Great Britain to be content with the shell, which would perhaps have been rather one-sided, though not when viewed through colonial spectacles.

The unexpected defeat of the Conservatives and the advent to power of the Liberals led by Mr. (now Sir) Wilfrid Laurier, changed all that. To begin with, the new Premier was a convinced free trader, though free trade in Canada and in the United Kingdom are two totally different things. Apart altogether from the dislocation of national industry that would have been caused by the entire sweeping away of a tariff which was the main source of the revenue of the Dominion, it would have been impossible to institute suddenly any system of direct taxation economically to embrace a small and widely scattered population like that of the Dominion. Free traders had consequently to be content with the comparative while the superlative was out of reach, and to accept reduction, rather than abolition, of customs duties.

It may be readily surmised that the love of United States protectionists for Canada was not in any way enhanced by its swerving round to free trade principles, which rather disposed them to lay a still heavier hand on the trade relationship between the two countries. But this was anticipated by Mr. Laurier and his Cabinet, which decided that after some necessary modifications in the Canadian tariff designed to ensure sufficient revenue for the carrying on of the Government, the real reduction should take the form of a rebate upon British merchandise and manufactures, to be participated in by such of the British possessions as reciprocated, but from the benefits of which foreign countries, including of course the United States, were to be excluded.

Thus the United States, when the Dingley tariff was finally passed in September 1897, were already confronted with the Canadian preferential tariff put into force 23rd April previous, which stipulated that from that date until the 30th June 1898—that is to the end of the following fiscal year—all goods of British production were to enjoy a rebate of $12\frac{1}{2}$ per cent. off the existing customs duties, and subsequently one of 25 per cent. Alcoholic liquors, tobacco in all its forms, and sugar, were specially excepted, though by a subsequent extension sugar grown in any of the British West India possessions was accorded the privilege. Owing to the existence, however, of certain commercial treaties between the United Kingdom on the one hand, and Belgium and Germany on the other, the exclusion of those two countries, and with them of all others under a favoured nation clause, could not be enforced until twelve months later, and only came into operation in the latter part of 1898.

Such is the history of this preferential tariff which has excited so much attention, and is being used as a basis of advocacy for the adoption of something similar throughout the entire British Empire. A study of it in its detailed working is thus absolutely essential.

To begin with, we have to realise that the object was quite as much retaliation against the United States as desire to promote trade relationship with the United Kingdom. Going back to 1868, the first year, that is, of Canada as a federal unit, and for which statistics of its foreign commerce as such are in existence, we find that the exchange of products between the two countries was about equal; Canadian imports from the United States were valued at $22,660,132 and exports to them at $22,387,846.[1] For several years following the

---

[1] The statistics in this chapter and succeeding ones where reference is made to Canada, are taken from the Annual Report of the Department of Trade and Commerce of the Dominion of Canada for the fiscal year ended 30th June 1901, and from the Provisional Annual Statement of the following year.

variation between the two was not very great, but
as far back as 1873 that divergence began which
has continued ever since. From that time, the
trade intercourse between the two countries exhibited
a remarkable absence of elasticity. In 1873, for
instance, the Canadian imports had increased to
$45,189,110. The highest figure they reached in
any subsequent year down to 1896, when they were
valued at $53,529,390, was $55,147,243 in 1883;
they fell as low as $28,193,783 in 1880. Exports of
home produce fluctuated even less; from $33,421,725
in 1873 they had risen to only $34,460,428 in
1896, the maximum and minimum of the interval
having been respectively $41,687,638 in 1882, and
$22,131,343 in 1878. Restrictive legislation on
both sides accomplished its purpose only too effectively, for while the United States were progressing
by leaps and bounds, with occasional, and sometimes
violent setbacks, their commercial connections
seemed to be extended with nearly every civilised
country in the world except the next door neighbour.
Nor need the fact be concealed that it was Canada
that was the real sufferer.

Canada might have gained a great deal by closer
commercial relationship with the United States, but
that, as we have already observed, was only possible
at the expense of independence which it was not at
any time willing to surrender. As it was, the
Dominion had little or nothing to lose in showing
that independence by setting the United States

openly at defiance. Both countries maintained a list of free imports which they considered necessary for their own industrial welfare, and from which neither could very well exclude the other, and the articles upon them have always accounted for a very large proportion of the interchange; indeed, had the figures just given been restricted to the dutiable section of the trade, the fluctuations would be found to be still narrower. It was only natural to suppose that from 1897 onwards, with the Dingley tariff in full operation on one side and the preferential tariff on the other, the relationship would have been further strained and trade fallen away to still smaller dimensions.

The Canadian Government anticipated this state of things, but a new epoch was opening in the development of the Dominion, and despite all the artificial barriers erected on both sides, commercial intercourse between the two countries grew by rapid strides.

But before dealing specifically with these particular trade connections, it will be advisable to follow the expansion of Canadian commerce as a whole. Like the portion with the United States, it had long given evidence of being very inelastic, and if the Dominion did not suffer so intensely from recurring periods of depression as its big neighbour, it never soared to its heights of prosperity either. It is just a question whether prosperity in the United States was not a bad thing for Canada, because it invariably attracted a certain proportion of the population who saw, or imagined they saw, greater opportunities for the display of their energies across the border. It is always a moot-point whether the state of political parties exercises internally, as distinct from internationally, any direct influence on commerce and industry. Each side claims that these flourish best under its own particular auspices. The Conservatives on their advent to power in the United Kingdom in 1895 were fortunate enough to catch the flowing tide after a long and weary ebb. Improvement in trade returns began immediately after that event, which was asserted to be the cause of it, whereas neither advance nor retrogression are actually reflected in these returns until some time after it has actually set in. But perhaps it was the anticipation of the advent of the Conservatives to power that first brought about the change. At anyrate the flow throughout the world soon became so strong that not even the many international complications in which the Government involved the country could arrest it.

Similarly in the United States the era of prosperity that set in shortly after the return of the Republican party to office in 1896 was claimed by it as the direct consequence. It was ignored that for once the improvement commenced in the Eastern hemisphere and travelled westward across the Atlantic, or that it then received its greatest impetus from a succession of magnificent harvests, more than one of them accompanied by scarcity in other parts of the world. But in Canada the change of Government that occurred much about the same time does appear to have exercised more than usual influence on the course of trade. The long succession of Conservative and Protectionist Ministries had got the Dominion into a rut from which it seemed unable to extricate itself, until the return of the Liberals inspired it with renewed hope and a fresh supply of energy.

The change of parties was not accompanied by that violent reversal of fiscal policy that was at one time anticipated; indeed it is surprising how small the difference is in this respect. The average *ad valorem* duty, for instance, collected on all dutiable imports into Canada in the fiscal year 1896, the last complete one under the Conservative régime, was 29·942 per cent. In 1901 it had fallen only to 27·427 per cent., a reduction, that is, of just 2½ per cent. Of course this does not quite reflect what actually took place, because on the more highly rated commodities like alcoholic liquors and manufactured tobacco (leaf tobacco is duty free and subject to excise), the rates remained unchanged, and the reduction on the remainder is consequently somewhat greater. But imports from the United Kingdom of these highly rated commodities are only limited, and after making allowance for the full rebates on everything else the decline in the average *ad valorem* duty between 1896 and 1901 was less

3

than 5½ per cent., from 30·20 per cent., that is, to 24·75 per cent.

Sentiment in this instance probably played an important part. There has been an atmosphere of greater freedom, a feeling that the financial arrangements of the Government were no longer designed for the benefit of a favoured few, but were being, and would be, regulated for the future in the interests of the whole community. The confidence such an idea inspired made everybody more enterprising: everybody, that is, except the small body of highly protected manufacturers who found themselves no longer the hub of the Dominion. And the result of this enterprise is very clearly shown by the figures of imports and exports for the last six years when compared with those immediately preceding.

	Imports of Merchandise for Consumption only.	Exports of Home[1] Produce.
1896	$105,361,161	$106,378,752
1897	106,617,827	119,685,410
1898	126,307,162	139,920,932
1899	149,346,459	132,801,262
1900	172,506,878	163,510,790
1901	177,700,694	177,431,386
1902	196,480,190	196,019,763

It would be easy to jump to the conclusion, as some people have done, that this is the direct result of the preference accorded to Great Britain, but unfortunately the real results do not confirm so

[1] These figures are admittedly short of the actual total, produce finding its way across the frontier into the United States without being reported. An estimate of this was formerly included in the returns, but this has now ceased.

flattering an explanation. Some figures of the
trade between Canada and the United States for
1896 and previous years have already been given
on pp. 29–30. Following these up, and comparing
with the totals just stated, we arrive at the actual
result for the later years.

	Imports for Consumption from United States.	Percentage of Total.	Exports of Home Produce to United States.	Percentage of Total.
1896	$53,529,390	50·80	$34,460,428	32·39
1897	57,023,342	53·48	39,717,057	33·19
1898	74,824,923	59·24	34,361,795	24·56
1899	88,467,173	59·24	34,766,955	26·18
1900	102,080,177	59·17	52,534,977	32·13
1901	107,149,325	60·30	67,983,673	38·32
1902	114,747,602	58·40	66,566,835	33·96

Both sets of figures are sufficiently remarkable
to call for further explanation. In the first place
it might be imagined that the great increase in
imports was due to the needs of Canadian manufacturing industry, and consisted principally of duty
free raw material. That did undoubtedly account
for a considerable part of the movement, but as the
following table shows, not by any means for the
whole of it :—

	Free Imports from United States.	Dutiable Imports from United States.
1896	$24,427,744	$29,101,646
1897	26,540,833	30,482,509
1898	36,760,963	38,063,960
1899	43,995,349	44,471,824
1900	48,182,616	53,897,561
1901	53,549,047	53,600,278
1902	54,561,118	60,186,484

It will be observed that the increase for 1901 was entirely in free goods, and the inference might have been drawn that the increased preference to 33⅓ per cent. was at length beginning to tell, but the total import of dutiable commodities was little in excess of the previous year, and the supply of these by the United States fell from 51·65 to 50·58 per cent., an inappreciable difference, and one that can be amply accounted for by other than tariff reasons. Any such inference, too, is absolutely destroyed by the figures for 1902, which show the further considerable gain in the total to consist almost entirely of dutiable goods.

Looking at the export side it would appear that the Dingley Tariff failed equally to keep out Canadian products as it was designed to do. The sharp rise in 1897 and the falling away again the following year are explained by the eager rush of imports into the United States from all the world over in anticipation of that tariff, which on the whole affected Canada less than any other country, as no serious diminution in the value of exports ever occurred, though rising prices may have affected the volume.

But the sudden jump in 1900, followed by another almost equally great in 1901, is accounted for by other than ordinary trade movements. Canada became a gold-producing country on a somewhat large scale, and the yields both of Klondike and British Columbia found their natural outlets in the United States, firstly because that country provided the nearest refineries and mints, and secondly because they afforded an effective set-off to the balance of trade between the two countries. In 1899 the value of gold-bearing quartz, dust, nuggets, etc., exported, amounted to only $3,272,702, whereas in 1900 it rose to $14,148,543 and in 1901 to $24,445,156, but fell again in 1902 to $19,668,015. Practically the whole of this found destination in the United States. Mining in all its branches has rapidly increased in activity throughout the Dominion, but with the exception of iron, no provision has yet been made for reducing the ores, which are accordingly disposed of in almost every case to United States smelters. Copper so increased from $917,394 in 1899 to $2,659,261 in 1901, lead from $895,769 to $2,272,830. Silver ore on the other hand marked a small decline from $2,630,280 to $2,379,950 in the same period. In 1902 copper showed a further slight increase, silver a corresponding decline, but the great fall in the price of lead, coupled with the high United States tariff and the indisposition of smelters to handle foreign ores, reduced the value of that metal to $889,310. The year 1902 did, therefore, witness some expansion of the ordinary export trade from Canada to the United States, but prior to that it was not any demand for Canadian agricultural products or manufactured goods that caused the considerable gains noted in the table.

Having followed the trade movement in the direction against which the preferential tariff was instituted, it remains to be seen what happened with the United Kingdom, in whose favour it was adopted. There is no denying the fact that from the very first it was expected to transfer the demand for such commodities as Canada required to import, from one side of the Atlantic to the other, but so far the anticipation has been completely falsified. The corresponding movement to that given on page 35 for the United States is as follows :—

	Imports for Consumption from United Kingdom.	Percentage of Total.	Exports of Home Produce to United Kingdom.	Percentage of Total.
1896	$32,824,505	31·15	$62,717,941	58·95
1897	29,401,188	27·58	69,533,852	58·09
1898	32,043,461	25·36	93,065,019	66·51
1899	36,931,323	24·72	85,113,681	64·09
1900	44,279,983	25·66	96,562,875	59·06
1901	42,819,995	24·10	92,857,525	52·33
1902	49,024,657	24·95	109,348,245	55·78

Again, however, distinction must be made between free and dutiable goods, and in this instance, unlike the United States, the bulk of the increase is in the latter.

	Free Imports from United Kingdom.	Dutiable Imports from United Kingdom.
1896	$8,458,326	$24,366,179
1897	9,183,766	20,217,422
1898	9,486,982	22,556,479
1899	9,409,815	27,521,508
1900	12,718,227	31,561,756
1901	11,118,341	31,701,654
1902	13,962,032	35,062,625

Not merely in total volume, but in relative proportion, the United States have scored the greatest gain in both classes. In the period it has taken to more than double the dutiable imports from that country, those from the United Kingdom have increased less than one-half, and for the latest year constitute but 29·55 per cent. of the total, absolutely the lowest figure recorded in the commercial history of the Dominion. Thirty years earlier, in 1872, the corresponding figure was 70·59 per cent.

Canada never having had much direct intercourse with any other countries than the two just dealt with, the volume of commerce outside them is comparatively insignificant. The official list of imports records fifty distinct countries of origin, and of exports forty-nine of destination, two of them in each instance providing for unenumerated, British and foreign, but for very trivial items. Indeed, the same may be said for most of those that are detailed, only some half-dozen, other than the two principal ones, exceeding $1,000,000 either way. Such trade as does exist consists very largely of specialities, and is carried on either through the United Kingdom or the United States.

But to certain British possessions the preferential tariff has been extended. The British West Indies, for example, enjoy the rebate of one-third of the duty on their sugar and other products, yet the Canadian imports still consist principally of European beet. That, however, must be attributed to the policy of

the United States, which by its system of countervailing the bounties still affords the best market
for all cane sugar, especially at the low prices which
have ruled ; but with the abolition of the bounties
on the one hand, and the increasing production of
sugar both in the States and their oversea possessions on the other, the West Indies may before long
supply most of the Canadian consumption.

East Indian tea, along with tea generally, is on the
free list, but only furnishes about one-third of the total
consumption.   That is due more to a matter of taste
than anything else, preference being given to the
green leaf of China and Japan over the black produce
of the Assam or Cingalese gardens, and efforts are
being made to popularise the Indian growths, which
in course of time may prove successful.   This is
perhaps an instance where the extension of the tariff
might help the movement.

The direct trade with Australasia, notwithstanding regular intercourse between the two continents
by means of the steamers owned and run by the
Canadian Pacific Railroad, remains comparatively
insignificant.   Canadian imports thence for 1901
were valued at $426,467, and fell in 1902 to
$156,735 ; the exports thereto for the latter year
were $2,940,290.   The fact is the two countries
produce very much the same things, and have less
real need of one another than almost any two
portions of the Empire, and the trade between
them is largely of a through or transit character.

On the other hand, the war had a distinctly stimulating effect on Canadian trade with British, that is, South Africa ; direct exports from a trivial amount having increased to $1,204,093 in 1900 and $1,085,033 in 1901, while the figures for 1902 rose to $3,842,070. It remains to be seen whether the connection having been opened up can be permanently retained. So far it has not gone much beyond horses and fodder, requirements that have ended with the war, but in view of the immense demand for agricultural, dairy, and hog products, so much of them hitherto supplied by the United States, there ought to be ample opportunity for the Dominion to build up a substantial business.

Of strictly foreign countries, Germany, Belgium, France, and Japan are the only ones worthy of attention. The first two, from a Canadian import point of view, owe much of their importance to the sugar trade for reasons already noted. France supplies wines and brandies, and also some sugar, and Japan tea, silk, and rice. In none of these instances is there any direct competition with Great Britain, but both Germany and France carry on a considerable miscellaneous business as well which does fall under that category. Some of the details of it we will deal with later, and for the present content ourselves with a comparison of the total imports from 1897 to 1902, that is, the last year of the old tariff conditions, and the latest of the new ones.

Canadian Imports from—

	Germany.	France.	Belgium.	Japan.
1897	$6,493,368	$2,601,351	$1,163,632	$1,333,865
1898	5,584,014	3,975,030	1,230,110	1,439,354
1899	7,392,106	3,889,295	2,318,723	2,018,107
1900	8,383,498	4,368,246	3,223,918	1,751,415
1901	7,020,100	5,397,793	3,828,450	1,619,102
1902	10,814,029	6,670,730	1,700,697	1,495,901

In each instance, therefore, there is improvement over the entire period notwithstanding the more difficult conditions of intercourse. The somewhat severe decline noted in the case of Germany for 1901, to be more than recovered the following year, is more apparent than real, there having been a falling off of $1,900,000 in sugar alone, partly owing to a decline in price, but also very likely to larger quantities than usual having been shipped through Belgian and Dutch ports.

Exports to three of the four countries also exhibit satisfactory increases,—to Japan they are insignificant, and even to the others fall considerably short of the reverse movement, leaving Canada mistress of the situation as far as the framing of a tariff policy is concerned.

Canadian Exports of Home Produce to—

	Germany.	France.	Belgium.
1897	$764,589	$683,955	$231,295
1898	1,419,096	1,015,612	803,655
1899	1,310,373	1,551,909	445,667
1900	1,108,163	1,372,359	859,715
1901	1,374,716	1,436,628	1,728,484
1902	1,298,654	1,300,798	1,363,098

These exports consist chiefly of grain and other agricultural and dairy produce. The movement to Belgium is the most marked, and that country owing to its more liberal tariff policy offers the greatest inducements, and there is no reason why this branch of trade should not grow to considerably larger dimensions.

Examining the Canadian trade of the last six years in the aggregate, the preferential tariff under which it has been worked appears to have been absolutely fruitless in diverting commerce from any other country to the United Kingdom ; indeed the most that is now claimed for it is that it has prevented diversion from the United Kingdom elsewhere. There may have been, indeed there are, some minor exceptions, but speaking broadly, Canada has been accustomed in the past to supply its various requirements from various sources, those wants have all materially increased, and the demands upon the original sources to a corresponding extent. It so happens that in the class of goods furnished by the United States there has been the greatest activity of all, and the United States have gone on supplying them disregardless of tariff considerations. It is more than likely that a change is pending in this respect, but for other reasons than the operation of the tariff.

How this contention is borne out by the facts is easily demonstrated. Every great trade revival has its own distinguishing characteristics ; the one that covered the end of the nineteenth and the beginning of the twentieth centuries rejoiced in two, and for that reason lasted longer, and was more accentuated, than most of its predecessors. A new industry, that of electrical construction, which had been budding for some time previously burst into full bloom. An old one, iron and steel, assumed proportions that nobody previously ever dreamt of; the low cost to which production was reduced having led to substitution for wood in almost every conceivable direction. Under any circumstance Great Britain would have been utterly unable to cope with the demand; as it was, there was not an idle furnace or an idle hand in the country that need have been in that condition. The problem was not to find new customers, but to supply the wants of old ones, many of whom had to be turned away.

The United States and Germany were not only later comers in this industry, but their national resources, owing to extent of territory, were much greater and far less drawn upon. That development in them should be at a greater pace than in the older country was but in accordance with natural law, and it was upon them that the bulk of the new demand fell.

Canada, in company with almost every other comparatively new and undeveloped country, found itself in need of great supplies of these, materials. Ability to execute orders promptly, coupled with geographical situation, settled the question in favour of the United States as we see by the following figures :—

Imports of Iron and Steel into Canada.

	Total Value.	From United States.	From United Kingdom.
1897	$10,785,576	$7,700,448	$2,705,678
1898	17,106,207	14,478,515	2,206,631
1899	19,848,433	16,758,924	2,716,422
1900	29,649,178	23,288,895	5,739,600
1901	27,107,419	23,054,350	3,387,553
1902	33,282,629	24,594,486	6,395,972

The great jump in 1900 was due to a very considerable extent to the enormous rise in values ; time was of greater consequence than price, and orders were placed where they could be quickest executed. It was not until 1901 that activity in this particular industry in the United States overtook Great Britain, and there has, in consequence, been some transfer of the trade. Steel rails, for instance, are imported into Canada free of duty, and in these, if in anything, the United States should enjoy a decided advantage. In 1901 they supplied 107,637 tons as against 15,710 only by Great Britain, but for 1902 the figures were respectively 58,995 and 44,583, while Germany came in with 17,532 tons.

But Canada has recently taken a new departure, and it looks only like a question of time that it will be able to supply the United States and Great Britain with iron and steel, and so turn the tables

completely. The day is not far distant when it will
at least furnish most of its own requirements, and
the loss will fall of course principally on the United
States, which will rapidly reduce their position
relatively to Great Britain, though the preferential
tariff will not be the cause.

Already the production of crude iron in the
Dominion exceeds the home demand for it, and
though the latter will increase, the former is more
than likely to keep pace. Whatever exports of pig-
iron there may have been prior to the fiscal year
1901/2 were not worth recording; for that year
the figure amounted to 113,438 tons, of which no
less than 100,519 tons were shipped to Great
Britain. This branch of industry, therefore, is
undergoing a revolution.

If iron and steel have hitherto constituted the
backbone of the trade with the United States,
textiles have occupied that position as regards the
United Kingdom, and it is in these that the most
marked increase has occurred. It was the textile
manufacturers of the Dominion who offered the
strongest resistance to any reduction in the tariff,
whether by way of preference to Great Britain or
in any other direction. As far as cotton spinning
and manufacturing are concerned, the result has
positively proved beneficial, judging at least from
the movement of raw material, the whole of which
has to be imported from abroad, principally from
the United States. Throughout the long spell of

high protection little or no expansion in this industry appears to have taken place ; in 1887 the import of raw cotton amounted to 31 million pounds weight, by 1896 it had only increased to $33\frac{1}{2}$ million pounds, and the intervening fluctuations were not very considerable. Since then progress has been rapid as appears from the following :—

Imports of Raw Cotton.

1897	.	.	.	.	39,365,733 lbs.
1898	.	.	.	.	58,203,660 ,,
1899	.	.	.	.	51,809,661 ,,
1900	.	.	.	.	54,912,849 ,,
1901	.	.	.	.	49,064,959 ,,
1902	.	.	.	.	64,225,764 ,,

The larger figures were perhaps in excess of actual consumption, but no such average over six years was ever before attained.

This has not prevented a corresponding, or even greater increase in the trade in manufactured goods, as will be seen from the following table which includes everything that is dutiable.

Imports of Cotton Manufactures.

1897	.	.	.	.	$4,051,361
1898	.	.	.	.	4,710,794
1899	.	.	.	.	5,984,188
1900	.	.	.	.	6,506,569
1901	.	.	.	.	6,927,992
1902	.	.	.	.	7,451,759

British goods have always constituted the bulk of this particular item, but with such large prefer ences in the duty as 25 and $33\frac{1}{3}$ per cent, the latter representing an advantage of 8 to 12 per cent. on the actual value of the goods, it might have been supposed that they would have driven all competition from the market. So far from this being the case, the United States as well as European countries have materially increased their trade, and an analysis of the foregoing figures gives the following results :—

	Great Britain.	United States.	Other Countries.
1897	$2,693,114	$1,119,147	$239,100
1898	3,086,068	1,332,533	292,113
1899	3,906,676	1,679,428	398,084
1900	4,474,687	1,509,312	522,570
1901	4,879,909	1,463,686	584,397
1902	5,108,513	1,608,369	734,877

From the point of view of actual consumption these returns mean a greater increase than appears on the face of them, because the export of home manufactures, which was valued at $949,861 in 1897, fell steadily to $575,125 in 1901, though it increased again to $958,963 for 1902, owing principally to the fact that quite a trade is developing with Australasia and Newfoundland, no doubt at the expense of Lancashire. Thus, in 1897, the shipments of goods to these countries were valued respectively at $77,389 and $16,916, while for 1902 the figures had grown to $436,837 and $49,370. China has always been regarded in the Western hemisphere as the dumping-ground for any excess production of cotton goods, and Canada in 1897 got rid of $628,896 worth in that way, at what sacrifice in value it is impossible to say.

At anyrate the trade was hardly a legitimate one or a determined effort would have been made to retain it, whereas by 1901 the shipments had fallen to the insignificant figure of $30,841, ample proof that satisfactory markets were afforded elsewhere. Canada, like the United States, however, looks to the Far East as an eventual outlet for its trade, and the fact that the value for 1902, principally for piece goods, increased to $148,745 indicates that the Dominion may soon become a keen competitor in this branch of industry.

As far as other countries are concerned, the marked increase under that head is accounted for principally by Switzerland, and is not a genuine gain. The goods consist largely of the embroideries for which that country is famous, but which are mainly purchased by Canadian dry goods buyers through the London warehouses. Formerly they were shipped along with other things as British, but now discrimination has to be made and the $16,622 of 1897 went up to $284,120 in 1902. Smaller increases are probably accounted for in the same way by France and Germany, the former having risen in five years from $55,181 to $119,162 and the latter from $111,303 to $192,878.

The bulk of the import, however, consists of piece goods, and it is in these that competition is strongest between British and United States manufacturers, and in which consequently, any preference in the tariff ought to tell most effectively. Values

4

have fluctuated so considerably in recent years that quantities afford the surest clue to what has actually occurred. Canada itself has made very rapid strides in one branch of the industry, namely printing and dyeing, which may be accounted for by the fact that it gets an additional 10 per cent. of protection, the nominal duty being 35 per cent. as against 25 per cent. on plain fabrics. This has had a very marked effect as far as the United States are concerned, the full 10 per cent. being in force, but less in the case of Great Britain, where the differential amounts to $6\frac{2}{3}$ per cent. only. The following shows the actual movements :—

Imports of Piece Goods.

	Bleached and Unbleached Calicoes. Yds.	Printed and Dyed Calicoes. Yds.	Miscellaneous Fabrics. Yds.	Velveteens, Plushes, etc. Yds.
1897	3,209,883	27,102,139	1,306,984	1,020,284
1898	4,654,819	31,304,955	1,566,233	1,009,705
1899	8,577,047	35,510,093	1,896,537	1,000,400
1900	9,278,833	34,825,977	1,903,325	949,949
1901	18,083,452	30,799,539	1,469,140	1,246,900
1902	14,464,353	36,168,662	2,212,914	1,585,253

Splitting the first two items, the figures are still more significant.

	Bleached and Unbleached.		Printed and Dyed.	
	Great Britain. Yds.	United States. Yds.	Great Britain. Yds.	United States. Yds.
1897	1,724,902	1,450,403	17,700,558	8,789,413
1898	2,447,151	1,962,014	20,738,967	10,014,061
1899	3,712,011	4,661,346	24,464,897	10,467,351
1900	5,748,158	3,335,974	27,070,851	7,215,079
1901	12,319,407	5,254,689	24,165,332	5,874,956
1902	10,151,591	4,001,721	27,393,747	7,944,635

Canadian cotton manufacturers have apparently not much ground for complaint at the way things have gone the last four or five years. But it is the woollen industry that claims to have been the hardest hit. The duty on almost every description of goods is 35 per cent., so that a reduction of one-third still leaves the very substantial protection of $23\frac{1}{3}$ per cent., a mere bagatelle it is true compared with what the United States manufacturer gets, but the latter is handicapped to begin with by a heavy duty on raw wool while the Canadian gets it free. The movement of the raw material is not quite so conclusive as in the case of cotton, because there is a considerable home production which is presumably increasing with the agricultural development of the country. Based simply on what is received from foreign sources, the result is admittedly not satisfactory from a Canadian manufacturer's point of view. The figures for seven years are as follows, but inasmuch as there is an export as well as an import trade, this must be included in order to arrive at the net results :—

	Imports of Raw Wool.	Exports.	Net Imports.
1896	8,992,244 lbs.	3,970,700 lbs.	5,021,544 lbs.
1897	5,704,194 ,,	7,857,657 ,,	2,153,463 ,, [1]
1898	11,785,899 ,,	1,172,034 ,,	10,613,865 ,,
1899	9,413,739 ,,	91,991 ,,	9,321,748 ,,
1900	8,054,699 ,,	2,213,863 ,,	5,840,836 ,,
1901	8,574,605 ,,	1,152,661 ,,	7,421,944 ,,
1902	10,360,738 ,,	1,973,772 ,,	8,386,966 ,,

[1] Net Export.

The extraordinary discrepancy in the figures of 1897 and 1898 is due to the disturbance caused by the Dingley Tariff, which transferred raw wool from the free to the dutiable list. The items given above, it must be borne in mind, are for fiscal years ending the 30th June, so that it was possible for Canadian wool growers to get a large part of their new clip across the United States frontier to meet the great demand that prevailed, while the gap thus created was filled later with foreign imported wool. Though allowing for this the net import is somewhat larger at the end of the period than at the beginning, it compares unfavourably with many years that preceded it.

As far as the Canadian woollen manufacturer is concerned, the competition he has to face is almost entirely British. The United States hardly count; it would be amazing indeed if they did, bearing in mind that everything they produce is based on dear wool. Of the total dutiable imports in 1902 valued at $10,946,856 they contributed but $354,598, though even that was an increase over 1897 when the item was but $218,396. Such trade consists probably either of specialities for which there is a regular demand, or for goods wanted in a hurry which there is no time to order from across the Atlantic. France maintains, and even extends its trade for the class of goods that are in demand in every civilised country in the world, and which a tariff, however high, never quite excludes. The value of the dutiable import in

1902 was $787,718, the highest figure reached ; for
1897 it was only $440,585. Germany, on the other
hand, while improving its position so long as the
disadvantage with Great Britain was no more than
25 per cent., has apparently been unable to withstand the increase to $33\frac{1}{3}$. In value Great Britain
has not made quite the progress that might have
been expected under the reduced tariff, but that is
owing to some extent to the severe decline in value
that occurred after the crisis in the market for raw
wool. The figures of interest, in addition to the
totals, are those for Great Britain and Germany,
which are as follows :—

Imports of Woollen Manufactures.

	Total Value.	From Great Britain.	From Germany.
1897	$7,125,748	$5,553,094	$853,592
1898	7,985,866	6,291,762	877,524
1899	9,803,203	7,605,467	999,634
1900	9,801,565	7,943,274	997,886
1901	9,944,105	7,940,370	818,048
1902	10,946,856	8,860,393	866,514

These three branches of industry, iron and steel,
cotton and woollen manufactures, though they represent less than one-half the total dutiable imports into
the Dominion, are those around which international
competition wages most fiercely, and which in consequence are likely to be most affected by tariff changes,
particularly of a preferential character. So far as
the figures given prove anything, it is that the
disturbance of trade has been very slight. It might,

of course, have happened that without the preference
Great Britain would have lost ground in its specialities to the advantage of some of its competitors, but
that is after all mere surmise. Still, it would have
been quite remarkable if in no branch of trade some
difference was not perceptible, and it is worth following the list to ascertain where anything of the kind
has actually occurred which may reasonably be
ascribed to this cause.

The first instance that presents itself is carpets,
nearly the entire import of which in 1897 was from
Great Britain and the United States. But from
$86,410 in that year, the former advanced to
$213,136 in 1902, while the latter fell from
$66,537 to $27,024. There was another force
besides the preferential tariff at work in this case.
The United States until 1897 enjoyed the advantage
of free wool, but after that was handicapped by a
home duty as well as the preferential tariff. Japan
increased in the interval from $2258 to $34,792, but
the demand in that case is a special one.

Drugs, dyes, medicines, and chemicals are mostly
on the free list and therefore not affected. The free
import increased from $1,792,033 to $3,645,266.
Nearly the entire gain was secured by the United
States, while Great Britain advanced only from
$640,341 to $756,945. This makes the movement
in the dutiable class all the more noteworthy, and
justifies the conclusion that here, at anyrate, the preference of one-third of the duty has operated most

effectively. For from $577,180 in 1897, the United States increased to only $772,875 in 1902, while Great Britain advanced from $224,517 to $560,397 in the same period, the larger figure a material decline too from the previous year. The items in this class are innumerable, and the result is highly creditable to shippers and importers who do not despise small things.

The earthenware and china industry has never been an important one to the United States except for the supply of home requirements. Still they managed to sell to Canada $242,055 worth in 1902 as compared with $62,528 only in 1897. Great Britain, nevertheless, received the lion's share of the increase, and advanced from $388,485 to $723,557. France and Germany likewise made substantial gains on a smaller trade.

In glass and glassware Great Britain has made an appreciable gain, but other countries have done so too. The British import increased from $186,008 to $387,883 under the preferential tariff. The United States always previously headed the list, but for 1902 with $526,134 had to give place to Belgium, which increased its trade to $530,378.

Flax, hemp, and jute manufactures have always been pretty nearly a British monopoly, and the fact that almost the entire gain has fallen to it is in no sense traceable to the action of the tariff. It is noteworthy, however, that since the present one has been in operation Germany has increased its supplies of such goods from $9959 to $39,343, and even France has gone from $9755 to $26,311.

Oilcloth records a large increase, the greatest part of which was secured by Great Britain, though an advance from $27,831 to $80,709 on the part of the United States is not to be despised. Compared with $124,697 and $367,045, however, it is still moderate.

The prosperity prevailing in Canada is nowhere more clearly reflected than in the greatly increased purchases of silk fabrics and manufactures, the $1,979,239 of 1897 having grown to $4,183,926 in 1902. Silk is not a strong point in British industry, and it is somewhat surprising to find that of the latter item no less than $2,430,664 was of that origin. Other countries, notably France and Japan, gained relatively far more, but this is notoriously an instance where prior to the preferential tariff goods purchased in London warehouses were passed as British, irrespective of where they were originally manufactured. The figures are consequently not of any great value as an indication of the changes that have occurred.

But as a set off against these few items, there is quite a formidable list of changes in the opposite direction; that is, of goods in which the preference in the tariff has not prevented the trade with foreign countries increasing far more rapidly than with

Great Britain. The United States, as might be supposed, have been the principal gainers, but in several instances continental Europe makes quite a good show. The bare enumeration of these must suffice, leaving everybody who is interested to inquire for themselves why this state of things should have come about.

The lower duty has not created a preference for English as against American literature, the value of British dutiable books and periodicals imported having actually decreased from \$204,921 to \$194,645 against the movement from the United States from \$537,780 to \$823,057. Promptitude of delivery after publication in many instances has no doubt a good deal to do with this, and the rate of postage is a sore point which an attempt is being made to rectify. Brooms and brushes are goods of a very different kind, but of the total gain from \$105,506 to \$227,326, Great Britain scored from \$12,322 to \$19,437 only, the rest falling to the United States, France, and Germany in considerable sums. While the import of buttons advanced from \$135,631 to \$218,962, the British share rose only from \$31,142 to \$36,951. English candles just maintained their ground at a bare \$12,000, while the American article nearly doubled from \$49,393 to \$86,282. Soap exhibits a disastrous result, the American increase from \$130,963 to \$234,200 being accompanied by a falling off in the British figures from \$107,023 to \$37,914. Possibly the erection of works near Boston by an important English manufacturing concern may afford some explanation of this. The demand for cement has grown enormously, but whereas in 1897 the British manufacture far out-distanced all competitors with a value of $109,887, in 1902 it was simply nowhere, the import of $126,672 contrasting with $588,525 supplied by the United States; Belgium coming very little behind with $113,603.

A reduction in the duty equivalent to over eight per cent. has not induced Canadian clock and watch dealers to transfer their patronage to British manufacturers. The United States trade advanced from $510,381 to $774,004, while Great Britain moved only from $20,217 to $24,966. Switzerland has largely increased its hold on the watch trade, having advanced in five years from $22,229 to $90,057. There is perhaps nothing surprising in the fact that Great Britain has hardly entered into competition for the supply of electric apparatus, and though the trade has considerably more than doubled, the United States enjoys virtually the monopoly of the total of $1,372,916, the few thousand dollars distributed among other countries not being worth taking into account.

To ship furs to Canada seems very much like supplying Newcastle with coal. Yet there is a large import as well as export trade in these, though the bulk of it is duty free. But in the dutiable section, where the rate is 15 per cent. on dressed furs, and

30 per cent. when manufactured into coats, capes, muffs, etc., the movements are :—

Great Britain	$176,565 to	$341,802
United States	38,953 ,,	178,579
France	15,489 ,,	126,521
Germany	139,726 ,,	359,019

Of other wearing material the total import of gloves and mitts increased from $511,464 to $651,309, but the British share fell from $228,060 to $199,603. France, Germany, and Austria were the gainers in this instance. Manufactures of gutta-percha, consisting principally of waterproof garments and boots and shoes, yielded an advance to the United States from $207,886 to $521,963, while the corresponding movement from Great Britain was only from $89,651 to $217,477. Hat, cap, and bonnet dealers distributed their favours more equally between the two countries, though with a decided leaning to the United States, as from $479,610 the value advanced to $858,964, while the British $692,613 rose to $844,290, and now stands second instead of first on the list.

Turning to a totally different class of goods, printing and writing inks are supplied in increasing quantities by the United States, while the demand for those of British manufacture is almost stagnant. The same thing is equally true of paints and colours. The British supply increased only from $209,485 to $242,075, while that of the United States advanced from $182,512 to $502,390, and of Germany from $90,841 to $216,671.

Varnishes and lacquers constitute a much smaller item, but while imports from the United States increased from $34,539 to $102,252, those from Great Britain showed the very modest movement from $23,499 to $34,671. The trade in paper of all kinds is passing at a more rapid rate than ever into the hands of United States manufacturers, for whereas in 1897 they supplied $685,997 as against $231,998 by their British competitors, in 1902 the figures were $1,471,779 and $361,692 respectively.

Manufactures of leather, including boots and shoes; furniture, and all kinds of wooden ware, musical instruments, and metal goods other than iron and steel, all tell the same tale in a more or less emphatic manner. Had the movement been limited to iron and steel, and perhaps one or two other classes of manufactured goods, some plausible reason might have been assigned for it, but as a matter of fact it is far too general to be dismissed in an offhand manner. Canada requires a multiplicity of goods of all descriptions to assist the development of its resources, and purchases them from the stocks nearest at hand to which quick resort can always be had. United States manufacturers may, or may not, be able to turn these out cheaper than their British rivals, but they are evidently determined not to allow a difference of five or ten per cent. in price to stand in the way. Something besides a preference in the tariff is evidently required to stimulate trade between the Dominion and the mother country, and this may possibly be found in increased and improved facilities of intercourse.

The tariff arrangements so fully discussed can only indirectly affect the export trade of Canada. Its needs can be supplied both by the United States and Great Britain, and it turns to the former as the most suitable and expeditious in the majority of instances. Its products cannot enjoy a natural market in the United States, because that country itself yields so large a surplus of them, and were the Dingley tariff swept away and free intercourse established, Canada could only expect to benefit in a very moderate degree. Its people very wisely seek to distribute their eggs among many baskets and open up markets wherever they are to be found. But after all, Great Britain is the natural market, and there is scarcely anything Canada produces which cannot be absorbed by it in far larger quantities than at present. That, of course, must lead eventually to the displacement of other countries, the United States particularly. What Canada has to do is to go on producing better and cheaper commodities than any of its rivals, and that it can do so everybody who knows anything of the country is ready to admit. Opportunities for development are consequently afforded in a way that most other countries may well envy. The first requirement is to steer clear of everything calculated to hinder progress, and one necessity of that is to supply itself with all that is wanted on the most favourable conditions from the most suitable markets.

With such a policy as that Great Britain cannot quarrel ; while as far as the Dominion itself is concerned, the increased absorption of its agricultural produce is bound to stimulate a return trade of some kind. The day may arrive, but is yet far distant, when Canada is able to rely mainly on its own resources, a point, however, that can never be reached as fully as in the United States.

CHAPTER III

The Foreign Commerce of Australia and New Zealand

The Drift of Australasian Trade—Influence of the Suez Canal—
Principal Products of the Country—Federation and its Effect on
Trade—The Continental Wool Trade—Gradual Extension to
other Commodities—Conditions of Commercial Intercourse—
Merchandise Marks Act—Financial Crisis in 1893—Wide
Fluctuations in Imports; and Changes of Distribution which
resulted—Export Movements—Recent Decline of Wool Pro-
duction—Growth of Direct Continental Trade—Trade Balances
with the United States—Special Situation of New Zealand—
British Imports of Australasian Produce—Relative Importance of
United Kingdom and Foreign Countries as ultimate Consumers
—Foreign Competition in Australian Markets—Trade with
China and Japan—South Sea Politics—Inter-Colonial Free Trade
—Australasia, Canada, and South Africa.

THE conditions under which Australia and New
Zealand exist are the very antithesis of those that
prevail in Canada. Completely isolated, and far
removed from the scenes of the world's greatest
activities, they can please themselves as to the
connections they form. Were proximity the chief
attraction, they would be drawn to the archipelagos
and mainland of what is known as the Far East, but
race and sentiment alike exercise a repellent influence which has not been overcome even in the
case of Japan, a country sufficiently advanced in

civilisation to be admitted into political partnership with Great Britain. But commercial intercourse cannot very well be carried on without personal intervention, and so determined are the whites of Australia to exclude what they call the coloured races from their shores, that they are willing to forego trade advantages that might afford them a foothold, and the extent of the connection, as we shall see on page 92, is very limited. The policy indeed has gone beyond exclusion and now embraces expulsion, for if recent legislation is not repealed every foreigner whose blood is not of European or American extraction will have to quit, no matter how long they have been domiciled.

The next choice is a far one, notwithstanding that it is on the same ocean. The Pacific States of the North American continent, though rapidly developing, have not yet reached that stage where their commerce goes much beyond supplying their own natural productions, receiving in exchange what they need for actual consumption. Of the first, Australia has more than a sufficiency of its own, and of the second wants much the same things itself, consequently the opportunities for direct trade are only limited. Australia must go still farther afield before finding suitable connections; not any considerable hardship, because the difference between 3000 and 6000 miles by sea is not as great as it looks, the cost of ocean as of land transport being largely regulated by terminal charges.

Apart altogether from sentiment then, Europe affords the fairest prospect. It wants what Australia produces, and is anxious to give in return just the things Australia requires. The Eastern sections of the United States are equally competent to supply many of these, and do not lack the desire either, but the difficulties attending a trade that is nearly all one way have hitherto handicapped them, though they are steadily and materially improving their position, assisted by the Australian output of gold, and consequent ability to pay in that commodity.

Now Europe covers a large and diversified area and embraces a vast population, and any country that could minister to the whole of it would be on the fair road to fortune. There are stages of civilisation, however, as well as fiscal restrictions, which impose a check on too extensive intercourse with any external territories, and the onward march of Australia, like that of many ambitious rivals, is stayed in consequence. As usual, Great Britain offers the widest field, and when all communication was by the Cape of Good Hope was also the most convenient in point of location. But with the opening, and steady absorption of traffic by the Suez Canal, this has changed, and Great Britain is now the country farthest removed. All bordering on the Mediterranean have to be passed on the voyage, and even those whose southern boundaries do not extend so far can be reached more quickly by overland route ; in fact the British mails are not put on board the steamers when they leave the last British port, but are despatched across the English Channel and on to Marseilles or Brindisi. The latter port does not offer any great facilities for cargo, but Marseilles or Genoa can be made distributing centres for Germany, Holland, and Belgium, as easily as London and Liverpool, while for Switzerland they are the natural ones.

Were Australia a great corn-producing country it might for these reasons prove a severe competitor with the American continent. But continental Europe is able generally to grow most of the corn it requires, and the deficiencies in Italy and Spain can be more economically supplied by Russia and the territories bordering on the Black Sea, or by Hungary, all of which invariably yield a surplus, while at present Northern Europe is better served through ports which are the outlets to waterways like the Rhine and the Elbe communicating with the heart of the Continent, and more particularly with its industrial districts. Australia's surplus productions, however, consist chiefly of raw materials for manufacture, especially wool and metals, and these are wanted in greater or less quantities everywhere. New Zealand, on the other hand, devotes more attention to perishable products which come into keener competition with those of Europe, whose peoples are eager for copper and wool, but chary about frozen mutton and butter. There is, consequently, a strong desire to establish direct commercial intercourse with Australia, but an indifference about doing so with New Zealand which throws the latter very much more into the arms of Great Britain, and explains, in a measure, the stronger affinity that seems to have sprung up.

For these reasons Australasia cannot be regarded as a commercial unit, but must be split into Australia and New Zealand.

But Australia itself has recently become a unit, and its five separate States, together with the adjacent island of Tasmania, will in future present a solid front to the rest of the world. So long as they remained separate, each treated the others as foreign territory and maintained its tariff against them just as with the outside world. One result of this was complication in the foreign trade returns, which always appeared very much larger than they really were. Important districts of New South Wales, for instance, are more conveniently situated to Melbourne or Adelaide as shipping ports than to Sydney, and their produce figured three times in the returns, once as exports from New South Wales, then as imports into Victoria or South Australia, and finally as exports again from those countries, while imports into the same districts were similarly recorded on the opposite side. But the countries of ultimate destination, or origin, are pretty well ascertainable, cargo clearing in a British vessel generally going to a British port; on a

German or French one, to the respective countries
to which they belong.

New Zealand has little or no direct intercourse
with any European State except Great Britain, and
must avail itself either of American or Australian
ports to get into contact with them. As a matter
of fact, there is a pretty extensive trade carried on
between Australia and New Zealand, and it figures
as trade with British possessions, though some of
it must ultimately be with foreign countries. The
different States of Australia cannot require a great
deal of New Zealand produce for their own consumption, while to ship to Great Britain *viâ* Australia will not ordinarily be a very economical
method. It must be assumed, therefore, that a good
deal of New Zealand produce is transferred at
Melbourne or Sydney to foreign steamers and passes
ultimately into foreign consumption. It is an important point to bear in mind for subsequent consideration.

Continental Europe was a consumer of Australian
products long before direct communications were
established. The merino breed of sheep is reared
in greater numbers in the countries of the Southern
Pacific than in any other part of the world, and
their wool is specially prized in the finer branches
of manufacture. These still maintain their strong-
hold in England, or to narrow the locality still
further, the West Riding of Yorkshire, at anyrate
as far as spinning is concerned, and the export of

fine yarns is quite a feature in the industry of that district. A great deal of what is actually spun on the Continent is from Australian wool imported into London and purchased at the periodical auction sales that are held there. But some is also imported direct, together with very considerable quantities of the commoner, or cross-bred varieties, and this constitutes the basis of the trade for which steamship lines have been created and liberally subsidised, Germany paying to the North German Lloyd Company the equivalent of £115,000 per annum, and France no less than £125,000 to the Messageries Maritimes, nominally for its own possession of New Caledonia, though most of the actual trade is with Australia.

So important have these countries become to the wool growers of Australia that periodical auction sales are now held at the principal shipping ports there, which are attended by the larger continental buyers or their accredited agents, who endeavour in this way to save the commissions and transhipment charges involved in passage through London. It also affords them opportunities for anticipating market fluctuations : in a period of rising prices they purchase in Australia several months in advance perhaps of the wool being offered in London ; in a declining one they await its arrival in London and get the advantage of the drop. Their calculations are not always correct ; several years ago, just before the tremendous slump in wool values, the best part of an Australian clip was purchased in this way at the top of the market, and must have left the wool growers with several million pounds sterling more in their pockets than had they consigned their produce to London in the old fashioned way. It was paid for presumably by bankers' credits, so that very little of the loss resulting from the collapse fell on the original owners or sellers.

The connection once opened up was not likely to be restricted to wool. The Australian tallow industry is not the important item it once was for two reasons; the succession of terrible droughts, or rather the prolonged single one, from which a great portion of the Continent, more especially the pastoral districts, has suffered, greatly reduced the flocks in numbers, and what are left are no longer killed for the sake of the skins and boiled down for the tallow, but are shipped abroad as frozen mutton. Copper and lead however are produced in ever-increasing quantities, and the first of these at least finds a ready market both in France and Germany. Gold may be left out of the question; as the only commodity enjoying a fixed value and worldwide demand it can be disposed of anywhere and under all circumstances, and its movement is controlled as much by considerations of exchange as of commerce.

It will be seen then that foreign countries are of very considerable consequence to Australian producers and shippers, much more for instance than they are to Canada. Great Britain might absorb most of the copper and tallow and other miscellaneous commodities, but could not possibly use all the wool. Some of this, the merino, continental Europe might have to purchase in any case, but a great deal of the cross-bred could just as easily be obtained elsewhere, and Australia cannot afford to offend such valuable customers.

But no country will trade with another all one way if it can help it, and both Germany and France sought as far as possible to discharge liability for their purchases by sales of their own productions, chiefly manufactured articles. So long as these eountries were content to purchase Australian wool in England, their indebtedness for it was to England and was discharged by the ordinary trade methods. Indebtedness to Australia for direct purchases can be, and for the most part still is, liquidated through London either by bills or credits, and in this respect there is not much to choose between the two methods of business. But there has always been a demand in Australia for certain continental manufactures, partly because they are specialities, but to some extent also, particularly as regards Germany, on account of their cheapness, and these were formerly supplied by British merchants and generally shipped from British ports.

Two forces operated to bring about a change in both respects. The adoption in the United Kingdom of the Merchandise Marks Act revealed to Australian consumers what previously many of them did not know, namely, that the goods they were purchasing were of foreign, not of British manufacture, and by tracing the origin they got into contact with the continental makers.   Where the British merchant was simply a middleman his services could be dispensed with, though British ships might sometimes still be necessary for transport, either from London or some continental port at which they called.   But by means of the direct services much of this was obviated also, and the trade became entirely German or French without any direct British intervention whatever.   Naturally every effort has been made to extend it, but while there has been considerable apparent expansion, it is necessary to bear in mind that it is not entirely at British expense.

So far as these movements are traceable they are shown in figures that follow.   Ten years ago both Australia and New Zealand had reached the culmination of a period of inflation, in the course of which large sums of money were borrowed for the promotion of all kinds of enterprises that were far in advance of the actual needs of the community. Many of these were undertaken by the various colonial governments, all of which, however, successfully weathered the storm as far as their finances were concerned, and none of them even tottered on the brink of suspension, much less tumbled over the precipice. Private enterprise, assisted by the banks which drew their funds very largely from British depositors, came to grief, and most of the banks with it, and 1893 will be ever memorable to Australians as the year when scarcely half a dozen of their financial institutions of the first rank emerged solvent from the crisis.

The previous inflation was attended by immense activity in the import trade of the various colonies, partly owing to the demand for materials of construction, but largely to the indulgence in luxury of many people who, on paper at least, were amassing large fortunes. With the collapse, all this expenditure was cut off as with a knife, and the period of severe economy, national as well as individual, that followed, was marked by immense shrinkage in the value of imports. Nor was that all ; the liabilities contracted with such light-heartedness had to be met where actual bankruptcy did not result, and as many of these were to British or foreign creditors, the only way of paying interest, to say nothing of principal, most of which was allowed to remain, was by the export of the products of the country which thus rapidly overtook the imports.

The trade returns for some years prior to this crisis are not consequently of any great value, as they represent much business that was absolutely reckless and carried through disregardless of ordinary business precautions. But during the interval that has since elapsed, altogether different principles have been enforced, and the trading community have turned whatever business has been possible on to the most economical lines. Trade returns, therefore, for the period during which the colonies have been gradually pulling themselves together again are of the utmost value, as they show distinctly the natural gravitations as distinct from forced or sentimental movements.

In most cases the culminating point of the imports was reached before the actual collapse, as credit became more and more restricted until that occurred, and the following table shows the highest values reached by each colony prior to 1893 and alongside them the figures for the subsequent year when they fell to the lowest level, showing how tremendous in several instances the shrinkage was :—

		Highest Import.		Lowest Import.
New South Wales	1891	£25,383,397	1894	£15,801,941
Victoria . .	1889	24,402,760	1894	12,470,599
South Australia .	1891	9,956,542	1895	5,585,601
Western Australia	1892	1,391,109	1893	1,494,438
Queensland . .	1888	6,646,738	1894	4,337,400
Tasmania . .	1891	2,051,964	1894	979,676
Australia . .		£69,832,510		£40,669,655
New Zealand .	1892	6,943,056	1895	6,400,129
		£76,775,556	.	£47,069,784

In Western Australia there was no falling off whatever, the goldfields were in 1892 just at the beginning of their development, and the commercial progress of the colony since has been rapid. The check in New Zealand was also very temporary, and the onward march was soon resumed, but with the others it was more or less prolonged, and years elapsed before the highest figures were again reached, indeed Victoria and South Australia have never touched them since.

Though it does not necessarily follow that the maximum and minimum total imports correspond with each of the principal countries affected, the figures of these do afford some guide to the commercial connections then existing, and for the years already given in each instance, the separate items were recorded as follows :—

Imports in Maximum year from—

	United Kingdom.	United States.	Germany.	France.
New South Wales	£10,580,230	£1,277,032	£773,016	£120,321
Victoria . .	11,414,682	991,009	606,673	181,490
South Australia .	2,876,548	319,005	322,244	18,624
Western Australia	592,496	29,774	243	1,524
Queensland .	3,121,246	157,321	40,186	22,057
Tasmania . .	655,006	16,868	1,029	...
Australia . .	£29,240,208	£2,791,009	£1,743,391	£344,016
New Zealand .	4,767,369	381,627	89,810	13,554
	£34,007,577	£3,172,636	£1,833,201	£357,570

Imports in Minimum year from—

	United Kingdom.	United States.	Germany.	France.
New South Wales	£5,983,489	£542,427	£345,364	£70,649
Victoria . .	4,830,956	333,928	284,658	57,939
South Australia .	1,857,989	241,886	171,579	20,323
Western Australia	733,001	25,170	34	1,154
Queensland . .	2,088,983	130,629	43,019	7,026
Tasmania . .	326,393	2,984	5	...
Australia . .	£15,820,811	£1,277,024	£844,659	£157,091
New Zealand .	3,992,359	394,233	78,034	12,696
	£19,813,170	£1,671,257	£922,693	£169,787

The total for these four countries it will be observed falls a long way short of the actual totals given in the table on page 74, but those include all the intercolonial trade. Nor can the figures be accepted in every case as absolutely reliable, because the same import may figure in the returns of two different colonies and not in the one only in which it was consumed. Stores destined for the Broken Hill mining district, for example, might be landed at Adelaide and included in the imports of South Australia as from the country of production. When crossing the border into New South Wales would they again be treated as from the country of origin, or as imports from South Australia? Such are the complications involved in the system prior to the establishment of the commonwealth.

Passing over the intervening period we now compare the figures[1] of the maximum and minimum

---

[1] Since the table following was compiled, the Board of Trade abstract for 1901 has been issued. Under ordinary circumstances Commonwealth trade would be treated as a unit the same as for the Dominion of Canada, but the regulations for the distribution of customs duties among the different states necessitates a strict account of the commerce of each, and the returns appear in the same form as before. There is no longer the same need, however, for strictness regarding purely intercolonial trade, and an increasing amount of this may escape registration and so affect the total. Under a common tariff the trade of each State is no longer of much interest to the outside world beyond showing the drift of things, and it will be sufficient to give the totals for comparison—

	Total.	United Kingdom.	United States.	Germany.	France.
Australia	£68,129,455	£25,237,032	£5,854,136	£2,799,956	£461,934
New Zealand	11,817,915	6,885,831	1,415,260	198,521	27,714
	£79,947,370	£32,122,863	£7,269,396	£2,998,477	£489,648

The feature is once more the rapid advance made by the United States.

with those for 1900, the last year, that is, under the separate State system.

Imports in 1900 from—

	Total.	United Kingdom.	United States.	Germany.	France.
New South Wales	£27,561,071	£9,923,117	£2,557,961	£1,105,664	£270,084
Victoria	18,301,811	7,055,028	1,461,880	778,056	207,783
South Australia	8,034,552	2,397,684	406,461	219,978	31,525
Western Australia	5,962,178	2,225,746	226,035	328,414	7,602
Queensland	7,184,112	3,100,706	357,124	270,783	39,714
Tasmania	2,073,657	628,663	25,253	3,942	...
Australia	£69,117,381	£25,330,944	£5,034,714	£2,706,837	£556,708
New Zealand	10,646,096	6,504,484	1,061,873	182,074	26,326
	£79,763,477	£31,835,428	£6,096,587	£2,888,911	£583,034

The most noteworthy feature of the Australian figures is the falling off in the imports from the United Kingdom and the gain from other countries, which betokens a certain amount of transfer of trade. This is fully confirmed by the returns of the actual exporting countries, which are useful for comparison as a check against any duplication on the part of the Australian colonies. Of course there must be discrepancies apart from different bases of valuation, for one thing because the year of shipment from one country and arrival in another differs over a certain period, and indirect shipments may be wrongly classified at one end or the other. Taking first the British exports to Australia, the following are the official Board of Trade returns for the years mentioned on page 74, though they are not in

every case the highest and lowest respectively
according to the British figures :—

British Exports to	Maximum Year.	Minimum Year.	1900.
New South Wales .	£9,872,187	£5,578,466	£9,357,426
Victoria . . .	8,761,588	4,344,848	6,314,729
South Australia .	2,620,158	1,714,793	2,172,145
Western Australia .	590,348	561,154	2,340,395
Queensland . .	3,017,665	1,848,293	2,726,034
Tasmania . . .	697,317	331,381	634,836
Australia . . .	£25,559,263	£14,378,935	£23,545,565
New Zealand . .·	3,884,829	3,443,688	5,899,292
	£29,444,092	£17,822,623	£29,444,857

The higher Australian valuations given in the
preceding tables are of course accounted for by the
addition of freight and other charges.

Foreign countries do not distinguish in their
trade returns between the different colonies, but
classify Australia and New Zealand as one country
of destination.

Exports to Australia and New Zealand.

From [1]	Maximum Year.		Minimum Year.		1900.
United States[2] }	(1891)	£2,768,350	(1893)	£1,546,300	£5,747,670
Germany	(1891)	1,474,350	(1893)	898,150	2,395,950
France	(1885)	304,000	(1893)	72,360	329,480
		£4,546,700		£2,516,810	£8,473,100

[1] Exchanges to £ sterling, $4.90, marks 20, francs 25.
[2] United States official returns for calendar, not fiscal, years.

The question next arises to what extent these increased foreign exports are pure encroachment on British trade or merely a reflection of increased purchases of Australian products by the respective countries.

But before proceeding to analyse the Australian export movement it is necessary to realise that it is more misleading than the import when judged by separate colonies. The following table for the year 1900 shows how the value of the exports was swollen by intercolonial trade and transhipment :—

Exports from	Total Value.	Value of Home Produce only.
New South Wales .	£28,164,516	£18,873,488
Victoria . .	17,422,552	13,918,556
South Australia .	8,191,376	3,770,983
Western Australia .	6,852,054	6,639,827
Tasmania . .	2,610,617	2,595,309
Queensland .	9,581,562	9,354,689
Australia . .	£72,822,677	£55,152,852
New Zealand .	13,246,161	13,055,249
	£86,068,838	£68,208,101

The value of the actual exports of Australia therefore, for 1900, was not £72,822,677, nor even £55,152,852, because of the smaller item no less than £19,540,093 was shipped to other Commonwealth States. A considerable, indeed the greater portion of this was eventually exported over sea as well, but a portion was retained for consumption in the States to which it was sent, and from an Australian point of view was not foreign trade at all, and under the Commonwealth ought not to be returned as such. On the other hand, the whole of the New Zealand export is to be counted as foreign trade, even when directed to Australia, as the country is entitled to, and actually receives, credit in full. But the oversea shipments of Australia would bring it at the outside credits for £50,000,000, or about two-thirds of the total value of its recorded exports. Of that sum too, upwards of £12,500,000 was gold, so that the available products which Australia had to dispose of abroad, animal, vegetable, and mineral, other than gold, did not exceed £37,500,000 for the year 1900.

Australian exports, as we have already observed, were not checked, but rather stimulated, by the financial crisis of 1893. The staple product however, wool, has been affected by another cause, drought, which has played terrible havoc, especially in what are become known as the Riverina districts, but fortunately for the growers the decreased quantity was accompanied by a great rise in prices, which at its height went a long way to compensate for the deficiency. New South Wales realised £11,738,607 for 240,019,494 lbs. of wool shipped in 1899, whereas the previous highest figure was £11,312,980 for 340,691,382 lbs. in 1891, but the whole of it was not in either instance actually produced in the colony. Several of the other colonies were less fortunate. Queensland showed a decline from 105,228,383 lbs. worth £4,262,471 in 1892, to 52,536,042 lbs. valued at £2,138,756 in 1901, and this was all home grown, while later returns will, it is to be feared, prove more unfavourable still in quantity if not in value. Victoria and South Australia suffered less severely, but still perceptibly, while on the other hand New Zealand not having been subjected to the visitation, maintained, though it has not of late years increased, its production of the fleecy staple, principally on account of the great expansion in the exports of frozen and chilled mutton which has checked the growth of the flocks.

The Australian export trade, however, is affected by other considerations as well as prosperity or adversity at home, such as the establishment of steamship lines. Germany first subventioned its service to Australia in conjunction with one to the Far East in 1885, and France was also by that time subsidising the Messageries Maritimes. The United States opened up direct communication across the Pacific with the Australian continent somewhere about 1882. The year 1886, therefore, may be taken as a starting-point to study this branch of the trade, followed by 1892 as coming just before the crisis, finishing with 1900 as the last year of the separate State system, with 1896 as a convenient resting - place between. The recorded

6

exports are, according to Australian returns, as follows :—

To United Kingdom.

From	1886.	1892.	1896.	1900.
New South Wales	£6,026,954	£7,653,915	£8,375,883	£8,273,272
Victoria . .	6,566,118	7,599,501	6,704,104	6,363,685
South Australia .	2,553,583	3,167,298	2,286,740	2,325,519
Western Australia	505,331	395,700	508,755	4,268,419
Queensland .	1,288,851	4,096,937	3,559,058	3,271,656
Tasmania . .	247,442	315,836	173,867	688,600
Australia . .	£17,188,279	£23,229,187	£21,608,407	£25,191,151
New Zealand .	4,587,434	7,483,618	7,541,981	10,259,342
	£21,775,713	£30,712,805	£29,150,388	£35,450,493

Exports from Australia and New Zealand.

To	1886.	1892.	1896.	1900.
United States .	£903,976	£2,316,651	£2,686,656	£5,236,180
Germany .	127,595	1,778,487	1,541,567	1,666,722
France .	318,606	1,858,657	2,425,581	1,927,043
	£1,350,177	£5,953,795	£6,653,804	£8,829,945

Imports into the United Kingdom from Australia and New Zealand, allowing for additions of freight and charges, do not greatly differ in the aggregate from the foregoing figures, but in consequence of overland movements from one State to a port in another, the details vary very considerably. But the imports similarly recorded by the other countries show very material discrepancies, as will be seen from the following :—

Imports from Australia and New Zealand.

Into United	1886.	1892.	1896.	1900.
States[1] .	£787,550	£1,696,440	£1,357,470	£1,074,070
Germany .	501,000	4,274,000	5,160,200	5,879,250
France .	344,000 [2]	2,334,720	3,076,840	3,673,520
	£1,632,550	£8,305,160	£9,594,510	£10,626,840

The wide difference between these two tables requires some explanation. Gold, as a natural product of Australia, is included in its export returns as an ordinary commodity, and the principal item of export from Australia to the United States usually consists of gold. The latter country, however, classifies the import as bullion, and separates it from the merchandise returns, so that the recorded import represents consumable products only, and is almost entirely accounted for by wool, sheepskins, and tin. The balance of trade being so largely in favour of the United States, Australia very simply and naturally liquidates it in gold as an exchange operation, which of course is a very different matter to Great Britain paying for its imports in gold which it does not produce.

Gold will not account for the great discrepancy between the value of exports to Germany according to Australian returns and the imports into Germany as recorded by the German official figures. One explanation of it is to be found in the exports to

---

[1] United States official returns for calendar years.

[2] French imports from Australia in 1884 were as high as £1,268,000, but this was something quite exceptional.

Belgium, which in 1896 were valued at £1,323,369, and in 1900 at £1,012,648, most of which were destined ultimately for the interior of Germany, and merely used Antwerp as the most convenient port. Other indirect shipments, probably *viâ* England, must also figure in the German returns, which after making due allowance for freight must be accepted as the approximate value of Germany's custom to Australia rather than the latter's own estimate of it. The same remarks, in a minor degree, apply to France.[1]

In what may be described as regular trade, the United States have been making very rapid progress in supplying their own goods while taking but little from Australia in return. The reverse of this is the case with Germany and France, both importing far more largely from Australia than they export to it. While, therefore, the adoption by Australia of a tariff that would place the United States at a disadvantage with the rest of the world, or even with Great Britain, might not curtail trade in a manner necessarily injurious to Australia, its effect, if applied to Germany and France, would obviously be in that direction, because increased imports from

---

[1] The export figures for 1901 are as follows :—

	United Kingdom.	United States.	Germany.	France.
Australia .	£25,194,923	£3,373,876	£2,552,458	£2,309,247
New Zealand .	9,295,375	519,079	10,470	36
	£34,490,298	£3,892,955	£2,562,928	£2,309,283

Less gold was sent to the United States, but on the other hand the direct exports to the Continent of Europe, more especially Germany, decidedly increased.

those two countries are accompanied by expanding exports to them.

It is here that some distinction is necessary as regards New Zealand, because the direct exports to Germany and France as well as to the United States fall short of the imports from them, and the increase of export trade appears to have been almost entirely with Great Britain. Taking the extreme periods under review, the following figures show the position :—

	Imports from		*Exports to*	
	1886.	1900.[1]	1886.	1900.[1]
United Kingdom	£4,481,101	£6,504,484	£4,587,434	£10,259,342
United States .	£337,322	£1,061,873	£247,400	£458,796
Germany .	44,549	182,074	...	24,186
France .	14,846	26,326	...	15,601
	£396,717	£1,270,273	£247,400	£498,583

But the trade between New Zealand and Australia must also be taken into account. For the year 1900 the returns record the following exchanges between them :—

	Exports to	Imports from
New South Wales .	£1,192,570	£1,052,792
Victoria . . .	514,231	552,013
South Australia . .	28,899	29,116
Western Australia .	59,891	2,811
Tasmania . . .	27,643	41,196
Queensland . .	35,348	99,050
Australia . . .	£1,858,582	£1,776,978

[1] The corresponding figures for 1901 will be found in the footnotes to pages 76 and 84.

As far as the last four colonies are concerned, most of the turnover was probably local; that is, the exports were destined for consumption, while the imports were natural products such as sugar and fruit. But with New South Wales and Victoria the movement was largely a transit one, and by this means a good deal of New Zealand produce eventually finds its way to continental countries, though in the trade returns it is classified as with British possessions, and consequently falls as trade within the Empire. The opposite might be true as regards the imports, particularly of manufactured goods, that is, the bulk might be of foreign, not of British origin. But New Zealand buyers are able to supply their wants much quicker from Sydney or Melbourne than from London, and purchases of anything required urgently are made in this way, as there are usually large stocks to draw upon. New Zealand, along with Australia, probably exports more merchandise to foreign countries, exclusive of the United States, than it imports from them, despite the official record to the contrary.

Nor is the dependence of either Australia or New Zealand on foreign consumers limited to what they supply direct. Nearly everything imported from Canada into the United Kingdom is consumed there; hardly anything of it figures in the re-exports of foreign and colonial merchandise which is such an important item in British trade returns. But the products of Australasia do enter into it to a very material extent, and though there is no method of distinguishing the actual countries of origin, it may be taken for granted that Australasian produce accounts for a very considerable percentage of the following items of British re-export for 1900 and 1901 respectively.

Wool	. .	£7,428,121	£10,649,470
Copper	. .	1,425,625	1,628,980
Tallow	. .	1,232,649	1,278,928
Gum[1]	. .	757,658	732,021
Sheepskins	.	643,736	611,059
		£11,487,789	£14,900,458

The total value of Australian exports for the year 1900 was £72,822,677, but as we have already seen this would mean a net export of merchandise of not more than £37,500,000, or about one half. Now according to the table on page 82 the total value of Australian exports to Great Britain was £25,191,151, and as this included about half the gold, the net value of other produce would be £19,000,000. This is probably below the mark, because the value of merchandise imported into the United Kingdom from Australia for the same year was returned at £23,800,820, but this included freight and other incidental charges excluded from the Australian figures which amount to a considerable sum. Suppose, however, that the real value

[1] £208,978 and £152,163 of these items was declared as Kowrie gum, and was therefore of New Zealand origin.

be taken at £20,000,000, and that of this 25 per cent. was subsequently re-exported, this would mean that of the net export of Australian products other than gold, £15,000,000 was ultimately consumed by Great Britain, and the remaining £22,500,000 by foreign countries.

New Zealand presents a striking contrast to this. Of the total exports of £13,246,161 exhibited on page 79, £1,439,678 represented gold bullion, and of the merchandise exports, after the further deduction of a small quantity of specie, amounting to £11,744,711, upwards of £9,000,000 was shipped direct to the United Kingdom. Nor would anything like the same percentage of this be re-exported as in the case of Australia, and it may be asserted that whereas Australia is ultimately dependent on foreign countries as outlets for at least 50 to 60 per cent. of its exports, Great Britain absorbs more than 75 per cent. of those of New Zealand.

Thus a preferential tariff enforced by the Commonwealth of Australia in favour of Great Britain would operate to the detriment of customers who consume more than half its produce. Some of them of course would not be affected in any case, because what Australia imports from them Great Britain cannot supply. But it is no secret that such a tariff would be directed primarily against the United States and Germany, which are the real competitors of British manufacturers in colonial as well as foreign markets, and it is necessary therefore to inquire as to what branches of trade would likely be affected.

The United States have made the most serious encroachments. We saw on page 78 that their exports to Australia increased from £1,546,300 in 1893 to £5,747,670 in 1900, whereas their imports actually declined in that interval. Several items of the former which show large gains may be dismissed as non-competitive, such as kerosene, timber, and tobacco. No tariff manipulation would be likely to affect these to any appreciable extent as far as Great Britain is concerned, partly because they are natural productions of America, and in the cases of kerosene and timber either on the free list or subject to very moderate duties. But there are other things which must be distinctly displacing British goods, and an enumeration of the important items showing in American currency the increases between 1893 and 1900, is as follows :—

United States Exports to Australia and New Zealand.

	1893.	1900.
Agricultural implements	$294,429	$898,282
Carriages, Street Cars, etc.	258,479	871,268
Machinery	280,551	2,306,866
Saws and Tools	258,056	445,776
Wire for Fencing, etc.	47,443	1,300,736
Iron and Steel	640,960	2,853,641
Boots and Shoes	5,756	1,338,416
Cotton manufactures	80,629	622,228
Paper	353,280	1,540,306

All the above, as well as some minor items not enumerated, could undoubtedly be supplied by British manufacturers, and it may be reckoned that quite half the trade done by the United States results in the displacing of them. But agricultural implements, fencing wire, and machinery are to Australia as much raw material for the development of their industries as raw cotton or wool to Great Britain; they must be purchased where they can be obtained cheapest and best, and in order that no unnecessary additions may be made to the cost, are admitted free of duty. Cotton goods were likewise placed on the free list, but finally subjected to the very moderate duty of 5 per cent., though in any case the American trade in them is so utterly insignificant compared with the British, that Lancashire has no occasion whatever to tremble. In structural iron and steel, rails, hardware, boots and shoes, and paper, the competition is much more serious, but the question is, what percentage of the duty, where there is one, would be necessary to transfer the trade? These articles are partially subject to duty, but the Australian tariff at its worst is not an extravagantly high one. A preference to Great Britain would bring the protectionist and free trade parties into bitter conflict, the first in resistance to any reduction in duties which they look upon already as too low, the second opposed to any increase on rates they deem too high, if not wholly unnecessary. And in the end it may be doubted whether any manipulation of the tariff that the Federal Parliament could be reasonably expected to undertake would affect £1,000,000 of trade as between Great Britain and the United States, for if 33⅓ per cent. off the Canadian duties has had such a slight result, 10 per cent.—the figure suggested at the Colonial Conference—off Australian ones, which in many instances are lower to begin with, would hardly be appreciable.

Though the aggregate value of German exports to Australia is less than half that of the United States, the competition they represent with British manufacturers is even more acute, as there is scarcely anything included that is not produced in British workshops. But the problem to be dealt with here is different, because as we have already seen Australia really exports to Germany more than twice as much as is imported from it, and it may be taken for granted that any attempt to displace the goods of that country will be met by prompt retaliation, and the possible loss, and certain contraction, of the best market Australia has outside Great Britain. Even New Zealand is on the wrong side, for its paltry export of £24,186 recorded on page 85 must be ultimately swollen by indirect shipments through Australia and Great Britain to something considerably more than the £182,074 imported direct from Germany.

France is not a serious factor in the problem. The value of French goods imported into Australia is in any case insignificant, and where they are not special productions, such as wines, brandies, and fruits, are of a nature not likely to be affected by tariff considerations. Neither Australians nor anybody else buy French productions because they are cheap; more often indeed the reason is that they are dear, which is part of the charm of a luxury.

There are no other foreign countries with which it is desirable, even if it were practicable, for Australia to endeavour to restrict or transfer trade by means of tariff legislation. Social, apart from economic reasons, may create a prejudice against China and Japan, but it is hardly likely to go the length of suspending commercial intercourse with them. Besides, as far as China is concerned, a large part of the trade is with Hong-Kong and is classed under British possessions, not foreign countries. How very limited that intercourse is will be seen from the following detailed figures for 1900 :—

	Imports from—			*Exports to—*		
	Hong-Kong.	China.	Japan.	Hong-Kong.	China.	Japan.
New South Wales	£67,928	£190,456	£122,041	£218,986	£68,004	£133,989
Victoria	110,396	84,202	82,019	76,515	107,424	3,524
South Australia	6,846	6,673	10,208	7,485	283,073	467
Western Australia	1,191	...	...	20,833	14,227	...
Queensland	71,130	35,741	34,690	59,858	54,530	32,169
Australia	£257,491	£317,072	£248,958	£383,677	£527,258	£170,149
New Zealand	20,953	...	...	13,577	...	...
	£278,444	£317,072	£248,958	£397,254	£527,258	£170,149

The largest single item in this list, South Australia's export of £283,073 to China, is accounted for by silver and lead, of both of which the Chinese Empire usually absorbs large quantities.

There are political problems in the South Seas as well as elsewhere calculated to affect trade relationships. Questions affecting New Guinea and the New Hebrides threaten collision with foreign powers, while some of the archipelagos lying between Australia and the Asiatic mainland have not yet attained their final destiny, and are not likely to reach it without the intervention of Australian politicians. New Zealand, again, is eager to embrace within its administrative area the Fijian group of islands and others in the South Pacific now under direct control of the Imperial Government. But with the outcome of such matters we are not at present directly concerned beyond stating that whereas very little trade is done with the archipelagos, nearly the whole of that of the British South Sea islands passes through the States of Australasia. The New South Wales coalfields account for most of the trade done with foreign possessions in the Pacific.

There is another aspect of the Australian tariff issue which must not be overlooked : the relationship with other parts of the Empire than the United Kingdom. Arrangements come to between them are less likely to create friction with foreign powers than if concluded with Great Britain.

The breaking down of all tariff barriers between the Australian colonies was a matter of purely internal legislation which may nevertheless exert a material influence on foreign trade. Previously, the local manufacturers of Victoria or South Australia enjoyed no advantage in any other part of the continent over those of Great Britain, or the United States, or Germany ; now, the Commonwealth tariff and internal free trade combined give them a distinct advantage on everything they produce that is dutiable. Against such legislation no foreign Government has any ground for complaint, nor would it have if New Zealand chose to join the Commonwealth or entered into special commercial arrangements with it, because though the countries are twelve hundred miles apart, they are looked upon as possessed of a natural, quite distinct from any racial or political sympathy for one another.

Serious proposals, however, have been made that the Australian Commonwealth should enter into a preferential trade agreement with the Dominion of Canada, and this would raise more far-reaching issues. When it is stated that for the fiscal year ended 30th June 1902 Canada imported from the whole of Australasia, merchandise to the value of $156,735, and exported to it $2,940,290, it is not difficult to guess on which side the idea originated. But both countries have something to gain were anything of the sort adopted, though the advantage would continue distinctly on the side of the Dominion.

In considering this part of the subject the Canadian trade returns afford much better information than those compiled by Australia, inasmuch as they are inclusive, far more concise, and permit of easy comparison with the United States which would be the country principally affected.

In the first place, it is not easy to see what Australia has to gain, as a trade of less than £35,000 requires a good deal of expansion to make it worth anything. No less than $116,961 of the $156,735 of the Canadian import just alluded to consisted of free goods, and as Canada requires them for its own industries in very considerable quantities, there is not much probability of making them dutiable for the sake of any trade arrangement. Dominion manufacturers needed in the year 1902 10,360,738 lbs. of foreign wool, of which only 295,402 was obtained from Australian sources, and it is incredible that the tariff of either country would be interfered with in an attempt to rectify such a divergence. Skins and tin constitute most of what is left, and as the Australian contribution of each is again but a mere fraction of the total, the same objection rules good. Some dutiable commodities required by Canada and produced in Australia will have to be discovered to make an agreement feasible.

As the greater part of the production of both countries is within the temperate zone, and consequently very similar in character, there is little room for interchange. Australia does ship some frozen mutton, but that is a trade Canada can have no special desire to stimulate. But tropical Queensland has no counterpart in the Dominion, the whole of whose requirements of tropical produce require to be filled from outside. Sugar can hardly any longer be regarded as one of these, and Canada, like all other importing countries, gets most of what it wants from the European beet-growing districts. But cane sugar is a tropical speciality, and in some respects preferable to the rival beet. Queensland produces it in quantities that already demand an oversea outlet for the surplus, and as it is a dutiable commodity in Canada a preference can easily be given. A trifling quantity is already imported from Australia, but as the total consumption annually exceeds 150,000 tons and reaches in value nearly $10,000,000, there is evidently room for an enormous expansion in this particular trade. The preference given by Canada to the British West Indies has not proved very effective simply because the United States have offered a better one, but both the West Indies and Queensland are likely ere long to welcome the Dominion as a consumer.

Queensland then is the only part of the Commonwealth that would stand to gain anything considerable, and the other States may not regard the arrangement with any particular enthusiasm. But they most certainly owe Queensland a turn. The people of that colony long hesitated about joining the federation, and their worst fears as to its results appear to have been justified, for not only has the fiscal legislation of the Federal Parliament proved inimical to their interests, but the exclusion of coloured labour has been directed more especially against them. If compensation can be found, therefore, in an arrangement with Canada, Queensland is entitled to it.

Canada on the other hand has much to gain. Australian wheat harvests are apt at times to be deficient, necessitating imports of grain, and to a greater extent of flour. This is necessarily a fluctuating trade, but in 1897 the United States shipped 1,829,591 bushels of wheat, and 318,073 barrels of flour across the Pacific, as compared with 100,805 bushels and 91,641 barrels respectively from Canada, and as they are both similarly situated as regards this trade in almost every respect, Canada with very little encouragement might secure the bulk of the business when it is available in quantity. Indeed it is with the United States almost exclusively that competition would be waged, and a recapitulation of the respective shipments of the two countries to Australasia will show how much room there is for it. The figures in each case are for the fiscal year ended June 30, 1901.

7

	Canadian Exports. Value.	United States Exports. Value.
Flour	$209,947	$16,641
Canned Salmon . .	182,282	343,540
Cycles	252,283	207,740
Agricultural Implements	441,761	970,900
Musical Instruments .	68,955	253,402
Cotton Manufactures .	234,734	694,435
Boots and Shoes . .	11,471	1,421,251
Provisions . . .	11,778	96,773
Timber. . . .	371,213	1,540,541
Manufactures of Wood .	91,162	919,916
	$1,875,586	$6,465,139
Total of all Exports .	$2,311,405	$30,726,687

Eighty per cent., that is, of the Canadian exports
are in direct competition with the United States,
and as the trade in them is still more than three
to one in favour of the United States there is plenty
of room to make inroads into it. Of course with
regard to several of the items the same objections
apply as to Great Britain. Agricultural implements are on the free list, and would not be
affected unless removed from it, which is not desirable. In such articles as bicycles, musical instruments, and boots and shoes, which are among the
more highly rated articles, a preference given exclusively to Canada would be objected to by British
as well as German manufacturers. But leaving these
out there is ample opportunity for an arrangement
covering breadstuffs, fish, provisions, and manufactures of wood, which would be unobjectionable

from any point of view except a United States one, and neither Canada nor Australia have any cause for considering that country. Both, moreover, are protectionist in their fiscal policy and likely to continue so, so that there is no principle at stake as would be the case with Great Britain. Besides, the addition of £1,000,000 to the trade returns of any of the British Colonial possessions means a great deal more to them than it would to Great Britain.

The war brought both Canada and Australia into close contact with South Africa. The political causes or effects of this do not call for consideration here, only the situation as it actually exists. Assuming, however, that the future fiscal system of South Africa will include moderate duties on most classes of imports, there is no reason why it should not be included in a commercial agreement between the other two. But in this instance the utmost care will have to be taken to avoid anything in the nature of European jealousies. Not much of what Canada and Australia are able to supply South Africa with comes into competition with European producers, either British or Continental. It is the United States again that would be principally affected, and in face of their own world-wide aggressive attitude they have no just cause for complaint if occasionally they are successfully check-mated.

With no other British possessions beyond its

own geographical sphere does there seem room for Australia to enter into any successful commercial arrangement. The dealings are necessarily limited to actual requirements, and are in most cases non-competitive, and there is certainly no inducement from any advantages likely to accrue to justify a departure from the ordinary trade relations that already exist.

CHAPTER IV

South Africa Before and After the War

No portion of the British Empire presents a more difficult problem in its fiscal and trade arrangements than the one about to be considered. Twenty-two thousand lives and two hundred and fifty millions of money were expended in bringing these to an issue, because whatever political differences were made the ground of the war, it was the economic ones that really caused it; the question of taxation in South Africa having been more inextricably bound up with industry and commerce than in any other part of the world in modern times.

Yet the real issues are extremely simple; there is scarcely another country to be found where they are more so. South Africa has no manufacturing industries clamorous for protection, nor does there appear much prospect under existing conditions of establishing any, as the labour required for them finds much more lucrative employment in other directions. Unlike most comparatively new and undeveloped countries whose inhabitants or settlers early turn their thoughts to the production of food as a means of subsistence, South Africa remains content to import a great deal of what is consumed of even the commonest necessaries of life, while for clothing there is entire dependence on foreign spindles and looms. For the great majority of the population therefore, European and native alike, absolute free trade in imports would be the most favourable policy, but as the country requires to be governed and the cost of administration must be raised somehow, this is subject to the limitation of imposing duties at least for revenue purposes.

Then again the political divisions of the country are purely arbitrary. Were ring fences drawn round the Rand and Kimberley, the fiscal policy that suited one part would be about equally applicable to all the rest. There is no need even to exclude Rhodesia, because it is not yet by any means certain whether that State will not have to depend for prosperity on pastoral and agricultural, much more than on mining pursuits. As far as trade and taxation are concerned, there are no obstacles, outside the districts named, to a uniform system throughout, always subject of course to the special needs of localities to be provided for out of local resources. The two exceptions, however, are so important, as to raise the question whether they are to govern South Africa, or whether South Africa is to govern them.

That this is no visionary sketch of the situation is proved by the fact that before the outbreak of the war there was already a customs union in South Africa, which embraced not merely most of the territories subject to the British Crown, but independent ones like the Orange Free State as well. Rhodesia had not formally adhered to it, but was for most practical purposes a constituent. As far as those under Crown Colony Government are concerned, it was not a difficult matter to bring about such union with one or other of the self-governing States, because after all the inhabitants would have very little say in the matter. The progressive government of the Orange Free State quickly recognised the advantages to be derived from union; Natal, on the other hand, was recalcitrant, and only joined at the beginning of 1899, less than a year, that is, before the war broke out. Yet Natal had on the whole more to gain than any other State, inasmuch as several of its productions were limited to its own area, the other States having either to purchase from it or from countries beyond the sea.

On such commodities, therefore, Natal really enjoyed protection to the extent of the import duties that were levied. But like most small self-governing communities, it objected to sink any part of its identity in a larger one, even though it might be ultimately to its own advantage.

The Transvaal Republic of course remained outside and rejected all overtures to become a member of the union. This was entirely on political, and not on fiscal grounds, nor were the inhabitants handicapped thereby, because on the whole the fiscal policy of the Transvaal was more liberal than that of the union. The excessive cost of living in Johannesburg, of which so much was heard before the war, but has been increased rather than diminished since, certainly did not arise from any extortion on the necessaries of life imposed by the Boer Government. Moreover, there was a considerable agricultural and pastoral population helping by its production and competition to keep down that cost to a reasonable level. If no real obstacle existed before, there can hardly be any now that the Transvaal has passed under the same political control as the rest of South Africa.

The causes of commercial friction between the Transvaal and British South Africa were in reality other than fiscal. As an isolated State without a seaboard of its own, it was compelled to draw its foreign supplies through one or other of the surrounding territories, and as these were not all

British, opportunity was afforded for showing preference, if not favouritism. And that is what
actually happened, every effort having been made
to divert trade that usually passed through Cape
Colony or Natal to the Delagoa Bay route. The
success attending this may best be judged by the
return of the value of goods imported from oversea
into the Transvaal by the three routes, which for
the respective years was as follows :—

	1896.	1897.	1898.
Cape Colony .	£6,035,920	£4,184,439	£3,188,876
Natal . . .	1,554,427	2,330,020	1,843,543
Delagoa Bay .	1,674,031	2,658,222	1,781,252

Guns, ammunition and military stores of all
kinds account for a good deal of what went over
the third route, but these, along with other Government stores, are not included in the above figures,
but were returned separately, if at all, among
goods purchased at Lorenzo Marques. Goods
purchased elsewhere in South Africa and imported
into the Transvaal were not necessarily always of
South African production, though in the case of
the British possessions this probably was the case
to a very great extent, and of the Orange Free State
almost entirely so. The figures for these are also
available for 1896 and 1897, and are as follows :—

Inland Imports from	1896.	1897.
Cape Colony . .	£1,981,309	£1,427,447
Natal . . .	1,446,606	1,280,629
Orange Free State .	944,325	871,738
Delagoa Bay . .	451,512	811,332

Of the last item, all but £350,805 was acknowledged to be on account of the Transvaal Government and consisted probably of military and railway stores.[1]

This diversion led more than ever to political complications through attempts to close the drifts, which meant the public highways, against the passage of merchandise from Cape Colony into the Transvaal, but were always ultimately defeated. A more legitimate method was employed in the making of differential railway rates, the Transvaal railways being more more or less under the domination of the State authorities, and irrespective of distance, conveyance over them was much cheaper from the Portuguese boundary to the interior than from the corresponding British frontiers. Though objectionable, this was not illegal, and is only what is constantly done by countries wishing to favour commercial intercourse with one neighbour at the expense of another. France before to-day has granted special railway rates on coal from Belgium in order to assist Belgian colliery owners to oust their British rivals, yet this has never been regarded as

---

[1] The provisional figures for 1902 have been published, and are interesting for comparison with above. They make no distinction, however, between oversea and inland trade.

Viâ Cape Colony	.	.	.	.	.	£6,376,000
,, Natal	.	.	.	.	.	5,412,000
,, Delagoa Bay	.	.	.	.	.	1,280,000
						£13,068,000

sufficient cause for official protest, much less for interference.

Nor have the altered conditions in South Africa by any means obviated this difficulty, though they are calculated to reverse it; that is, trade that would naturally flow through Delagoa Bay may be diverted to Cape Colony or Natal instead, which will be no less objectionable from the point of view of the consumer of the Transvaal Colony than the other was from that of the British Colonies affected. Cape Colony provides the longest, and other things being equal, consequently the most expensive route, and, in conjunction with Natal, levied a transit duty of 3 per cent. on nearly everything that passed through its territory, allowing of course, like the others, the actual customs duty to be collected at destination. The Portuguese on the other hand permitted transit goods to pass through their territories entirely free of duty. The first attempt towards remedying this drawback was made immediately after the conclusion of the war, when it was proposed to reduce the transit duty to 1 per cent. in exchange for the concession that all British South African produce was allowed to enter the Transvaal free, but the arrangement unfortunately broke down. This is one of the many difficulties the new administration has to overcome, and it may not be easy to do justice to the Transvaal under pressure of the demands of those interested in

British, as distinct from the Portuguese possessions. Quite likely, the latter may be commercially controlled to a very large extent by British capital, which should at least ease the situation and permit of greater freedom without charges of undue favouritism.

These problems of inward trade presented no such intricacies as to render them incapable of solution by negotiation and the exercise of a little patience. They must be kept distinct from the more serious one of the monopolies, which were not only indefensible on economic grounds, but would have been far more difficult to get rid of. The war at anyrate settled these, and they are not likely to be revived again in quite their old vicious forms. They were vested interests, which experience has proved to be the most difficult things in the world to destroy. They were not invented in the Transvaal, and are, not entirely unknown in Great Britain to-day. Though fewer than they were, it took centuries of political agitation to uproot some of the worst. The tendency of the present day, if not exactly to re-establish the old, is at least to create new ones, which will in time be no less galling to those who have to bear the brunt. Democratic institutions afford no guarantee against them; the most consistently Republican of nations, the United States of America, is the one that has fallen most completely under their thraldom. Whatever may be the final outcome there, surely South Africa has had sufficient bitter experience to be entitled to have everything of the sort carefully and rigidly excluded from its future internal and external arrangements.

The export trade of South Africa can hardly be said to present any problems at all. There are few countries in the world that have so limited a variety of surplus products to dispose of. Gold and diamonds it yields in abundance, but while both excite more envy and jealousy than anything else the earth yields, neither creates any of that particular strife identified with the industrial warfare waged everywhere with such increasing intensity. As a matter of fact, most of the gold raised in South Africa is sent first of all to London, but that does not help Great Britain to conquer the trade of the world. In this respect both the United States and Germany appear to be outstripping it, and though the former have gold supplies of their own to draw upon, the latter has absolutely none at all, yet gets all it requires, and actually holds in its banking reserves much more of the metal than Great Britain. Great Britain indeed makes no effort to retain what it gets, and allows it to flow out as freely as it flows in, only regulating the flow by an occasional movement in the Bank rate, which has absolutely nothing whatever to do with the question of production, and is rarely influenced by anything that happens in gold-producing countries other than the United States, where it is but an insignificant industry compared with most others.

Nor does the receipt of the metal in London or elsewhere ensure the return trade. That, to some extent, may depend on the political connection, and would doubtless do so to an even greater were any other country than Great Britain the virtual owner of South Africa. Were other countries largely to increase their export trade to South Africa, it is quite possible that some of the gold would go to them in payment direct, indeed this is actually occurring with the Argentine Republic; but were the whole of the gold to be divided in the first instance between the United States, Germany, and France, instead of being sent to Great Britain, British trade would not necessarily be affected to the slightest extent. The United States have not in recent years materially increased their exports to Australia because Australia sent them gold. Cause and effect were reversed; Australia sends the gold because the United States have increased their exports to it, though quite likely trade has been facilitated by this opportunity for liquidation. South Africa is sure of a market for its gold at all times and under almost any circumstances, and wants no artificial channel cutting to ensure its regular outflow.

This advantage arises from gold having a fixed value, a privilege shared by no other commodity. Indeed gold only enjoys it theoretically; it was worth less at the end of the war than it was at the beginning, because in the interval prices of nearly all other commodities rose. This, in the ordinary course of events, would reduce the profits of production in South Africa, and though in this particular instance there was expected to be a set off in economies not previously possible, it is becoming more and more doubtful whether they can be enforced. But in any case South Africa will not have to seek customers for its gold, nor will any possible competition that may arise for it affect its nominal value.

Diamonds are not by any means so favourably situated. Under ordinary circumstances the value would fluctuate for the same reasons that affect most other commodities; under the existing monopoly it is steadily maintained, and it is the output that is regulated. But there is no more object in diverting the trade in diamonds than there would be in gold, and were it to be decreed that all produced in British territory should be sent to London and distributed from there, that would probably only further tighten the grip of the present monopolists without any advantage to the community at large. It might, of course, be made the means of obtaining revenue, but that could be more easily and economically accomplished by levying a duty on the export. This is already done to the extent of $\frac{1}{2}$ per cent. of the value as a registration tax, which may at any time be substantially increased, the monopoly itself affording the best guarantee against fraud, so easily perpetrated when dealing with anything of great value occupying little space.

With gold and diamonds out of the way there is but little left. The food produced in South Africa is wanted for local consumption and leaves no surplus for export, nor can the British Empire look to it for a long time to come to furnish any of the deficiency of its supplies. Like Australia, however, it affords great pastoral facilities, and were it not for its mineral resources would be valued for these almost exclusively. The export of wool is thus a considerable item, but like other wool-growing countries it must eventually depend on many other consumers than Great Britain, even though the produce should, in the first place, all pass through British markets. Goats as well as sheep are a feature of the South African veldt, and their hair forms another fairly important article of commerce. The skins both of sheep and goats when killed, and the animals themselves when alive, go to swell the total trade, which all told does not often exceed £4,000,000, a striking contrast to Australia with its annual normal export of sheep products amounting to over £20,000,000.

South Africa has another speciality besides diamonds, namely ostriches, and the export of the feathers also yields a considerable sum. Just as rubies, or emeralds, or any other precious stones never quite outshine diamonds, so there is nothing that takes the place of the ostrich plume, and in this respect the industry is almost a monopoly. It is intended to keep it so too, as irrespective of whether there is any other country where the bird would thrive so well, every obstacle is thrown in the way of trying the experiment. An export duty, or, to use the correct term, a fine of £100 is imposed on every bird sent out of the country, and this makes experiments too costly to be undertaken. And lest some foreign bird should have the temerity to attempt to hatch an egg disregardless of consequences, a fine of £5 each is imposed on the export of these; a prohibitive tax in face of the extreme probability that when the egg was successfully transported elsewhere it would turn out to be addled. On the whole then, this particular industry may be regarded for the present as tolerably safe and not in need of the extension of favours by any other country. It depends on the general state of prosperity throughout the world and the ability to spend money on luxuries.

Except minerals, there is scarcely anything else of sufficient export value to be worth noticing. Gold and diamonds do not by any means exhaust these; copper has long been a product of the country, and the mines have proved exceedingly profitable to the owners, while rumour places Rhodesia as eventually one of the richest copper producing areas in the world. Coal, too, is everywhere found in more or less abundance, but when far inland can only be economically utilised for local purposes. In Natal, however, it is found sufficiently near the seaboard to be of use for export, and the demand for it is steadily growing. As

8

recently as 1890 the quantity disposed of in this way was under 10,000 tons, whereas in 1899 it had increased to 163,610 tons. Owing to the collieries being located in the portion of the colony where the war waxed hottest during the early part of the campaign, work was suspended during the closing months of 1899 and the opening ones of 1900, with the result that both output and export were reduced, the latter falling to 112,625 tons valued at £139,381. But with full resumption, the figures rose with a bound in 1901 and nearly trebled in value, the total production reaching 567,460 tons. This is a trade dependent largely on the expansion of South Africa which will result in increased steamship communication with all parts of the world. A successful attempt has also been made to bunker steamers at Delagoa Bay with Transvaal coal, but this trade is necessarily somewhat limited.

Under any circumstances South Africa does not require preferential treatment from any country with which it is accustomed to trade. It would be no use, for instance, for Great Britain to impose a duty on foreign diamonds and ostrich feathers and admit those from South Africa duty free. And South Africa might have more to lose than to gain from such a favour shown its wool and sheepskins, because it might result in a restriction of the number and importance of the markets now freely open to them.

Whether there is anything to gain by according such treatment to any of the countries from which it imports, is a question not quite so easily answered. There cannot be anything in reciprocity, which is generally supposed to be the only basis for preferential trade, though the Dominion of Canada has conclusively disproved this. But sentiment in such matters counts for a good deal if properly applied. The Canadian preferential tariff, as we have previously had occasion to discover, whatever else it may have effected, has not prevented the imports from Great Britain falling to the lowest percentage of the total ever recorded, yet it has probably gained for the Canadian producer and exporter far more tangible advantages than if Great Britain had responded by reciprocal action. The idea caught hold of the public mind, and whereas previously everything from the Western hemisphere was American, now there is discrimination between Canadian and American, and the former is always supposed to possess the better flavour. Canada has thus been a distinct gainer, first by securing a reduction in the price of many of its imports through rebate in duty, and next by the greatly increased popularity of its own commodities. But the result might have been very different if, instead of paying less through a rebate, it had had to pay more by an increase of already existing duties.

South Africa, unlike Canada, has nothing to gain in meal or in malt as far as any increased demand for its products is concerned. But it may secure, nevertheless, by tariff arrangements, material advantage for itself, and at the same time confer it on other constituent parts of the Empire. Food is the first and most essential want of the country, and is likely to continue so for an indefinite period to come. Within the customs union this necessity is used for the purpose of raising considerable revenues, the duties levied being high. Wheat and other breadstuffs including maize are rated at 2s., and flour at 4s. 6d. a cental, cured meats such as bacon and hams 2d. a pound, fresh meats 1d. to 2d., butter and cheese 3d.; raw sugar, 3s. 6d. cane, 5s. beet, per 100 lbs.; while a commodity like tea is charged 6d., and coffee in the berry $\frac{3}{4}$d., roasted or ground 2d. The *ad valorem* rates in these instances work out at tolerably high figures, 30 per cent. and upwards, and are in striking contrast with the $7\frac{1}{2}$ per cent. on most manufactured articles that are not actually free. At first sight this appears altogether unjustifiable, and the policy pursued by the Transvaal Republic in rating these commodities at $7\frac{1}{2}$ per cent. only was much more lenient. It is true there were on some articles nominally heavy specific duties as well, but these, except for luxuries, were nearly always in abeyance, and consequently exercised no real influence except for purposes of agitation.

Taxation of the commonest necessaries of life is both unsound and unwise, unless under very special circumstances, but a little consideration of the prevailing conditions in South Africa may possibly afford evidence that such exception in this case does actually exist.

In a densely populated country like Great Britain, or one with densely populated areas like the United States, dear food must, under the most favourable circumstances, be accompanied by great hardship to the poorer section of the community, and any artificial addition to its price is absolutely inexcusable. The submerged portion of the great cities, whenever there is no work for it, or, as more frequently occurs, when it does not desire work, cannot be turned out to get its living on the land; in Great Britain because there is no suitable land available for it, even were it suitable for the land, and in the United States for the second rather than the first of these two reasons. But a country like South Africa not only possesses an abundance of land, but has few dense centres of population in which to breed an anæmic element. Loafers there are sure to be wherever there is a town of any magnitude, but the only legislation to which they are supposed to be entitled is of a penal character, and it matters very little to them whether bread is dear or cheap; the price of beer is of much greater interest.

Again, in a country like the United States accession to the land means an increase of surplus production, and as such accessions when coming from town populations are more likely than not to be in times of commercial and industrial depression, addition to the surplus is anything but desirable from the producers' point of view. But in South Africa, where there is a standing deficiency, increased production creates no such surplus, and is consequently disposed of without difficulty. The town dweller in such a country, therefore, who finds himself deprived of regular employment can have recourse to the land, which is everywhere within easy reach, and at least produce his own food. The occupation may be uncongenial, and, in a country where black labour is used in the menial departments of agriculture, not altogether desirable, but it removes him beyond the fear of starvation whatever the cost of food may be.

The wages of labour employed in non-food producing occupations is therefore a very important factor in settling the economic price of food. If they are very low, as in India, food is wanted at the cheapest rate at which it can be obtained; if very high, as in South Africa, this is of much less consequence. The high cost of living in the Transvaal necessitated high wages, but it is absurd to contend that a $7\frac{1}{2}$ per cent. import duty on foodstuffs was the cause of either. With a wage for the most ordinary skilled labour averaging from 20s. to 25s. a day, and a demand for unskilled white labour at 5s. a day and all found, a halfpenny on a four pound, or even a two pound loaf, does not count, especially as the labourer has usually only himself to feed, his wife and family, if he have them, living very likely elsewhere under much more economical conditions. Two shillings a cental on breadstuffs and twopence a pound on meat become no hardship to such a man, whereas the barest impost on the necessaries of another earning half his daily wage in a week, and with many mouths dependent on him, results in positive starvation.

From the South African working man's point of view indeed, it is a question whether this somewhat higher cost of food caused by the duty is not a positive advantage. Were it reduced, it would afford his employer the excuse for reducing wages to an even greater extent, and as a matter of fact the question of the cost of living is regarded much more seriously by the capitalists who recognise that this tax, whatever it amounts to, falls on them, than by the working classes, who while elsewhere generally the victims, are in this instance rather the beneficiaries. Sir David Barbour in his report on the finances of the Transvaal and Orange River Colony dated Bloemfontein the 29th March 1901, clearly recognised this, and advocated the abolition of all duties on food purely from the point of view of industrial, or in other words mining interests. He was actuated probably by two motives, a strong prejudice in favour of doctrinaire free trade ideas, and a wish to reduce the cost of gold production to the lowest possible point, quite as

much on the economic ground of its being sound
policy as from any desire to further enrich the
capitalists.

So long as conditions remain much as they were
before the war, there is no reason why a moderate
revenue should not be raised from foodstuffs, levied
on something like the basis already existing within
the customs union.   In one paragraph of his report
Sir David Barbour writes : " But strong objections
are entertained in the Transvaal with reference to
the tariff in force in the union on the ground that
it favours the rural population at the expense of the
urban and mining population, and for other reasons.
The objections appear to me to be well founded
and I cannot recommend that the Transvaal should
join the customs union at the present time." But
a good deal has happened since this was written.
The sentiment of almost the entire British population at that time was in favour of the industrial,
and opposed to the agricultural interest, represented
entirely by the Boers.   The commission was intrusted
to Sir David Barbour under the impression, so em-
phatically asseverated in the autumn of 1900, that the
war was over and the Boers entirely defeated and
at the mercy of their victorious foe.   Under those
circumstances financial aid such as that granted by
the actual terms of peace ultimately agreed upon
would have been scouted, and more likely than not
heavy taxation imposed instead.   The necessities
certainly were not so great then as they subse-

quently became, but a grant of £5,000,000 and of
free loans to a further unlimited extent, prove the
importance attached by the British Government,
entirely endorsed by the nation, to the re-establish-
ment of agricultural prosperity at the earliest
possible moment.

But what is the use of spending and lending
so freely, if from the very first the recipients of
the bounty are to be subjected to the keenest
competition from all the rest of the world? Production is hardly likely for some years to come
to be on the most economical basis, if for no other
reason than that the high remuneration of industrial
labour affords strong counter attractions to the work
of the farm and the veldt. South Africa, moreover,
or to localise it more exactly, the Transvaal Colony,
has to find money for developments which will
simply be thrown away if not rendered properly
effective in the end. This means that taxes must
be raised, and from industrial and not agricultural
sources, as no war taxation is to be imposed on the
land. Inasmuch, therefore, as a moderate tax on
food will not, in the near future at anyrate, press
severely on the consumer, it seems to be in the
interest of the colony itself that one should be
levied, because not only will it be a source of
revenue, possibly a substantial one if the population
increases at anything like the rate that is anticipated, but it will at the same time be calculated
to raise the profits of agriculture to a nearer level

with those of mining and other undertakings in which they are likely to be large.

This is all the more desirable where a great industrial community is located in the heart of a continent. The cost of transport across five hundred or a thousand miles of mostly undeveloped country is itself no inconsiderable item, and it must eventually be in the interests of such a community to stimulate the production nearer home, even if to begin with the process is somewhat expensive. And a comparatively high cost of living will not be without its negative advantages if it deters the invasion of the colony by a horde of adventurers, eager to pick up a living by dishonest, in preference to honest means. It would not be the first experience of the sort the Transvaal has had to undergo.

The self-governing communities of Cape Colony and Natal are not likely to be willing to alter their tariff in the interests of the Transvaal, more especially as the Orange River Colony in its previous state of independence found no objection to it. A customs union of the whole of South Africa therefore, desirable in every respect, can only be effected by the accession of the Transvaal on something like existing terms, and there is no reason why the higher duties on foodstuffs should be allowed to block the way to a speedy accomplishment that will benefit most people concerned who are British subjects. Two shillings a cental on grain and twopence a pound on meat ought to, if they do not actually, afford a very substantial measure of protection to the home producer, when taken in conjunction with the high cost of transport, though the great distances in South Africa tell against the local farmer as well as his foreign competitor unless he is somewhere within easy reach of the consuming centre, or railway communication with it.

Thus the tariff on foodstuffs may well be halved in favour of countries within the British Empire, and this would almost certainly mean a corresponding reduction in the price to the consumer. Canada produces far more breadstuffs and hog products, and Australia and New Zealand more dairy produce and dead meat than are sufficient to supply the whole of the requirements of South Africa, and South Africa would consequently continue to enjoy the full benefits of unrestricted competition. What the other colonies would gain would not be so much increase in price of what they had to sell, as the assurance of an important market at current market rates, because their foreign competitors would have to accept less by the amount of the rebate in the duty to get in.

Were the countries within the Empire unable to supply the whole of such requirements the case would of course be different, as the cost to the consumer would then be based on that paid for the deficiency, which would at once enable the

British producer, or more likely some middleman, to secure the extra profit represented by the difference in the duty. As this would be almost certain to result in recrimination, anything of the sort is to be avoided, and such concessions in the tariff should only be made where there is no risk of this happening.

Until just before the war, direct commercial intercourse between South Africa and the outlying portions of the Empire, other than India, was exceedingly limited. Canadian exports, for instance, never reached $250,000 in value, and were generally only about half this figure. But Canada is by no means favourably situated geographically, whereas Australia is, and accordingly did a good deal better, the exports before the war having already exceeded £750,000, exclusive of gold, in a single year, and trade was rapidly expanding with the establishment of a regular line of steamers the latter part of 1898. Military exigencies caused a material improvement in both instances, as was observed in the chapter dealing with Canada, but the returns are hardly likely to be repeated as regards the Dominion since the war is over, unless the newly subsidised steamship service proves particularly successful. The foundation has certainly been laid for more permanent intercourse, inasmuch as from merely nominal figures, the shipments of breadstuffs and provisions rose in the respective years to $162,802 and $122,792. These are still a very long way behind the United States, whose corresponding supplies in the two years were valued at $4,839,298 for the first and $4,206,353 for the second, so that there is room for considerable expansion.

The improvement in the figures for Australasia was still more marked, but this is accounted for to a large extent by specie, South Africa instead of continuing gold producing becoming suddenly, though temporarily, gold absorbing, and a considerable portion of the coin required for financing the war was shipped direct from Australia. Still the disputes regarding the meat contracts for the supply of the army, in which Australia took so prominent a part, are hardly likely to be forgotten, and prove at least that that country is well able to furnish what South Africa requires in this way, though as far as cereals are concerned the ability is more doubtful, at any rate until the drought is permanently broken. The actual figures of the trade under recent conditions are of very little value, because whatever is done in future must be under totally different ones.

The trade between India and South Africa has always been a natural one, and, consisting principally of rice and gunny bags, is not likely to be subject to the vicissitudes of the tariff.

To what extent the Transvaal was formerly responsible for the import of foodstuffs was shown in a special article on "The Trade and Shipping of South Africa" in the *Board of Trade Journal* for December 1898, the figures having been compiled from official sources. They include a great deal of South

African, as well as foreign produce, but there is nothing to distinguish between them, though all the cattle may be taken as of local origin. Cape Colony and Natal found the Rand a profitable customer for their products, while the bulk of the exports of the Orange Free State, other than diamonds and wool, had their destination there, enjoying indeed special tariff privileges, thus establishing that close bond of union which no disaster was capable subsequently of severing.

Transvaal Imports for—

	1895.	1896.	1897.
Butter	£87,728	£122,245	£158,867
Cattle	484,761	488,569	714,068
Cheese	20,589	27,308	28,702
Eggs	24,163	39,969	51,813
Jams and Confectionery	19,164	26,393	31,626
Meal, Grain, Flour, and Corn . . .	304,626	372,150	360,574
Mealies (Indian Corn) .	189,306	481,840	273,506
Pork	17,015	51,943	60,568
Provisions and Groceries	180,855	263,309	299,253
Other Foodstuffs . .	143,460	324,680	348,675
	£1,471,667	£2,198,406	£2,327,652

But what is actually produced in South Africa and shipped from one State to another does not affect the purely foreign commerce. Much of the food imported from oversea is consumed elsewhere than in the Transvaal. Cape Colony, Natal, and the Orange Free State dispose of so much of their own produce that they are compelled to make good the deficiency created for themselves with foreign supplies, the extent of which will be seen from the succeeding table. The years are not identical with the preceding one, except in one instance, but go to a later date. For ordinary trade purposes 1899 is the last that is of any use; even that was affected by the war, though it was too late for any striking figures resulting from it to have appeared in the South African returns until the year following. The import valuations for the three years during which activity in the mining industry was at its height were as follows :[1]—

	Cape Colony—			*Natal—*		
	1897.	1898.	1899.	1897.	1898.	1899.
Butter . . .	£196,759	£163,771	£137,236	£50,514	£87,142	£85,195
Cheese . . .	58,134	70,658	67,181	..	..	22,245
Flour and Meal .	67,269	73,738	64,070	174,329	239,244	177,662
Wheat . . .	652,656	837,285	503,911	..	28,058	4,938
Maize and Indian Meal . . .	137,089	171,580	173,678	100,891	48,650	114,156
Rice . . .	79,603	85,290	85,085	52,146	102,389	101,337
Meats, salted, cured, and preserved .	181,428	193,989	245,027	83,091	88,424	122,869
Meat, chilled .	..	..	120,389	..	28,555	46,666
Fish, preserved .	89,453	104,277	103,851	..	19,527	39,225
Milk, preserved .	174,247	149,078	160,290	..	75,349	74,420
Sugar . . .	423,382	432,660	525,979	..	..	..
Tea	79,051	101,169	74,418	13,288	18,451	18,643
Coffee . . .	337,349	241,192	244,332	56,419	42,044	37,888
Confectionery and Preserves . .	98,488	93,826	98,408	23,753	62,169	53,741
	£2,574,908	£2,718,513	£2,603,855	£554,431	£840,002	£898,935

What were the sources of supply of these commodities? One does not usually expect to find Great Britain among the exporters of agricultural

[1] The statistics are taken from the regular abstracts and tables published by the Board of Trade unless some other source is specially designated.

and food products, yet in this instance it occupies a very conspicuous place in the list. The explanation is, that they were largely re-exports of foreign and colonial merchandise, and that facilities of steamship communication as well as the general importance of the trade connection between the two countries made this often the most economical method of obtaining supplies. This will no doubt undergo considerable alteration in the future as direct communication with other parts of the world is opened up, and British exporters are destined to lose a good deal of that portion of their trade. A preferential tariff, too, like the one suggested, would greatly accelerate the movement, as it would be necessary to divide the sheep from the goats, that is, colonial from foreign produce, which is not so easily done when both are supplied from the same source. Only the details for 1899 are given in this instance.

	United Kingdom.	Australia.	United States.	Sundries.
Butter	£25,386	£146,332	£3,418	£19,731 [1]
Cheese	18,130	...	...	62,968 [1]
Flour	1,312	88,195	129,188	...
Wheat	6,751	217,230	283,935	...
Maize and Meal . .	...	...	153,112	124,208 [2]
Rice	13,154	...	...	168,081 [3]
Meat, salted and preserved . . .	141,616	44,540	155,031	...
Meat, fresh . . .	...	158,462	...	...
Fish, preserved . .	119,953	...	11,890	...
Milk ,, . .	219,319	3,443	...	6,871 [1]
Confectionery and Preserves . . .	127,139	...	3,670	2,177 [1]
	£672,760	£658,202	£740,244	

[1] Holland.   [2] Argentine Republic.   [3] India.

The most noteworthy feature of this table is the rapid decline in the butter trade with the United Kingdom and Holland in favour of Australia. In the years 1897 and 1898 respectively, not to go back any further, the imports from Australia were valued at £70,240 and £89,324, whereas from the United Kingdom the figures were £90,994 and £98,232, and from Holland £26,756 and £27,652. Holland enjoys almost a monopoly of the market for cheese, and for obvious reasons will be difficult to displace unless Canada or some other country can successfully imitate the special make and flavour. The wheat in the two previous years, when the imports were much larger, was nearly all from the United States, but Australia has an excellent chance of competing when it has a surplus, and Canada ought to be able to make headway. Cape Colony takes nearly all the breadstuffs it wants in the form of wheat, Natal as flour, where it is for the time being admitted for local consumption duty free, and for 1897 and 1898 the same state of things existed as with wheat.

Natal produces annually some 25,000 tons of sugar, sufficient to supply its own requirements and leave a surplus for the Cape as well, but the latter gets most of what it wants from the island of Mauritius. The proportion of refined sugar imported is only small, and is obtained from the regular beet - producing countries. Despite the

9

direct connection between South Africa and India, most of the tea is imported from the United Kingdom, and what is obtained direct from country of production is of China growth. Natal also grows a little, the production having reached about 1,500,000 lbs. The great bulk of the coffee is in the raw state and imported from the Brazils.

To show how important this re-export business is to Great Britain, the figures follow of the shipments of British and foreign commodities respectively :—

Exports to Cape Colony.

	1897.	1898.	1899.
British Produce and Manufactures	£9,976,849	£9,144,420	£8,380,547
Foreign and Colonial Merchandise	789,319	720,714	627,484
	£10,766,168	£9,865,136	£9,008,031

Exports to Natal.

	1897.	1898.	1899.
British Produce and Manufactures	£3,407,088	£3,055,390	£2,989,578
Foreign and Colonial Merchandise	214,285	227,141	211,671
	£3,621,373	£3,282,531	£3,201,249

It is certain, moreover, these figures do not represent the real values, as the amounts included in the British returns for such things as provisions, condensed milk, grain and flour are suspiciously large, and owe their British origin more, probably, to the labels and marks on the packages, or to some finishing touch given them, than to actual production within the United Kingdom.

It will be apparent from the foregoing figures that a South African preferential tariff, so constructed as to place all countries of the British Empire on an equal footing, is likely in the first place to be detrimental to Great Britain itself. It may lead to an increased consumption of Australian and Canadian breadstuffs and provisions and dairy products at the expense of the United States, but these colonies will supply them direct, instead of, as at present, largely through the intervention of British exporters, who no doubt realise the advantages of closer imperial union, and will not permit the sordid interests of their pockets to interfere with their patriotism.

But what about the very large sum of British produce and manufactures given in the preceding table? Where these do not consist of consumables; drinkables as well as eatables, they are mostly subjected to very moderate duty, when not actually on the free list. Seven and a half per cent. *ad valorem* was the prevailing rate throughout the South African customs union, as well as under the laws of the Transvaal Republic, and as a means of protection would be laughed to scorn in every protectionist country. Whatever may be the object of the duties on foodstuffs, a moderate revenue is all that is aimed at from those on manufactures, and while concessions of a shilling a cental and a penny a pound would in most instances be very substantial, and prove effective in diverting trade, $2\frac{1}{2}$ or $3\frac{3}{4}$ per cent. on more or less high-priced goods would not necessarily do so to anything like the same extent. We have seen already that in the case of Canada $33\frac{1}{3}$ per cent. of much higher duties, working out at 8 to 12 per cent., has not succeeded in accomplishing this, and though no country may be quite so favourably situated to South Africa as the United States are to Canada, there is often a much wider difference than $3\frac{3}{4}$ per cent. between distant active competitors. The only way of placing British manufactures on a secure basis therefore, would be by materially increasing the maximum rate of duty, and then allowing a rebate of one-half, raising it say to 15 per cent., and leaving British goods at $7\frac{1}{2}$ per cent. But this could not possibly benefit the South African consumer, and would in all probability hurt him, as he would almost certainly be called upon to pay on the basis of the higher duty. In the case of foodstuffs he would get off cheaper and have every reason to be satisfied; with other goods at higher prices he would grumble, if he did not actively protest.

Nor is it difficult to understand why this

should be so. It may be just as true that Great
Britain manufactures more than South Africa can
consume as that Canada and Australia produce
more food than it can eat, and the competition
in each instance, therefore, ought to be equal.
But it is not. In the one case, cereals and meat
are produced, totally irrespective of when and
where there will be a demand for them, and in
the full assurance that somebody will need them :
in the other, more or less careful inquiry is made
as to possible outlets before goods are manufactured at all, even when this is not done on
specific order. In the first instance then, competition is eventually free and open as long as there
is not positive scarcity or monopoly, while in the
second, calculation is carefully made of the utmost
price that can be exacted. It is only when
surplus stocks have to be cleared that the consumer comes by his own, and then tariffs are not
of much consequence.

Further, in this class of imports it is necessary
to distinguish. It consists partly of goods for
immediate use which require constant replacement,
and those for more permanent forms of industrial
development. In a country situated like South
Africa, a slight addition to the cost of clothing may
be little more of an evil than of food ; it is likely on
the whole to be somewhat more widely felt, because
it will affect all engaged in agricultural pursuits, and
therefore indifferent about the price of food as far

as their own individual consumption is concerned. But the country could perhaps stand a trifling addition to the cost of its clothing, especially with the possibility that one of the nations supplying it might from time to time be able to do so on the former terms.

But a change in the tariff in this direction would benefit Great Britain very little, if at all, simply because it already has very nearly a monopoly of what is supplied, and any rise in price following an increase in duty would be calculated only to diminish the existing demand. On a commission of inquiry sent to South Africa after the war by an industrial association, the Manchester Chamber of Commerce was invited to appoint one of the delegates, but declined on the ground that it was already thoroughly and adequately represented out there, and possessed all the information likely to be obtained that could prove in any way useful. It might have added, and probably only refrained from doing so for diplomatic reasons, that its members, or others whom they represented, had nearly all the trade as it is, and that any publication of facts was more likely than not to help envious competitors to a share of it. This applies to a still greater extent to the other textile industries, and a comparison of the imports of these, and of wearing apparel, for 1899, will show at a glance what an immense preponderance Great Britain has of the trade.

Imports of Textiles and Wearing Apparel.

	From United Kingdom.	From Germany and Belgium.	From United States.
Apparel and Slops . .	£963,972	£13,783	£15,861
Haberdashery and Millinery	1,507,580	32,856	3,619
Boots and Shoes . .	692,401	25,918	26,785
Hats and Caps . . .	120,685	...	...
Hosiery . . .	286,939	5,318	3,496
Cotton Piece Goods . .	592,648	25,798	5,498
Blankets and Rugs [2] . .	140,223	23,956	...
Woollen Manufactures .	348,215	9,310	...
Linen do. . . (including sailware)	63,895	...	3,837
	£4,716,558	£136,939	£59,096

No other countries figure in the list for anything worth naming. It is extremely likely, however, that some of the goods imported from the United Kingdom are of foreign manufacture, but the value of such given in the British re-exports is very trifling.

Food and clothing thus constitute between them by far the most important of the requirements, and industrial expansion on the Rand or elsewhere will add to them at a more rapid rate than to any other class of imports. Machinery is wanted once ; a railroad, when built and equipped, requires renewal so gradual that it may be many years before the original outlay on it is duplicated, but what the miners and the railway employees and the tens of thousands dependent on them and their industries consume,

---

[1] Includes other leather manufactures for Natal.
[2] Principally for native use, the duty being 20 per cent.

must be replaced daily and monthly and yearly. They have other wants that do not recur either so regularly or so frequently, such as household utensils and the multiplicity of the smaller articles of domestic use which are drawn from all quarters of the globe. Some of these, like kerosene, must be obtained from one or other of the few countries of actual production, and so far the United States have enjoyed the preference. The Burma oilfields, however, are much more conveniently situated, and if they show capability in quality and price in competing with the American product, a similar opportunity is offered as with foodstuffs for affording it some advantage, as there is an import duty of threepence a gallon. The consumption is not relatively nearly so large as in many similarly situated countries, as nowhere else in the world are the centres of population more splendidly equipped with modern appliances, and the electric light has already largely banished oil and candles, to say nothing of more primitive methods of illumination, from the interior of the dark continent.

Most of these household and domestic requisites, however, are manufactured articles as distinct from natural productions, and the supply of them is open to the competition of all the countries now struggling so desperately for industrial pre-eminence. A list of the more important shows once more that, so far at least, Great Britain stands in no need of special advantages to secure the bulk of the trade.

Imports for 1899.

	From United Kingdom.	From Germany and Belgium.	From United States.
Earthenware and China .	£112,601	£19,563	...
Glass and Glassware .	105,756	46,856	£9,182
Soap	132,852	1,320	2,448
Candles	81,539	2,526	4,496
Paints and Colours .	83,273	...	11,022
Furniture . . .	292,360	23,820	43,162
Musical Instruments .	35,558	41,160	11,212
Paper and Stationery .	301,678	20,285	18,082
	£1,145,617	£155,530	£99,604

European and American manufacturers will undoubtedly endeavour to make inroads into what almost amounts to British monopoly in the more important articles of regular and constant use just enumerated, but it will be the British manufacturers' fault if they succeed. Where cheapness, irrespective of quality, is the first consideration, a little headway may occasionally be made, but South Africa is not likely for some little time to come to make that a prominent condition of trade, because where wages and profits are high, the real economy of value as distinct from price is pretty certain to be studied. Unfair methods of competition may in some cases be introduced, but when this has actually happened, or is seriously threatened, it will be time enough to talk about checking them.

Sentiment, however, does not at present attach so much importance to the trade in foodstuffs and

clothing and articles of domestic use as to industrial
plant of all kinds. In the first instance, the
items as a rule are individually insignificant, and
quite a lengthy invoice may only total a few hundred
pounds. In the second, a single contract may run
to a very large sum, and men like to think in big
figures. There is something fascinating in the idea
that a single mine or small group of mines will cost
a million sterling to equip before it can be counted
on to yield a penny of profit to the shareholders,
and in comparison with this, supplying stores looks
mean business.

Yet most of the million will go in wages, and
most of the wages will be spent at the stores, so
that those who do supply the latter will in the
long run get the bulk of the money and derive
the chief benefit. But in driving plant, mining gear
and machinery of all kinds, electric installation, and
everything applicable to the mechanical side of the
industry, international competition was already keen
before the war, and is likely to be keener in the
future. And when added to this is the certainty
of considerable railway extension, the attraction for
those huge amalgamations of industrial concerns
which have become the order of the day are too
strong to be resisted. If they can secure the contracts for the thousands of tons of rails, or the dozen
locomotives, or the fifty head of crushing stamps,
anybody that likes can have the orders for the yards
of calico or hundredweights of butter and bacon.

On the other side as well, the capitalists regard with the greatest concern the outlays that have to be made in large sums. They watch, no doubt with great jealousy, everything that tends to make the cost of living dear and wages correspondingly high, but they must recognise that moderate duties on food and clothing only affect this to a very slight extent on the scale prevalent in South Africa. They would consider it a much more serious matter were they called on to pay a duty of $7\frac{1}{2}$ per cent. on £50,000 worth of plant and machinery, than if their workmen had to pay double that rate on a suit of clothes; in the one instance the money would come straight out of their pockets, in the other it is an addition to ordinary working expenses for which allowance must be made in all their calculations. The large sum taken from them in a lump is looked upon as an exaction; the higher wages necessitated by the smaller ones are grumbled at, but accepted as for the time being inevitable.

There was no grievance so strongly resented as the dynamite monopoly. Had the extra cost it involved been merely a working expense resulting in a reduction of profit, a good deal less would have been heard about it. But great quantities had to be used in the process of development and before profits were attainable, and it was the addition to capital outlay that rankled. The same thing would occur if, by monopoly or import duty, cost of equipment in any direction were substantially raised.

This is recognised in almost every country any way similarly situated to South Africa. Where-ever machinery or tools are wanted in considerable quantities, and no means of supplying them exist at home, they are looked upon as the raw material of industry, and treated accordingly. It is not surprising therefore, to learn that throughout South Africa machinery of all kinds, tools, structural iron and steel with very few exceptions, agricultural implements, fencing wire, and very nearly every-thing requisite for mining and agricultural equip-ment, is admitted either entirely free or at merely nominal rates of duty.

Yet it is exactly in this class that competition has hitherto proved most successful, and the supply most widely distributed. Nor is it merely relative cost of production that decides the issue. Invention in the engineering industry is always affording one competitor an advantage over another : to-day it is something new from the United States, to-morrow from Great Britain, next week from Germany or France, that appeals to the manager of some big undertaking and is adopted by him ; and to impose any check on enterprise of this nature is flying in the face of all conceived ideas of progress.

The figures that follow are again for 1899, though the shadow of impending trouble naturally checked this branch of enterprise, which was not nearly so active as in preceding years. Still, for the present purpose the latest particulars are the most valuable, inasmuch as they show the relative standing of each competitor at the furthest stage of the struggle.

Imports for 1899.

	From United Kingdom.	From United States.	From Germany and Belgium.
Agricultural Implements .	£73,880	£58,332	£25,458
Carriages and Carts . .	14,787	32,663	...
Iron Pipes . . .	138,420	130,921	5,393
Sheet-iron (Corrugated and Galvanised) . . .	268,599	...	...
Iron Fencing Wire . .	101,709	73,077	25,336
Other Iron and Steel . .	160,384	2,311	3,561
Machinery . . .	877,843	405,947	134,239
Railway Material . .	603,548	136,127	32,636
Telegraph Material . .	64,090	...	6,435
Hardware, including Cutlery, Tools, Ironmongery, etc.	883,267	101,593	83,520
Cement	78,139	...	49,517
	£3,264,666	£940,971	£366,095

These figures represent the imports through Cape Colony and Natal only, and would be affected more than those of any of the other groups by what passed to the Transvaal through Delagoa Bay, as apart from the partiality of the Boer Government for that route, it was largely utilised for heavy goods, such as mining machinery and railway plant. Very scanty information is available of the details of the trade, but in the report of the British Consul at Lorenzo Marques for 1898, there is published the countries of origin of the previous year's imports in transit, which were as follows —

United Kingdom and Colonies .	£1,195,344
Holland	843,585
Germany	325,920
France	93,401
Italy and Portugal . . .	35,725
America	149,776
All others	10,840
	£2,654,591

British goods maintained the lead in this instance as well, though nothing like to the same extent as by the other routes. Germany was probably responsible originally for a large share of the goods credited to Holland, Rotterdam being the most convenient port of shipment for some of the Westphalian iron industries. No corresponding record appears to exist for 1899, but the figures were doubtless considerably reduced.

Hardware includes a good deal that would be more rightly classified along with domestic requisites, but it is impossible to separate items of so miscellaneous a nature. It must also be taken into account that the year 1899 was a very exceptional one in the iron and steel industry. British manufacturers proved utterly incapable of meeting the demands made on them, and orders, which in the regular course they would have secured, were placed with foreign rivals. Contracts to the extent of at least £500,000 are known to have gone to the United States, including one very large one for pipes, through sheer inability on the part of

any British works to fulfil them within reasonable
time. As this state of things no longer prevails,
it is quite likely that a larger proportion of
many of the items in the table as they come
to be renewed, will fall to the share of British
trade.

Here, if anywhere, Great Britain has something
to gain by preferential treatment. Though most
of the articles included in the list are free as
regards British South Africa, and subject only to
nominal duty when destined for the Transvaal, as
most of them were, it is not that which afforded
the United States and Germany their advantage,
because they were under no fiscal disability in
anything else, and enjoyed equal privileges with
Great Britain and all the British possessions. But
to place the latter in a position of superiority now
would necessitate the imposition of duties that
either never existed, or were only levied at very
low rates, and thus to renew in another way the
very handicap of which such bitter complaint was
made in the days of the Boer Republic. It would
substitute one group of monopolists for another,
and in the eyes of the Rand mining industry at
least, it would make very little difference that
the new ones are British while the old were
Dutch or German.

These four groups—food, clothing, domestic
requisites, and industrial material—by no means
exhaust the imports into South Africa, but what

is left is difficult to classify. It will be found also, that when not obtained from the United Kingdom, some special circumstance generally favours, if it does not compel, the supply from elsewhere. Thus about £600,000 worth of timber was imported, and it is natural to look to Sweden and Norway for that part of it used in the mines. About a fourth of the total was of United States origin, and there is no reason why Canada should not have a look in there, especially as all timber is dutiable at from a penny to three halfpence the cubic foot.

Chemicals, drugs, and blasting compounds also figure for considerable sums. Of the first two, British manufacturers and shippers had by far the largest share for 1899; £226,296 against £21,751 for Germany, and £25,441 for the United States. The notorious dynamite monopoly, however, drew its compounds and materials largely from foreign sources. The supply of glycerine valued at £135,183 was entirely from Germany and Belgium. Of dynamite, gun-cotton, and cyanide of potassium, £90,419 was of the same origin, but there were imports valued at £200,590 recorded as British. The greatest part of it was probably only in transit, and not manufactured in Great Britain at all, but, under the new order of things, there is likely to be a change in this respect at least, and this particular industry may pass largely, if not entirely, into British hands.

It is universally admitted that if South Africa is ever to refund any considerable portion of the immense sum expended on the war, it can only be through its mining industry. The Transvaal is generally spoken of alone in this respect, though why the almost equally important diamond mines of Cape Colony should be excluded is difficult to understand. They have hitherto almost entirely escaped direct taxation of any kind, and the powers that control them secured such preponderating political influence that they were able to regulate the financial laws very much to suit their own interests. It is quite certain, however, that a tax merely on realised profits, either of gold or diamonds, will not go a very long way towards paying for administration, let alone liquidating any war indemnity that may be imposed. The very highest figure at which the annual profits of the Rand mining industry was ever returned fell short of £5,000,000, and despite the sanguine forecasts that have been made, it is doubtful whether they will ever greatly exceed this. The rich outcrop mines are being rapidly exhausted, and though the actual production of gold in a single year may exceed anything yet obtained, it will be at nothing like the same percentage of profit.

To limit the tax on the industry to £500,000 therefore, which is the utmost that the recently imposed 10 per cent. on profits would have yielded

10

in the past, is to allow it to escape on ridiculously easy terms. The amount is less than many single individuals draw from South Africa as annual income, and there is little wonder at the jubilation they exhibit. In any event, such a tax will hardly be felt by them, because their profits are drawn almost entirely from capital manipulation, and not from dividends, most of which find their way into the pockets of a crowd of more or less genuine investors scattered throughout Western Europe.

The principal source of government revenue should be the same as of the capitalists' profits, and nothing substantial is ever likely to be recovered until this is attempted. Exactly how it is to be done is hardly within the province of a work devoted entirely to trade issues to discuss, except to the extent that it can be accomplished through trade. And that will not be by the placing of any burdens on the instruments of the industry itself, such as a more or less heavy customs duty on plant and machinery would inflict. That would be penny wise and pound foolish policy, because cost of equipment is bound to decide to a considerable extent whether or not a mine is worth working. To impose a duty of say 10 per cent.—and in view of the Canadian precedent hardly anything less is worth considering—on such equipment in favour of British manufacturers may be taken as equivalent to raising the capital outlay to that extent, and in the more expensively worked mines, or those producing low grade ore, may make all the difference as to whether or not they are actively opened up and developed. If they are neglected, less labour will be employed, and the very branches of trade in which Great Britain now excels correspondingly curtailed.

These arguments of course equally apply to the high cost of living, which is just as reprehensible when brought about by artificial means. But this is not due anywhere in South Africa to extravagant import duties; far more onerous exactions in the United States have not prevented the attainment of abounding prosperity there, and a South African gold or diamond mine that cannot afford to pay wages that will allow the employees to contribute something to the revenue of the country on the necessaries they consume, had better be left unworked, quite as much in the interests of investors as of everybody else. Furnish equipment on the most economical terms the world can offer without fear and without favour, and transport it at rates that leave but a moderate profit; but there is then no reason why the State should cut down every item of subsequent expenditure in order that workmen's wages may be reduced and managers' and directors' fees and remuneration augmented.

That the Transvaal under its Republican Government did not suffer materially in this respect may easily be judged by a comparison of its inward trade and customs revenue with those of Cape Colony and Natal. As obviously no complete returns for 1899 are possible, the figures are given for the year 1898, when the Rand mining industry was at the zenith of its prosperity, though as a matter of fact the trade of the Republic was past it. The reckless extravagance of former days had given way to more sober living, the equipment of the mines was in most instances complete, and the internal monopolies accounted for the home production of some things previously imported. The maximum import was reached in 1896 with a value of £14,088,130 and a customs revenue amounting to £1,355,486.

	Total Imports.	Customs Revenue.	Rate per Cent.
Transvaal Republic .	£10,632,895	£1,058,224	10
Cape Colony . .	12,041,246 [1]	1,911,138	15¾
Natal . . .	4,385,139 [1]	427,766	9¾

As Cape Colony and Natal have identically the same tariff, the discrepancy in the percentage needs some explanation, the probable cause being that more dutiable commodities like sugar, or of merchandise paying the higher duties, were imported at the Cape than into Natal. The fairest method is consequently to combine the two, when the average rate will be found to be 14¼ per cent.

[1] These amounts are arrived at after deducting imports declared in transit for countries outside of Cape Colony and Natal respectively, principally for the Transvaal Republic.

More generous treatment than that shown by the former Boer Republic can consequently hardly be expected under existing conditions by the new British Colonies. It may be more equitably adjusted, and Sir David Barbour's advice that the duties on alcoholic liquors might well be increased has already been acted on. But the normal rates on almost everything were so moderate that on this score at anyrate there was very little legitimate ground for complaint.

If the fiscal system of South Africa generally is to be brought more into accord with that previously existing in the Republic, there is no reason why this should not be done by affording the products of the British Empire a preference. This can be effected, as we have seen, mainly on articles of food where duties are comparatively high, and where the consumer has the opportunity of benefiting by the reduction, even if it be only a partial one. In personal and domestic requisites where rates are already moderate, there is little room, as from a British point of view there is little need, for concessions, and it will be most unwise to establish them by increasing existing duties, or imposing such where they are not already in operation.

South Africa is not a country whose fiscal system requires to be adapted to the needs of a vast impoverished community always tottering on the brink of starvation. But it does need intelligently adapting to the possibilities of development under economic conditions, and this will not be attained if heed be given to the demands of the citizens of any one country merely on the ground that, as such, they have been compelled to contribute through taxation to the cost of the war. That must now be regarded in the light of a national outlay, to be reclaimed to as great an extent as possible in tangible form, but to the enormous degree in which this is likely to prove impracticable, by the stimulus afforded to national as distinct from any specialised industry. And this will be best accomplished through multiplying the wants of the population as well as the population itself, by giving it opportunity of free and unhindered expansion in every direction that is presented.

It is impossible to bring this chapter to a conclusion without uttering a word of warning as to the future, especially as the anticipations regarding it are so intensely sanguine. With the enormous depredations requiring to be made good, and which are being partly met by the British Exchequer, it is impossible to draw any sound inferences from the trade of 1902. So far as the figures are available, however, they are sufficiently extraordinary to strike attention—

	Imports.	Exports.
Cape Colony	£29,575,000	£16,381,000
Natal	13,317,000	985,000
	£42,892,000	£17,366,000

To appreciate the meaning of them it is necessary to contrast them with those for 1899, which were but slightly affected by the war, beyond the inclusion of nearly £4,000,000 in specie imported for military requirements—

	Imports.	Exports.
Cape Colony	£19,207,549	£23,662,538
Natal	6,713,507	1,885,580
	£25,921,056	£25,548,118

In the earlier period, that is, imports were paid for by exports—for the previous year 1898, there was actually an excess of £4,500,000 in the exports —in the latter there was upwards of £25,000,000 to be provided out of capital expenditure, exclusive of Delagoa Bay trade which must have been nearly all imports. Only a moderate portion of this sum, moreover, represented real capital outlay at all; most of it was for consumable stores, either food or clothing.

It will take a great deal of gold or other South African produce to repay that, and if repeated on anything like a similar scale two or three years n succession, the interest alone will amount to a serious item. Either imports must greatly diminish, which will entail a corresponding cessation of trade activity in Great Britain and elsewhere, or the exports must expand at a far more rapid rate than they afford evidence of doing, otherwise South Africa will be threatened with economic collapse and early bankruptcy. And what further aggravates the situation is the extravagant cost all industrial enterprise entails as compared with other countries, which is bound to tell sooner or later in the returns.

CHAPTER V

THE FOREIGN TRADE OF INDIA

UNLIKE most British possessions, and especially the
self-governing ones, the welfare of India depends
far less on external trade than internal development. It is true of them all as it is of Great
Britain and every other civilised country in the
world, that internal trade is many times the volume
of their foreign commerce, but there are various
degrees of the dependency of one on the other.
Nobody can doubt, for instance, that were the
United Kingdom suddenly deprived of £100,000,000

of its exports, internal resources and turnover would be diminished to several times that extent. A gradual diminution might not be attended with such serious consequences, or for that matter with any at all, because the necessary readjustment could take place as it went on.

With countries like Canada and Australia, foreign trade is the source of economic life, and prosperity or adversity varies almost in direct ratio to the surplus and price of their products available for export, which is the best means they possess of obtaining the resources necessary for the development of their territories. But if in these instances it is one of the principal organs of vitality, to India foreign trade has never yet been much more than a mere excrescence. This is less on account of any want of variety or abundance of natural resources than of the extreme poverty of the vast majority of the people. In the most prosperous year of their existence many of them can hardly hope to be consumers of anything, save perhaps cotton clothing, produced fifty miles from their own villages, let alone of luxuries imported from oversea, while the subsistence they extract from the land is so meagre that there is seldom much, if anything, to spare for sale outside their own immediate neighbourhood. Indeed a good deal of what is every year exported from India to foreign countries is a token of want rather than abundance, and has been parted with to meet the pressing demands of the money-lender, to satisfy some urgent personal need, or more rarely to gratify a special taste or curiosity.

It is necessary, therefore, to examine Indian trade returns from a totally different standpoint to those already dealt with. They affect directly but a small minority of the inhabitants of that Empire, and the indirect influences are not always easy to trace upon the large majority. To those that are concerned, the results are no doubt very much the same as in other countries, and as these increase in number and wealth, commerce assumes an added importance to which it is not really entitled. And this may have very deleterious consequences, because the greater may be sacrificed to the less, particularly when those representative of the second class wield a disproportionate amount of influence.

In illustration of this the trade in cotton piece goods may be referred to. It is the most important branch of commerce there is in India, and in its rapid expansion years ago, undoubtedly killed a great deal of local industry. The theory of course is that the population gained by the introduction of cheaper clothing, and to some extent this is true. The vast majority of Englishmen are ready to admit that unlimited supplies of cheap foreign food have been an inestimable boon to Great Britain, but there might be some doubt on this point were two-thirds of the British population producers of food. Of course the number of native cloth weavers was never

more than a small fraction of the whole community,
but then India has never afforded much diversity of
occupation, nor the means of readily changing from
one to another of those that actually exist, and there
is consequently no comparison between the benefits
that might accrue to Great Britain from an industrial revolution and what would be experienced in
India.   Great Britain affords a standing proof of
these to the least observant in the well-being of
its working population to-day compared with fifty,
or even twenty, years ago, and if there is still a
frightful amount of the most abject poverty, very
little of it can be attributed to the national industrial system.   On the other hand, outside the
India Office, whose mandate for some years past
has been to pronounce India more prosperous than
at any previous period of its history, there is an
almost general belief on the part of those able to
form an unprejudiced opinion that the movement
has been backward, and that social and material
conditions are decidedly worse than a decade ago.

Still it is impossible to stop the wheels of the
world's progress to remedy a grievance such as
this, granting even that it could actually be proved
to exist.   But what is to be thought of the sacrifice
of the Indian population to the needs of the mercantile class in conjunction with those of the Government?   Yet this is what happened with regard to
the Indian import duties on cotton goods.   No
Government in its senses would dream of raising

revenue by taxing an important home industry unless it were of the nature of a public or private monopoly such as opium or intoxicating liquor. But an easy and very usual way of raising it is by means of import duties, and these were imposed on cotton goods. An equivalent internal duty on all goods manufactured in India would have been defensible in theory at least, however unwise or unjust in practice, but to pick out just those descriptions that were supposed to come into direct competition with imported fabrics was a frank declaration that India was to have its internal industries regulated for the benefit of foreign trade.

Free trade principles, with which almost everybody engaged in Indian commerce is imbued, refuse to sacrifice the home consumer for the benefit of the home producer. How can they sanction the sacrifice of the home consumer and the home producer alike to the foreign producer? It was not the fault of the first two that the Government had to raise more revenue by some means or other, and the Government did not profess to wish to obtain it from the Indian cotton industry, yet it imposed an excise duty in the sacred name of free trade, designed to restrict one branch of trade for the advantage of another. What is the difference in principle between the United States Government imposing a duty to protect the home producer against a foreign rival, and the Indian Government one to protect the foreign producer against the home rival? Somebody replies that both are thereby placed on an equality. But what right has any Government to create an inequality that did not, and need not, exist, and then set to work to redress it by unfair and restrictive legislation?

There is another case in point. India possesses what every economist denounces in every other country where it is found, an inflated currency. The difference is that most countries that fall victims to it cannot help themselves; in India it was deliberately adopted, and enormous efforts and sacrifices were made to maintain it. What is the difference between insisting that five silver dollars, say, shall be worth the equivalent of one pound sterling, when they are not, and that one pound sterling shall be worth no more than fifteen rupees, when it actually is? Again the answer is, that the first is done to maintain the value of silver, which is wrong, the other, to ensure the maintenance of gold in some particular position in which self-interest has chosen to place it, which is right. We hear a great deal about shibboleths, and idols, and other Hebrew and heathen symbols, but in modern days gold is a god upon whose altars, if it become necessary, every principle of economics must be sacrificed.

And sacrificed they most assuredly were in India. No pretence was ever made that the gold standard was adopted for the benefit of the native population. The excuse certainly was urged that increased taxation would be necessary if it were not adopted, but that taxation was nevertheless imposed after the gold standard was introduced, and has not been remitted since. It was, in short, considered advisable in the interests of those twin sisters, the Indian Treasury and Foreign Commerce, and nothing else counted, and to say that it has done what it was never intended to do, benefited the community at large, is to fly in the face of overwhelming evidence to the contrary.

As if to emphasise all this, the Indian Government has recently taken to publishing its financial and trade returns in sterling, thus departing from the immemorial custom, not only of India but of all other countries, of expressing them in the actual currency of the country. Such manipulation will no more compel the use of British money, either actually or by denomination, by the people of India, than similar action, if it were possible, would induce Canadians to abolish cents and dollars for pounds, shillings, and pence. If anybody doubts such a contention they have only to consider the position of the metric system in England, the vast majority of whose inhabitants using any system at all are by this time educated and supposed to possess a fair amount of ordinary intelligence. Yet the displacement of yards and miles for metres and kilometres, of ounces and pounds for grams and kilograms, is virtually an impossibility. The English farmer has never yet become reconciled to the abolition of measure for weight in the sale of his grain, and where the latter has actually been adopted, it has more often than not been under the designation of the former in the retention of the bushel. Anybody offering him so much per hundred kilograms for his wheat or his hay would run serious risk of being handed over to the police as a dangerous lunatic at large.

That the metric is greatly superior to the nondescript English system has nothing whatever to do with the question. French and Spanish are in many respects superior languages to English, yet no Englishman advocates the abolition of his mother tongue because the others are useful in commerce. He acquires them in addition, and the comparatively small proportion of the nation that is ever brought into contact with foreign trade finds no difficulty in absorbing metric weights and measures as well as their own. Similarly, every Indian or Anglo-Indian engaged in foreign commerce knows the value of pounds, shillings, and pence as well as of rupees, annas, and pice, and encounters no difficulty in converting one into the other. Besides, if a change be advisable, why adopt the antiquated British system at all ? rather go at once to the simpler decimal one of dollars, or francs, or marks, or any other nomenclature that may be selected. The only result of the absurd arrangement now in force is that well-paid officials are employed in dividing a great number of statistics by fifteen, in order that anyone who wishes to understand them may have the trouble of multiplying them again by the same figure before he can do so. Such a departure is almost brutal in the frankness of its acknowledgment that the foreign commerce of India is carried on for the benefit of the people, mostly foreigners, principally engaged in it, utterly disregardless of the native community as a whole.

There is no present intention of discussing either the fiscal system or the currency policy of the Government of India, and these allusions have been introduced simply to show on what a very different basis foreign trade exists in that country to most others. The annual returns of the commerce of the United Kingdom, of the United States, of Germany, and of a host of other countries, are regarded as a barometer of the progress and prosperity of the nation. As far as India is concerned, these afford no true indication of the industrial weather apart from other considerations which may not in any way directly affect them.

As a set off against what we have been discussing there is at least one instance of the imposition of a restraint on foreign trade apparently for the benefit of the native producer. This is to be found in the addition to the duties on imported beet sugar to countervail the bounties paid by exporting countries. But there has always been a great deal of doubt whether the initiative in this step was taken by the Indian Government,

11

or whether it was instigated by the British Government at home with Imperial rather than Indian objects in view. The policy, as a policy, was right enough, provided action was taken to make it properly effective. But this never seems to have been done. It is not generally realised that India is the greatest sugar-producing country in the world, and that as far as cane sugar is concerned it usually yields more than all others put together. But it is all consumed at home and consequently makes no impression on the world's supplies, nor affects market values; only when the latter are very high is there an inducement to export on anything like a considerable scale.

Methods of extraction and preparation, too, are almost everywhere so exceedingly primitive as to make anything to be found in the West Indies modern alongside them. There has consequently always been a demand in India for sugar of a superior quality to what is produced there, and until quite recent times this was supplied in sufficient quantities by the British island of Mauritius, where methods of manufacture are of a more approved type. There are plenty of people in India well enough off to purchase a superior to an inferior article where difference in price is not very great, and still more to prefer the one to the other when there is no difference at all, and this is practically what happened when the price of refined beet sugar fell some years ago to very low figures.

No doubt this low price was to some extent attained with the assistance of bounties. But the sugar supplied a demand that the native product did not, though it is universally admitted to be capable of doing so. Yet no steps of any consequence have been taken with that object in view.

The reason assigned is that this is a matter for private enterprise, and in most countries it would be so. But with a population so intensely conservative, not to say ignorant, as that of India, almost every movement of reform must be initiated, if not actually carried on in its earlier stages, either by the Government or under Government guarantee, unless, that is, there is a prospect, amounting almost to certainty, of substantial immediate returns. The only people likely to take action in such a matter are the mercantile community, British or native. But they only take a hand in industrial enterprise calculated to stimulate foreign trade, and improvement in sugar production might curtail it. They profit at present by the import of beet sugar and its sale to the consumer, while the trade in home-grown sugar is in other hands. This view is very likely a shortsighted one, because under true economic conditions India might become a far more important sugar-exporting country than it has been an importing one.

The object in imposing these countervailing

duties, however, was in a measure accomplished. It frightened the bounty-paying countries which feared what was done in India might prove the forerunner of similar action in Great Britain, especially since the reimposition of a revenue duty on sugar. The result is to be seen in the Brussels Conference, and of what appears at the present moment to be the entire abolition of the bounty system as far as all the chief exporting countries are concerned. But to believe that this was aimed at principally for the benefit of the Indian sugar growers is to tax credulity too far.

When the Indian Government determined to establish the gold standard it went about things in a very different fashion. It imposed fresh taxes, created artificial stringency in the money market, borrowed to an unlimited extent to maintain its own resources, and actually threatened a wholesale destruction of the ordinary currency, all utterly disregardless of the wants and interests of the natives. But in the interests of the sugar growers whom it is supposed to be championing, it does nothing that does not imply a threat to countries whose competition is dangerous as well as unfair in the markets of the United Kingdom.

In every country there is a certain amount of legislation in the interests of trade. Almost invariably it is designed to benefit internal industry and help the home trader, but enough has probably been said to show that hitherto these have not been the animating motives where India is concerned.

In the light of these facts we shall more readily be able to understand the movements of Indian foreign commerce. The first question that naturally presents itself is how the balance is adjusted. A backward and undeveloped country like India usually requires a great amount of capital, not in the shape of coin or money of any kind, but of commodities. If the former was all that India wanted, its people probably possess among them sufficient accumulated treasure to meet all requirements so far filled, but partly from suspicious dislike—gradually disappearing—and partly because it was not treasure that was really needed, most of what has been borrowed has been obtained from British lenders. When a movement of this sort is active it often means that imports considerably exceed exports. Twenty years ago and less, notwithstanding the fact that the United States were immensely indebted to Europe, it sometimes happened that their foreign trade showed an excess of imports, a state of things that would now be regarded by an American with horror, and he points to the excess of exports, running into the hundred millions in pounds sterling, as the best proof of the wealth of his country, though he very likely fails to realise that the very different state of things existing a quarter of a century ago was the real foundation of to-day's prosperity.

But under normal conditions, that is, when development has made a certain amount of progress and is being continued by slow degrees, such a country will exhibit an excess of exports, provided out of the profits or earnings of past development, and used to pay interest on capital outlay. That is the position occupied by India, and to say that the excess of exports usually shown is a tribute to Europe is entirely misleading. There are what is known as the home charges, varying annually in amount, and averaging from £15,000,000 to £17,000,000, but even these do not constitute tribute. Part of it does, no doubt, but money to pay interest on loans for railway construction, irrigation purposes, and other public works is not, unless they are unremunerative, and even then such payments may be but investments until the time they become so. But what is paid for the maintenance of the India Office and all its various ramifications in London, or for the pensions of retired Indian officers and officials resident in Europe, is a tribute, exacted from India in produce rather than in money, and to this extent India is handicapped. No self-governing country pays such tribute to another. France and Germany, it is true, are taxed for the support of officials and cost of administration in oversea possessions, but a moment's consideration will show that this is quite the reverse principle to the one operating in India. But the amount so paid by India is a mere trifle compared with the total raised by taxation, and the advocate of true economy is likely to find more methods of enforcing it in the affairs of internal administration.

In proof of the contention that Indian foreign trade is only partially, indeed slightly, regulated by internal considerations, we have the fact that India's excess of exports varies but slightly from one year to another, and that a season of plenty or one of famine makes comparatively little difference in the totals. Merchants lay themselves out to do a certain amount of trade, and if it is not forthcoming in one direction, look for it, and generally find it, in another. This excess too does not generally greatly differ from the amount of the Council drawings upon the Indian treasuries, and as these are for the purpose of covering the home charges, the fact of their being met by a corresponding export of Indian produce tends to confirm the mistaken idea of tribute. How these compare will best be shown by the figures that are available.[1]

[1] Indian trade returns are made up for years ending on the 31st March, the same as the financial accounts. The figures appearing in this chapter are taken from the usual abstracts and reports published regularly by the Board of Trade and India Office. I have adopted the plan, however, of converting them in every instance into tens of rupees. Despite all edicts to the contrary, most Anglo-Indians still regard ten rupees in the light of the £ sterling when mentally making comparisons on a large scale, not of course in business calculations. And they are justified in so doing, because the internal value of the rupee has undergone no such revolution as is depicted by the fall in the gold value of silver to not much more than one-third of its so-called par equivalent, nor even to the extent of the purely fictitious value set on it by Government enactment.

	Excess of Oversea Merchandise Exports.	Net Imports of—Silver.	Gold.
1896–97	Rx.32,120,468	Rx.5,856,000	Rx.2,291,100
1897–98	28,270,610	8,473,500	4,908,500
1898–99	44,341,132	3,980,800	6,503,400
1899–1900	38,264,323	3,576,700	9,440,600
1900–01	31,135,995	9,507,200	842,100
1901–02	42,994,062	7,192,834	1,937,641

	Net Excess of Exports.	Council Drawings.	Net Imports of Government Stores.
1896–97	Rx.23,973,368	Rx.25,787,000	Rx.4,253,745
1897–98	14,888,610	14,812,800	4,284,864
1898–99	33,856,932	28,076,400	3,642,935
1899–1900	25,247,023	28,480,100	4,485,481
1900–01	20,786,695	19,983,800	4,267,169
1901–02	27,032,428	25,120,400	6,831,159

The Council drawings are affected by the rate of exchange ruling, and also by borrowings both in London and India, and the two sets of figures given above must not be regarded as dependent the one on the other. Their seeming correspondence may be due to accident rather than design, though as the bills are usually bought by the Indian banks to cover exports of produce, when they are in short supply or withheld from the market the adjustment has to be made with either gold or silver bullion, or occasionally left over perhaps on current account to the following year.

The merchandise figures are given to represent actual commerce, and have excluded from them the movements of Government stores. These are mostly on the import side of the account, and consist principally of material for the construction of railways and public works provided out of capital raised for the purpose. The policy of this exclusion may be questioned, because if such works were undertaken by private enterprise the figures would appear as ordinary trade, so they are shown separately. Another point difficult to decide is whether silver should or should not be included. It is the currency of the country, but has always been more or less a merchandise commodity, and is now distinctly so, and subjected to 5 per cent. import duty. Since the closing of the mints only Government has the privilege of importing for coinage purposes, and when this is done, occasionally on a large scale, trade returns are affected. The separate movements are also given for each year.

An excess of exports of course necessitates that being the larger side of the trade account, and to this extent at least the more important, which entitles it to chief consideration. The first thing that strikes an inquirer is that the export trade of India is not to any large degree one of surplus products. In almost every country of the first rank, agricultural and manufacturing industry are primarily devoted to the supply of home requirements, and it is only what is left over that becomes the basis of foreign commerce. It is not often an industry is found that has been created, and is maintained principally, much less exclusively, for that object.

Something of the kind is to be discovered in

the Australian pastoral industry, scarcely any of
the wool it yields being wanted at home, and all
but a slight percentage of it going for export.
But the corn and meat and dairy produce of the
United States and Canada are first devoted to
home requirements, only the surplus being
shipped abroad.

Most of the industries of India, however, can
be sharply divided between home and foreign.
The agricultural is in every way the most extensive and important, and of the land under
cultivation something like five-sixths is devoted
to the growth of food of various kinds, and only
the remaining one-sixth to the raw materials of
manufacturing industry. Among the chief food
products of the country are millet and pulse, and
of these there is virtually no export whatever.
Wheat is grown principally in the more temperate
climate of the northern provinces for consumption, and in an ordinary year to provide a
surplus, rarely exceeding 10 per cent. of the
crop, for export. Throughout the large and
thickly populated area of Bengal, and more or
less everywhere on the eastern side of the
continent, rice is the staple food, and again it
is grown for home consumption and does not
yield any great surplus for export. It is Burma
that grows rice for that purpose, and though part
of the Indian Empire, is really separate from the
continent.

For the millet there is no foreign demand whatever unless it is for bird-seed, and for the pulse very little. Wheat is not at any time a very important crop relatively speaking, but rice is the mainstay, not only of India but of a great part of Asia. Though largely exported to Europe, it is not as an article of food; it would take a great many more rice puddings than are eaten to account for what is annually shipped, and the bulk of it is used for distillation, or starch extraction, or some other industrial purpose. It costs in an average season so little to produce that there is serious risk of the foreign demand drawing off more than can be spared and leaving the home food supply deficient. China insures against this by prohibiting the export altogether. India guards against it by imposing an export tax equivalent to about fourpence a hundredweight. Such taxes are not as a rule desirable, but this one fulfils the double purpose of providing about half a million sterling a year for the Indian treasury, and preventing the rice getting beyond the reach of the poorest of the population and subjecting them to starvation. So far from being condemnable, therefore, it is a question whether in years of scarcity, to say nothing of famine, it ought not to be increased, and thereby prevent rice rising to a high level of price by checking the export. But rice exporters are an important section of the Indian mercantile community and it is not considered judicious to interfere too seriously with their trade, even in the interests of a starving population.

Of the last six completed years three have been given over to famine, but as crop years and fiscal years overlap, it is difficult to estimate the effect on the export movement in any one. The previous five years, however, were free from this curse, and tolerably free even from severe scarcity, and a comparison of the export movements of wheat and rice for the two periods is interesting. No conclusive arguments can be drawn from them because the crops outside as well as within famine areas vary in size from year to year, but one thing may be safely asserted: if the population of India had been properly and sufficiently fed in the famine years there would have been little or no surplus of either grain for export.

Export in Hundredweights of—

	Wheat.	Rice.		Wheat.	Rice.
1891–92	30,306,700	33,166,929	1896-97	1,910,553	28,281,227
1892–93	14,973,453	27,938,325	1897–98	2,392,607	26,834,552
1893–94	12,156,851	24,649,723	1898–99	19,520,496	37,946,886
1894–95	6,890,130	34,442,600	1899–1900	9,704,087	32,278,438
1895–96	10,004,171	35,161,968	1900–01	50,021	31,343,788
Total .	74,331,305	155,359,545	Total .	33,577,764	156,684,891
Annual Average	14,866,261	31,071,909	Annual Average	6,715,553	31,336,978
			1901-02	7,321,818	34,034,647

India's normal consumption of wheat may be taken at from five and a half to six million tons; much the same, that is, as in the United Kingdom. Both acreage and yield, however, are on the decline; for the famine year 1899 1900 the latter was less than five million tons, which explains the almost entire disappearance of exports the year following, indeed imports actually exceeded them more than tenfold, being 559,357 cwts., principally from Australia. Only once within the decade has the total crop been returned as having reached seven million tons.

Of the rice export about two-thirds is of Burma growth, about one-third of that crop, on an average, being shipped, while much more goes to other parts of India. This contrasts strikingly with the rest of the country, which in a fair average season probably does not export more than two per cent. of its food production, showing how very near the population is at the best of times to the brink of starvation. It may be asserted without fear of contradiction that there are tens of millions who never have enough to eat, and were everybody adequately fed conti-nental India would be a food importing, not exporting, country, unless it were to increase its yield very materially.

Canada desires an import duty on grain in the United Kingdom in order that it may be afforded a preference, with the belief, more or

less well founded, that it would promote the
cultivation and export of wheat from which the
Dominion would benefit. Any measure calculated
to artificially stimulate the export of foodstuffs,
and especially of wheat, from India, would be
detrimental to that country, and the interests of
the two possessions are thus diametrically opposite.
Yet to grant Canada a preference and deny it
to India would hardly be possible, because the
Indian export merchants would be up in arms
against such differential treatment. In other
words, British preferential treatment would put
Indian foreign trade and Indian native interests
in this respect into direct conflict.

India cannot be regarded then, under the most
favourable circumstances, as a food exporting country.
Its principal supplies for foreign trade are the yield
of industries specially devoted to it. The tea
gardens of Assam are not cultivated and picked
for the Indian, but for the foreign consumer.
Linseed, rapeseed, and sesamum are grown to
supply Europe and America with oil for industrial
purposes, and the bye-products to fatten their cattle,
though they may be used to some extent in India
for the latter purpose as well. Cotton and jute
were grown a quarter of a century or more ago to
supply foreign spindles and looms, part of the
product finding its way back again in the form of
manufactured goods, but in modern times the existence of the raw material has led to the establishment

of important manufacturing industries at home, chiefly with the aid of foreign capital.

This side of the export trade, affording as it must a vast amount of employment, can hardly but be beneficial, providing, that is, it does not draw labour off anything that will better promote internal development and prosperity. That must to some extent depend on wages, which are not in many instances too high. The native cultivator grows his own food, and as long as he has enough for himself and his family, the market value as far as that portion is concerned is a matter of total indifference to him. But the facilities afforded for the export of whatever surplus remains raise that portion in value to somewhere near the price in the outside consuming markets, less, of course, the charges of transport, and it is this price which has to be paid by the non-food-producing labourer who works in tea gardens, or cotton plantations, or in the cotton and jute factories. A wage substantially higher in amount than that earned by the ryot may thus in reality be materially lower in effective purchasing power, and the labourer would be better employed producing for home, or his own individual consumption, than for export.

There are several items of export scarcely affected by any of the foregoing considerations. The hides, skins, and bones of animals are not wanted in India in anything like the quantity produced, and naturally gravitate to foreign markets. The increase of this trade is a marked feature of every season of famine; the number of cattle killed for want of fodder or dying from actual starvation being excessive. This alone always helps to make up the deficiency in exports in a famine year, thus giving as the very result of disaster the appearance to a superficial observer of apparent prosperity. The most recent famine had another unusual result of this kind. The copper utensils with which most Indian domestic establishments of any consideration are supplied, had to be parted with for food, and the value of the metal having attained an unusually high level, most of them were exported. India's direct distress may thus be the means of swelling the volume of its foreign commerce.

Wool is another commodity of similar character. The climate of India does not render its general use for clothing a necessity, and the only woollen industries of any consequence that exist are associated with carpet manufacture. Most of this staple produced there is consequently sold for foreign consumption.

Of the trade in opium, important as it is, little need be said. It is a Government monopoly, and both crop and price exercise a very important influence on the finances of the country. Happily this is a branch with which neither Europe nor America have much to do, the distribution being confined almost exclusively to the continent of Asia.

In every year then, whether under conditions of comparative prosperity or of adversity, India has a considerable quantity of commodities to dispose of, some of which could be put to much better use at home, others for which no economic demand at present exists there. These go to some extent to discharge indebtedness, but principally to pay for imports. The measure of that indebtedness ought to be the excess of exports; really it is something greater, because a year rarely if ever passes in which part of the import, other than Government stores, does not represent invested capital, and is not called upon to be paid for with exports at all.

Having considered the nature of the exports it remains to be seen how they are distributed. In this respect Indian commerce is extremely cosmopolitan. Whereas in the case of New Zealand something like three-fourths of the exports find their way to British consumers; of Canada, excluding gold and other minerals, nearly two-thirds; and of Australia very nearly one - half; —less than one - third those of India arrive at that destination. Of one or two things, opium for example, none at all is sent. Of raw cotton scarcely any is now wanted by British manufacturers, whose trade has gradually drawn them off to the superior staples of the United States and Egypt, grown under conditions of moisture as distinct from temperature which India does not afford, and cannot consequently hope naturally to

12

compete against. This is of little consequence as long as the Indian consumption itself goes on steadily increasing and there is a growing demand for China and Japan of raw material or manufactured goods. That for continental Europe is gradually being curtailed for much the same reasons as Great Britain.

Jute in its raw state is peculiarly an Indian product and is drawn upon by every country using the fibre. It is not every country, however, that has a jute industry, though nearly all require more or less large supplies of sacks and bags for transporting their produce, both inland and across the seas. The demand for gunny bags and cloth is therefore much more widely distributed than for the raw material, and there is scarcely a country that can in any way get into contact with India that is not a customer for these goods. Calcutta is the keenest competitor Dundee has ever had, and the direct export of manufactured material has increased of late years very rapidly. The following figures selected from the returns of the last decade illustrate this :—

Exports of—

	Sacks and Bags.	Gunny Cloth.
1890–91	98,749,416 No.	29,854,029 yards.
1895–96	168,247,453 ,,	114,180,818 ,,
1900–01	202,908,199 ,,	365,214,990 ,,
1901–02	230,126,651 ,,	418,566,614 ,,

Burma rice is popular wherever this grain is used for food or any other purpose. It is shipped in large quantities to the United Kingdom, but in still larger ones to other markets, both east and west, as it is the food staple of everybody of Asiatic origin in whatever part of the world they happen to be located. Of the oil-producing commodities, earth nuts and sesamum find an almost exclusive market in France; rapeseed enjoys the special patronage of German seed crushers; while linseed is wanted more or less everywhere, and has an extensive market in Great Britain. Hides are less widely distributed; but if the British is the largest market for the dressed article, the United States and Germany are the biggest customers for them in the raw state.

The relative importance of India's customers for exports is best shown in tabular form, the figures representing percentages of the total for each of the respective years of all countries usually taking up to 5 per cent. :—

Exports to	1897–98	1898–99	1899–1900	1900–01	1901–02
United Kingdom .	31·1	29·3	29·2	30 1	25·1
China . . .	12·9	11·6	13·3	11·3	14·5
Germany . .	7·6	7·5	7·1	8·8	8·4
United States .	6·3	4·9	7·2	6·9	6·9
Straits Settlements .	4·6	5·2	5·2	6·6	5 2
France . . .	6	7·1	6·3	5·7	7·3
Japan . . .	4·4	4·8	6	2	5·7
Egypt . . .	4·2	6·3	5·1	4·3	4·4

The trade with the Straits Settlements is almost entirely transit, and its redistribution, along with that entered for Egypt consisting principally of rice cargoes to await orders, would affect most of the foregoing percentages to some slight extent. The contraction shown in 1900–01 by China and Japan was only temporary, and arose from the falling off in the shipments of raw cotton, yarn, and piece goods owing to the failure of the cotton crop.

The distribution of the import trade is in one instance at least, that of the United Kingdom, in remarkable contrast to the foregoing, and there is no better way perhaps of introducing this side of the subject than by giving for it a similar table to the last :—

Imports from	1897–98	1898–99	1899–1900	1900–01	1901–02
United Kingdom .	67·1	68·8	68·9	63·8	64·5
China . . .	2·4	2·5	2·2	3·3	2·2
Germany . .	3·5	2·5	2·4	3·4	3·7
United States .	2·1	2	1·7	1·6	1·4
Straits Settlements .	3·5	2·9	2·7	3	2·9
France . . .	1·3	1·5	1·4	1·4	1·7
Austria-Hungary .	3·1	3·5	3·4	4·1	4·8

This is just the reverse of what one would expect to find in the natural course of things. India being so largely indebted to Great Britain for interest and other fixed charges, and its exports being annually considerably in excess of imports, what more reasonable than that the discharge of the indebtedness should be made in that way ? Yet the financial balance, instead of being liquidated, is aggravated by the trade balance. Were pure theory to be applied to remedy this, it would no doubt seek to stimulate Indian exports to the United Kingdom by some fiscal arrangement designed with that object. But as a matter of fact British consumers and manufacturers get all, and often more than all, they want from that source as it is, and the extent of the imports from India, relatively small though they are, have already adversely affected other trade relationships. Indian tea, for instance, has almost entirely displaced the China leaf, and in so doing has thrown the balance of trade between the two countries so immensely in favour of Great Britain that it requires very skilful exchange operations to settle it. This might be of less consequence were the Chinese currency a stable one in relation to those of most of the countries with which it has commercial intercourse, but depending as it does on the fluctuations in the value of silver, liquidation may often be possible only at considerable sacrifice, and nations like Germany and the United States which have a more evenly balanced trading account gain distinct advantage in consequence.

Great Britain might, of course, increase its imports of linseed at the expense of Russia, and of hides to the detriment of the Argentine Republic. But it would hardly care to encourage a trade in the coarse cotton fabrics produced by Indian looms, even were there any considerable demand for them, and Dundee would certainly object to any fiscal arrangement likely to increase competition in the jute manufacturing industry. Besides, the present arrangement suits Great Britain admirably. Its trade with most other countries results in a great excess of imports which have by some means or other to be paid for. Where any of these particular countries are indebted in other ways to a corresponding extent, the settlement is a very simple matter. Nobody imagines this to be the case with the United States or France. But if both, while selling more to Great Britain than they purchase from it, buy more from India than they sell to it, the one is a set off against the other, and Great Britain repays itself for part of what it sells to India, by imports of what it requires from the United States and France. So far then from being a hindrance to trade, this apparent divergence is an incentive to it, and any policy that sought to encourage the shipment of Indian produce to Great Britain instead of to such countries as are accustomed at present to take it would be thoroughly unsound.

The converse proposition is to stimulate British exports to India. This might be done in two ways : either by increasing the present volume of Indian imports, or by securing part at least of what is now supplied by foreign countries. The first method is decidedly objectionable, and it could only be detrimental to the interests of Great Britain and India alike to force on the latter more than was required for actual consumption. It would savour of the methods pursued by Spain in bygone days towards its South American possessions, when the measure of outward trade was not colonial requirements, but what Spain happened to want to dispose of. Nor would it be wise to undertake permanent enterprises with too great haste, because unless there is some prospect of them earning an adequate return on the capital outlay they could only tend to sink India into still greater depths of economic depression.

And as regards the second method there is but little opportunity. A country that already enjoys two-thirds of the trade of another necessarily finds it hard work to encroach on competitors who have no more than a trifling percentage of it. Two-fifths of the imports into India comprise cotton manufactures, and when any set of manufacturers have more than 95 per cent. of any particular trade they may be credited with monopoly. That is the position Great Britain, or to narrow it further, Lancashire, holds to-day, and it has to guard against encroachments rather than make them. Its principal ground of complaint is that the trade is not expansive as the following figures pretty conclusively prove :—

Imports of Cotton Piece Goods into India—

1891–92	1,882,884,360 yds.	1896–97	1,998,962,052 yds.
1892–93	1,808,340,594 ,,	1897–98	1,861,849,513 ,,
1893–94	2,129,704,914 ,,	1898–99	2,070,777,269 ,,
1894–95	2,259,427,320 ,,	1899–1900	2,191,342,906 ,,
1895–96	1,717,507,439 ,,	1900–01	2,002,820,214 ,,
Total	9,797,864,627 ,,	Total	10,125,751,954 ,,
Average	1,959,572,925 ,,	Average	2,025,150,391 ,,

1901–92 . . 2,189,714,365 yds.

This can only be remedied, however, by steady improvement in the condition of the people, and the British cotton manufacturer is the last man in the world likely to gain anything by a policy of forcing trade. The native manufacturer, it is true, is a keen competitor, but hardly in anything so far except the cheaper fabrics, and if India became wealthier the first visible effect would be increased demand for cotton goods of all descriptions, but more especially the better qualities, which are almost entirely imported.

Of other goods there are necessarily some of which Great Britain is not a producer. The contest for the trade in kerosene has been waged for some years between the United States and Russia, and the latter has finally come off victorious; partly because its sources of production are nearer at hand, and partly because the quality, being inferior, is cheaper, a most important factor with so poor a country as India. Burma, however, is now in turn threatening Russia, and the day may not be far distant when India not only supplies its own wants, but becomes a competitor with, instead of a consumer of, the production of other countries. The dread of something of the kind has moved that powerful American corporation, the Standard Oil Company, to seek to obtain control over the output of these oilfields.

Then there are others not exactly dependent on demand or supply, such as salt and coal. The

consumption of salt in India is an even better
barometer of the condition of the people than spirits,
or beer, or tobacco, or tea in the United Kingdom.
These are, to some extent at least, luxuries, though
people do not always deny themselves indulgence
on account of the empty state of their pockets. But
salt is a necessary of life, more so in India than in
England, where proximity to the sea imparts a
certain brackishness to the atmosphere.

The barometer is not the import, for India has
supplies of its own, and produces on an average about
one million tons per annum, or something like three-
fourths of the annual consumption. The tax upon
consumption is so heavy as to be equal to about four
times the value, inclusive of oversea freight and
charges. The use of it is thus necessarily restricted
to the narrowest compass in all but the better class
households, and the impost is admittedly the most
severe of any levied throughout the country. That
consumption would immensely increase with the
abolition, or even the lightening of the duty, goes
without saying, and were the means of the people to
expand, this also is one of the first ways in which it
would be likely to show itself. Irrespective of this,
there ought of course to be an increase of consumption in proportion to increase of population, which
though small of late, is nevertheless progressive.
This affords, as perhaps nothing else does, an insight
into the condition of the people, and the following
shows the figures for the last ten years :—

Salt consumed in Maunds (1 *Maund* = 82·2857 *lbs.*).

1891–92	.	34,851,228	1896–97 .	35,788,366
1892–93	.	35,451,290	1897–98 .	35,121,723
1893–94	.	34,028,156	1898–99 .	35,769,581
1894–95	.	34,550,872	1899–1900	35,996,018
1895–96	.	35,186,983	1900–01 .	35,727,000
		174,068,529		178,402,688
Average		34,813,706	Average	35,680,538

As the yield of the salt duty averages nearly
Rx. 9,000,000 per annum, or about one-seventh of the
total taxation and land revenue of India, it will be
realised how heavily it must fall on an impoverished
people. The corn tax recently imposed in Great
Britain is estimated to produce about £2,500,000;
but if one-seventh of the taxation revenue were
derived from it, the amount to be raised under
ordinary conditions would be upwards of £17,500,000,
that is, the tax would have to be increased seven-
fold. It appears then that the Indian peasant
is taxed on one of the principal necessaries of
life to what would be the equivalent of nearly
ten shillings a quarter on wheat in the United
Kingdom.[1]

Another remarkable feature is that in Bengal,
which is almost entirely free from visitations of

[1] Announcement has been made of the intention to reduce the salt
tax for the fiscal year 1903–04 by 8 annas per maund, equivalent to a
total of about Rx.1,750,000. Probably the revenue will not suffer to
this extent, as some increase in consumption is likely. The step is
one of the most commendable the Indian Government has taken for
many years.

famine, and where population is more dense and increases more rapidly than in any other part of the continent, the consumption of salt is actually on the decline, whereas in Bombay where the reverse conditions have latterly prevailed, there is a steady increase. This can only be accounted for by Bombay being the chief centre of manufacturing industry as distinct from commercial enterprise — Calcutta, the main outlet for Bengal, being still the leading port both as regards the import and export trade of India. The wage-earning industrial class is compelled to consume more food than the agricultural peasant, and there are a greater number of well-to-do people whose resources do not limit them to bare subsistence. This is one more evidence of the benefit to the minority engaged in industry, or directly affected by it, though it may be at the expense of those who are otherwise occupied.

Even the one-fourth, more or less, of this condiment that is imported depends on extraneous circumstances. Apart altogether from value, the bulk of Indian exports is much greater than that of the ordinary class of imports, and vessels would only be likely to secure full cargoes outwards. For the other voyage, salt or coal is usually more profitable than ballast, but as India is rapidly developing its own coal supplies, and becoming in some instances an exporter, that is almost every year of less importance. But with so heavy a tax on salt narrow fluctuations in price do not signify, and a year when India's produce shipments are heavy almost invariably signifies a large import of salt, carried in the vessels required for transport. Thus the most important, as far as bulk is concerned, of British exports to India, is really directly dependent on the Indian export season.

Beyond these, India annually requires a large assortment of goods for industrial purposes and general consumption. Very little is raw material in the generally accepted meaning of the term; India has no manufactures worth speaking of which are not based on material of home production like cotton and jute. A good deal is for constructive purposes, especially for railways, and most of the remainder is destined for the consumption of the European population, or at best of the wealthier natives. Outside cotton piece goods and salt, the general native population may be said to have little or no interest in the import trade.

As the great majority of the Europeans are British, it is scarcely surprising that they look to the United Kingdom for their supplies, and it is remarkable how small have been the inroads of the most enterprising of foreign nations. Buying so largely as they do from India, one would expect to find both the United States and Germany bidding for a full share of what they are proving themselves well able to supply in competition with British manufacturers, but whatever attempts have been made in this direction have not, so far at least, met with any conspicuous success. Austria stands well up in the list, but owes its place to the beet sugar trade, having made this branch of its foreign commerce a speciality, and in addition to the State bounties, assisted latterly by the cartel system, has established a steamship service to the East with specially cheap freights, and having ports on the Mediterranean has been able to outdistance its competitors of northern Europe. This is a trade outside the scope of Great Britain, and one with which under ordinary conditions it would have no cause to seek to interfere, though as we have already had occasion to observe it has instigated the Indian Government to do so.

But as regards general manufactures, Great Britain manages to hold its own extremely well. It will be remembered that not long ago there was considerable controversy concerning the supply of American locomotives for Indian railways, the orders having been given on the ground that British makers were unable to supply them within a reasonable period. Whether that was really so or not, it appears to have been generally agreed that the American engines turned out, apart from prime cost, exceedingly expensive, especially as regards consumption of fuel and need of repairs. Another experiment was subsequently made, and Germany secured a considerable order on tender, said to be 20 per cent. lower in price and 25 per cent. more expeditious in time, than that of any British manufacturer. It remains to be seen whether the outcome will be any more satisfactory. Possibly a fair amount of trade in the other machinery and iron and steel industries passed temporarily to foreigners for the same reasons, home manufacturers for a time having been quite unable to cope with the demands made on them. Other branches of industry were scarcely so pressed, and in a few of the more important it is interesting to follow the movements over a period of years.

Value of Total Imports—		*Value of Imports from*—		
		United Kingdom.	Germany.	United States.
Iron and Steel—				
1890–91	Rx.3,034,494	Rx 2,572,060	Rx.54,620	Rx.146
1895–96	3,848,601	2,444,794	69,599	537
1900–01	4,572,631	2,939,247	151,717	156,240
1901–02	4,863,919	2,836,155	216,661	73,237
Machinery—				
1890–91	Rx.2,063,863	Rx.2,045,946	Rx.5,186	Rx.1,580
1895–96	3,237,401	3,187,817	31,230	1,598
1900–01	2,257,559	2,166,436	15,500	36,240
1901–02	3,005,881	2,887,362	19,854	69,310
Railway Plant and Rolling Stock (exclusive of Government import)—				
1890–91	Rx.2,001,853	Rx.2,001,175	...	Rx.18
1895–96	1,520,585	1,504,380	...	85
1900–01	1,341,120	1,258,026	...	48,559
1901–02	1,542,579	1,393,068	...	29,817

Hardware, Cutlery, Tools, etc.—	United Kingdom.	Germany.	United States.
1890–91 Rx.1,197,614	Rx.1,033,916	Rx.55,794	Rx.3,398
1895–96 1,483,475	1,167,315	148,740	6,595
1900–01 1,841,473	1,281,120	232,709	38,827
1901–02 1,706,637	1,187,242	257,877	42,224

Woollen Manufactures—

	United Kingdom.	Germany.	United States.
1890–91 Rx.1,818,213	Rx 1,361,344	Rx.224,041	...
1895–96 1,445,517	939,644	260,403	...
1900–01 2,112,576	1,328,352	537,261	...
1901–02 1,969,499	1,199,274	558,900	...

Wearing Apparel and Boots and Shoes—

	United Kingdom.	Germany.	United States.
1890–91 Rx.1,349,898	Rx 870,401	Rx.22,187	Rx.1,154
1895–96 1 594,280	889,248	65,074	2,400
1900–01 1,539,777	870,600	134,996	6,129
1901–02 1,694,145	887,206	102,063	7,278

Paper and Stationery—

	United Kingdom.	Germany.	United States.
1890–91 Rx.703,318	Rx.489,892	Rx.26,340	Rx.189
1895–96 744,588	447,542	72,194	2,351
1900–01 769,875	504,893	40,636	17,954
1901–02 850,020	497,877	86,085	14,710

These returns show that Germany is making some headway, but that the United States have hardly yet begun to make their competition felt whatever they may be destined to accomplish in the future, and in no instance is their percentage more than a beggarly one. One or two countries that Great Britain does not usually regard as dangerous rivals have entered the lists. The missing item in the table for iron and steel is accounted

for by Belgium, and though Belgian competition
at times is keenly felt in the home markets, there
has not so far been a great deal of evidence of it
abroad. Austria, too, is quite unexpectedly found
claiming a share of the Indian demand for goods
it produces besides sugar, but has not usually
shown itself able to dispose of abroad in any large
quantities. It is very likely, however, that part of
these, as well as some of the sugar, are of German
origin. The shorter sea voyage and cheap freights
offer inducements to South German manufacturers
who can ship *viâ* Trieste that would not exist over
the longer land, and much longer sea route, by
Hamburg, or Bremen, or the Rhine outlets.

An examination of the details of the minor
articles of merchandise, far too numerous to do
more than refer to casually, reveals the predominating proportion supplied by Great Britain whenever
they can be produced there. Indeed it is remarkable
how many goods of foreign origin, incapable of
being economically produced in Great Britain at
all, only find their way to India through British
ports and British merchants, whereas with most
other outlying portions of the Empire of any consequence, direct trade in them has been opened
up. For the same reason, it may be that foreign
competition in the more important articles is keener
than appears from official records, and part of the
imports returned as British may actually be of other
origin.

Without artificial incentive then, the foreign trade of India has drifted into channels that best suit its own interests and those of Great Britain at the same time. India could not possibly be so excellent a customer for British merchandise and manufactures were it not that worldwide opportunities are enjoyed for disposing of its own products without restraint. Deprived of these, some of its chief industries, agricultural as well as manufacturing, would be severely crippled. Continental Europe for instance, is rapidly following the example set by Great Britain in discarding East Indian cotton : the greater earning power of its various peoples, together with the cheapening of production, enabling them to use the superior fabrics manufactured from the American or Egyptian staple, and in future it will only be when there is a deficiency of these that any large demand for the mostly inferior growths of India will be experienced. The cotton operatives of Europe situated one day under such circumstances, may then repeat the prayer of the Lancashire operative during the cotton famine caused by the American war, who in the middle of an eloquent appeal to the Almighty for supplies of the raw material, added as parenthesis, " But O Lord, not Surats, not Surats."

This one very important source of such wealth as India enjoys would have been largely dried up had it not been for the appearance of a new customer in Japan, whose rapid progress in civilisation has made it an immense consumer of cotton fabrics, though it has not attained that state of wealth where indulgence in the more expensive ones is possible to any considerable extent. Just as Germany, France, Austria, and Italy took the place of Great Britain, so now Japan has followed them, and may be expected for many years to help to maintain the Indian cotton planter.

India requires equally ready access to the consumers of the whole world if the industries built up and dependent on foreign trade are to continue to prosper, and none of them could now be destroyed without making the general condition of the country worse than it actually is. It thus requires absolute freedom in its export trade for everything but food products, nor does it want that trade attracted to Great Britain by artificial tariff arrangements while it has the whole world for its customer.

It is equally essential that its import trade should have imposed upon it as few restrictions as possible. India wants the necessaries of life and of industry at the cheapest prices procurable, and experience proves that hitherto no country has been able to supply them on these terms so well as Great Britain. But there is still a great deficiency of many of the simplest of modern appliances without which nowadays a country can hardly hope to make progress. Modern agricultural machinery is hardly yet known throughout India,

and it is impossible to believe that were it largely
to take the place of the existing primitive methods
of culture, the production of food in a nominally
favourable season would not be immensely increased.
Something like one-third of the cultivable area
is still waste land; much of it, no doubt, inferior,
but still capable of substantial yield if properly
tilled, and above all irrigated. The pressure
of population on the existing cultivated area is
perhaps the most serious problem the country
presents, and anything calculated to distribute it
more widely is bound to help to raise India to a
higher level of existence. If another country can
provide the best and cheapest inventions, Great
Britain should not stand in the way.

Any scheme then, that brought India within
the circle of a so-called imperial tariff, must be
to its detriment rather than its benefit. Indeed, it
would more likely than not be used in an endeavour
to cripple or destroy some part of its existing trade.
India's coalfields are now supplying countries in
the East where formerly British fuel enjoyed the
monopoly. Indian cotton yarn has almost displaced
Lancashire spinnings in the markets of China, and
Indian piece goods are competing as far west as
Africa, imports of them into Zanzibar and other
ports on the Eastern littoral reaching far into the
interior of that continent. Calcutta bags and
gunny cloth rival the productions of Dundee in
every market of the world, and the industry pro-

mises eventually to exceed in importance that of cotton manufacture.

India has quite sufficient risks to face in the ordinary course of events, without being artificially handicapped in addition. One of its most valuable natural products, indigo, has lately been threatened with extinction through the discovery, long sought after, of a manufactured substitute, which at length rewarded the patience and perseverance of German chemists. The effect has been a fall in price of the natural dye as well as a great supersession of it, but it is still a question whether it will pay to go on producing it in anything like the former quantity in face of the competition of the synthetic substitute. As far as the inferior qualities are concerned, this already appears to be decided in the negative.

Can it be conceived that were India's fiscal arrangements placed to any considerable extent under the control of British legislators, they would not be regulated with an eye to British interests ? Intense jealousy of India is constantly cropping up in everything affecting fiscal or industrial legislation for that country, and no Factory Act can be introduced there which does not induce sharp criticism and the demand that it shall be made as stringent as possible in the interests, less of the native operative, than of the British manufacturer. With the opening of the Far East, India's opportunities ought to be illimitable, but are sure to come into conflict at many points with Western Europe.

To give Great Britain under such circumstances the control over Indian foreign trade and internal industry that would be secured by a common tariff, would be an unpardonable iniquity.

Consideration of this subject has been limited to the oversea trade. There is also a growing, and already considerable, overland trade with the native States fringing on the northern and western boundaries of India, but their inhabitants are scarcely yet sufficiently civilised to engage in commerce on any large scale. The Asiatic instinct for barter is no doubt strong in them, and this leads them to collect such natural products as their territories yield, to exchange for what many of them regard as the luxuries of India. This is a trade that ought certainly not to be interfered with more than the revenue laws imperatively demand, and is likely, too, to encourage oversea commerce, because in many instances it proves to be European merchandise that is the most eagerly sought after.

After a lengthy period of stagnation, and a shorter one of retrogression, arising from the severe famines of the last few years, Indian foreign trade has, according to the latest returns, taken a decided step forward, and for the year ended 31st March 1902 the exports exceeded in value anything previously recorded. This is all the more satisfactory because the principal increases are not in articles that drain India of commodities it stands so much in need of for its own consumption. Gains

of Rx.7,765,233 in oilseeds and of Rx.4,298,692
in raw cotton show the extent of the recovery in
two directions where production is chiefly for foreign
use, and another of Rx.5,146,105 in cotton yarn
marks the rehabilitation of an important industry,
temporarily overthrown by scarcity of raw material.
The increase of Rx.3,245,610 in wheat and flour represents very nearly the total value as well, and while
satisfactory to the extent that it shows the crops to
have returned to more normal size and conditions, is
not, for reasons already given, to be regarded with
any great amount of favour. On the other hand the
very large decrease of Rx.3,251,952 in hides and skins,
raw as well as dressed, can only be regarded with
mixed feelings. It affords an idea of the dearth of
cattle as a result of the famine, but also engenders
the hope that by careful preservation of what are
left the herds may in the course of a few years again
increase to their former numbers.

Figures showing trade totals will be found in the
Appendix, but to enhance their interest they are
given here in more consecutive detail. They refer to
merchandise only, but are inclusive of Government
stores.

	Imports.	Exports.
1891–92 . .	Rx.69,432,383	Rx.108,173,592
1892–93 . .	66,265,277	106,595,475
1893–94 . .	77,021,432	106,503,369
1894–95 . .	73,528,993	108,913,778
1895–96 . .	72,936,753	114,334,738
1896–97 . .	76,117,373	103,984,096

	Imports.	Exports.
1897–98 . .	Rx.73,647,035	Rx.97,632,781
1898–99 . .	72,101,528	112,799,725
1899–1900 . .	75,304,480	109,083,322
1900–01 . .	80,894,589	107,763,415
1901–02 . .	88,732,387	124,895,290

But mere magnitude of trade is no real test of Indian prosperity, and to be properly appreciated the figures must be studied in relation to internal conditions as well as the external influences that have helped to produce them.

CHAPTER VI

CROWN COLONIES

Nature and Influence of their Populations—Dominance of the White
Race in Government and in Trade—Ownership of the Land.
THE WEST INDIES :—Natural and Political Affinities—Draw-
backs arising from Restricted Area—Importance of the Sugar
Industry—Success of Cocoa Cultivation—Obstacles to Fruit Cul-
ture—Dependence on Foreign Food Supplies—Endeavours to
Negotiate Commercial Treaties—Advantages Offered and Sought
by United States—The Jamaica Subsidy and Fruit Industry—
Absurdities of the Fiscal System—Trinidad and Venezuela—
Generally Unsound Economic Conditions. WEST AFRICA :—
Activity of Foreign Nations—Resulting Political Complications—
Limited Character of Export Trade—Importance of Foreign
Countries as Consumers of the Products—Disadvantages of
Climate—The Spirit Trade—Cotton Piece Goods—Hardware—
Working Expenses of Trade—The Gold Mining Industry—Chaos
of the Present Tariff System—Basis of Readjustment—Trade
Clearing Houses—Transit Dues—Coinage and Currency—Free
Trade. THE FARTHER EAST : CEYLON :—Competition with India
—Different Distribution of Trade—The Tea Industry—Plumbago
—Cotton Goods. MAURITIUS AND SEYCHELLES : Transfer of
Landed Estates to East Indian Cultivators—Sugar Trade with
India and South Africa—Vanilla and Cocoa Nut Industries.
HONG-KONG :—Purely a Trade Centre—Increasing Competition
of Foreign Countries. STRAITS SETTLEMENTS :—Natural Products
—Importance as a Transit Station—Absolute Fiscal Freedom—
Currency—Partial Dependence on British Free Trade.

INDIA is the greatest of the Crown colonies; so great
in fact, as to be dignified with the title of empire.
But in form of government and methods of administration it is akin to the scattered possessions of the

British Empire, and not to the large self-governing communities we have been dealing with. One result of this, as we have seen in the case of India, is the tendency to regulate trade as well as finance in the interests of the minority which governs, and not of the majority which is governed, and this is undoubtedly one of the causes which keep many of these possessions in so backward a condition.

The theory is that the populations they contain are neither fit for self-government nor the management of their own business affairs. They belong to the coloured and so-called inferior races, which white mankind has always chosen to believe must be kept in a state of tutelage, if not of actual bondage, with the result that their capabilities have rarely been tested. Yet there is no just ground for the assumption that these are really inferior. It is only the pick of the white races, mentally and physically, that settles for any length of time in the tropics, where the British Crown colonies are nearly all located, and it is only sheer force of will that prevents rapid decadence. Climate in the long run proves irresistible, and even if the emigrant overcomes it, the next generation, to say nothing of succeeding ones, is certain to succumb to the enervating influences. The negro on the other hand passes down his physical fitness unimpaired, and were his mental faculties equally developed they might be equally retained. Every now and again one does emerge from among his fellows and proves his right to rank among the best and most intelligent of mankind, though unfortunately this is too often accompanied by an inclination to despise the race from which he has sprung and to which he belongs. There are very few coloured men, who having become educated and gained some social position, do not seek to ally themselves with the race with which intellectually they feel most in sympathy. All the more honour to the handful that does devote its talent to the raising of its fellows nearer the level it has itself attained.

But in this little assistance is ever rendered by the governing power. Political legislation and administration are devoted almost exclusively to the welfare of the dominant race, and sometimes even the crumbs that fall from the table are carefully gathered lest they should benefit the subordinate, and unfit it for the sphere to which it is supposed Providence has ordained it. Nor does Christianity often attempt much more, at anyrate where there is a permanent white element, but contents itself with saving the soul without elevating the mind beyond the stage necessary to realise some of the mysteries of religion.

Tropical colonies thus fall into two distinct classes. In the first pretty nearly everything has come into the possession of the white race; the land belongs to it, the produce it yields is its perquisite, while the children of the soil are but little

removed from the condition of slavery ; indeed for
some reasons that state would be preferable, because
the slave generally possesses an intrinsic value
worth conserving. The owners either become themselves residents, or, where they can afford it, appoint
permanent agents to represent them who speedily
assume all the authority attached to ownership, and
locally at least become despots. As a rule their
influence is more baneful than that of the real
owners. The latter may now and again be animated
by sentiment, or humanitarianism, or some other
feeling the indulgence of which means expense : the
agent cannot afford to indulge out of his own
pocket, and does not often feel justified, if he would
be permitted to do so, out of his employer's. The
main object kept in view in nearly all such cases
is to extract the greatest amount of profit with the
least possible outlay.

In the second class, ownership if not actually
declined is not sought after with any zest on a
large scale : the object is trade, and the soil and
its cultivation are left to the aboriginal community.
India is an instance of this ; the great sums of British
capital invested there going almost entirely into
enterprises that were foreign to the native inhabitants before the incursion of Western civilisation.
But the white man has permeated India in a way
not attempted elsewhere, and the invasion has not
always proved entirely beneficial. In some of the
minor possessions he has remained content with

keeping on the edge; and has left the profits of production and of internal trade in the hands of the people themselves. Sharing in the spoils, they are stimulated to greater exertion, and possessions of the second class are generally more progressive and prosperous than the first. They enjoy the further advantage of fresh energy constantly instilled at the base of operations. The same commercial firms may exploit them for generations, but regularly with fresh blood. It is the junior partners and men who hope to become partners, to whom the colonial management is usually intrusted, and who are invariably relieved before the deadening influences of climate become permanent. Success greatly depends on the energy they can instil into the local community, and this is sometimes effectively accomplished.

Intelligent application of these broad principles will enable us to realise more fully the forces at work in the outlying portions of the British Empire subject to Crown Colony Government. For the purpose of more definite consideration these may be divided into three groups: the first situated in the Western Hemisphere, and designated the West Indies; the second in West Africa, no longer confined to a narrow strip of coast; the third scattered over what is usually termed the Farther East, and embracing everything east of the Cape of Good Hope.

I.—THE WEST INDIES.[1]

These possessions lie in a part of the world where Great Britain has long ceased to be the paramount power, and where it has been compelled to relinquish much of its commercial influence. Were they scattered upon the mainland as they are over the Caribbean Sea, it would be impossible to retain ownership; they would be compelled in their own interests, as well as for the safety of the surrounding territory to become identified more closely with it. But as islands they are able to maintain their political integrity, though that has not prevented them gravitating in their commercial relations to the Western continent with which they have a natural affinity.

There is one exception, British Guiana, better known to many people under the designation of one portion of it—Demerara, which forms part of the South American mainland, and has in consequence involved Great Britain in complications with neighbours. Fortunately none of them are politically or commercially powers of the first magnitude, though there is one such nearly always ready to take part in any dispute that arises; the Venezuela boundary question, for instance, very nearly resulted in a quarrel between Great Britain

[1] For a succinct account of the causes that have led to the depressed condition of these colonies I would refer my readers to a previously published work, *The British West Indies and the Sugar Industry*, which deals with social and economic, rather than trade, issues.

and the United States. But islands have their boundaries set by nature, and as long as jurisdiction is not divided no questions of ownership can well arise. With the exception of Jamaica, and possibly Trinidad, none of those in the West Indies any longer subject to European control are sufficiently large to permit of this; most of them are smaller than an ordinary sized English county, and some with hardly the area of a decent sized English parish. Such restriction must necessarily be detrimental to development, but ought at least to afford that measure of happiness supposed to accompany absence of history.

But it also detracts from their value as industrial units in a modern sense. They were all very well when the prevailing idea favoured getting everything out of a country and putting nothing back again; but now the aim seems to be to put as much as possible in and never mind what comes out. The West Indies afford little opportunity for development on a European, or African, much less an American, scale. When people can walk across an island in the cool of the day they hardly need a railway to carry them, and the only use for it in many places is to convey the produce of plantations to the nearest shipping port, which, needless to say, does not require plant or rolling stock of a very high order. In the largest as well as most populous of the British islands, Jamaica, a trunk line has been in existence many years, but impoverished rather than enriched the people who invested their money in it. Under the most favourable circumstances all that can ever be wanted there in future is a series of short branch lines connecting with it from such points as are of any consequence. For most purposes good roads and a constant steamship service round the islands furnish the best means of regular and cheap communication.

Bridges and other great engineering works are for the same reasons superfluous; anything of the sort that is needed can only be on a comparatively insignificant scale. Even the products of the soil, with one important exception, require no costly implements or machinery to cultivate or manufacture into a fit state for consumption, and there is only one industry in which any considerable amount of capital can be economically sunk. That particular one, namely sugar, is and has been over a considerable period in the direst distress, and even where the inclination may exist, want of resources prevents the expenditure sufficient to benefit the interests most directly concerned.

Supposing the prospects were as bright as until lately they appeared gloomy, there would be a strict limit to artificial development. Where ideas in other parts of the world are accustomed to flow in millions, they rarely in the West Indies get beyond a few modest thousands, and an expenditure of one or two millions sterling would accomplish almost everything that could be dreamt of on an important scale. Trade is consequently restricted to those regularly recurring branches, which though the most profitable in the long run, are not as a rule the most eagerly sought after.

The British West Indies have, during nearly the entire period of their connection with Great Britain, been essentially a one-horse concern as regards production. Sugar dominated everything: and as sugar until some twenty or thirty years ago was only another way of spelling wealth, everything was sacrificed to it. When the evil days of the bounty system and over-production ensued, therefore, the islands were left without other resource, and only in British Guiana and Trinidad were efforts made to save the industry by the adoption of modern methods. They were partially successful at least, inasmuch as neither of these possessions has until quite lately, like nearly all the rest, had to fall back for periodical assistance on the Imperial Exchequer, and as neither enjoys as great natural advantages as some that have suffered far more severely, it may be safely surmised that had the same means been adopted throughout, the distress would have been much less intense. Gradually, other industries have been introduced, and in one or two instances sugar is no longer the mainstay: in one at least it has entirely disappeared as a commercial factor.

This is the island of Grenada where cocoa is now as completely monarch as sugar was in former days. It has been a case of transferring all the eggs from one basket to another, and so far the result has been excellent, as the world's production of cocoa still lags behind the demand, and prices which must leave a handsome margin to the grower are the result. But whereas in most countries this would mean the rapid accumulation of wealth, in Grenada it seems for some reason only to raise the population a trifle above the low average of the neighbouring islands. Trinidad grows more cocoa than Grenada, but it is a much larger island with a more varied production, though such prosperity as it enjoys is derived principally from this particular cultivation.

Jamaica in recent years has taken a departure in another direction, and now relies mainly on its fruit crops, but as it is larger in area, so its productions are more diverse than any of the others and consist of nearly everything associated with a tropical climate. Many of the smaller islands are equally suited to fruit culture, but difficulties of rapid transport have hitherto prevented this being turned to profitable account.

This brief survey of the capabilities of the West Indies shows that their production is almost entirely limited to food; the only exceptions worth noting are the gold mines in British Guiana, and

14

the pitch obtained from a lake in Trinidad. A land so situated might be expected in the first place to feed its own inhabitants; but here it is otherwise, for not only do these islands export nearly everything of the kind they grow, but as a natural consequence import most of the food they consume. Of vegetables and fruit they have abundance : more perhaps is eaten than is good for health, but breadstuffs, dairy produce, fresh meat, and even fish, are obtained in large quantities from outside. This at least increases the foreign trade of the West Indies and makes it, what rarely occurs, of greater importance than the internal. And no doubt the truest economy will be for them to go on selling to the foreigner, which in this instance includes the British, much of what they produce, buying from him in return most of what they consume.

To achieve this successfully the utmost possible freedom of trade is essential, yet no portion of the British dominions has endeavoured more sedulously to bind itself down by treaty or arrangement to exclusive dealings. This may be largely the misfortune rather than the fault of the West Indies, which have suffered so heavily from the most remarkable fiscal legislation of modern times, over which they have had not the slightest control. Having failed to persuade Great Britain to afford them the necessary protection, some of them have more than once tried to sell themselves, commercially at anyrate, to the United States : indeed some of the white estate proprietors would have been only too glad to transfer themselves politically as well from the Union Jack to the Stars and Stripes, though after the experience Cuba has passed through they very likely realise by this time that it would have been a mistake. Certainly as regards their sugar, finding a market for which was the sole inducement to such a transaction, they would hardly have been any better off than under existing conditions.

Because for some years the United States have afforded them that market, and nearly all the sugar they have produced has found its destination there. This is owing to the circumstance of the European bounties having been countervailed by the Dingley tariff, not exclusively to the benefit of the West Indies, but of all cane sugar producing countries, of which the West Indies being in such close proximity were among the first to be able to take advantage. Experience proved that this was not enough to prevent a continuous fall in prices, as persistent over-production in Europe ultimately regulated market values. Canada likewise extended its preferential tariff to British West India sugar, but as no account was taken of the bounties, and the concession in duty proved less than the countervailed bounties, it has so far been of little effect. The result is that the entire export of some of the islands, and a large portion of that of others, has gone outside the British Empire, in other words to the United States. However this may be regarded from a sentimental point of view, there is nothing to deplore in it from a West Indian one, because assuming the United States to be consumers of West Indian produce, they afford the nearest and, other things being equal, the most natural market for it. There is no reason to suppose that had Great Britain offered equal facilities, this particular trade would have been diverted.

This movement is accentuated as far as Jamaica is concerned by the fruit trade, practically the whole of which, until quite recently, was conducted with the United States. With the subsidising of a line of steamers to Great Britain specially in the interests of this industry, a change is occurring, but this it must be remembered is an attempt to open out a new channel, not to divert an old one, and if successful should result in more or less substantial increase in the value of the exports of the island. The service was only commenced in the spring of 1901, the main condition of the subsidy being that at least 20,000 bunches of bananas should be purchased and exported each recurring fortnight. This means rather more than half a million bunches a year, but inasmuch as the shipments to the United States have already reached over ten million bunches in that time, it will be seen what a big margin there is to fill up.

The contract minimum has so far been pretty regularly exceeded ; for the first complete year the quantity actually carried was nearly 650,000 bunches, while another branch of the service has more recently been opened with Manchester, and promises to absorb even larger quantities. There has, however, been some amalgamation of the interests of the American and English fruit companies, and though this may facilitate the smooth working of the trade, the removal of competition is hardly calculated to benefit the native producer. As a matter of fact the 1s. 6d. a bunch export value credited in the official trade returns is generally considered to be in excess of what actually accrues in hard cash to the island.

Irrespective of tariff preferences, British Guiana and Trinidad both find a market for their sugar in Great Britain, partly owing to the fact that it is prepared in a way to make it regarded as a luxury, and so to command a specially high price, and partly because for that very reason it is at a disadvantage in the United States markets where there is a differential import duty against refined sugar. Great Britain too is the principal market for cocoa, though a large quantity is exported to France, famous for its confections of chocolate. Coffee, arrowroot, spices, and a few minor products likewise find their way across the Atlantic to a greater extent than to its western shores.

With the exception of sugar West Indian pro-

ducts stand in no need of preferential treatment
in Great Britain or elsewhere. What they do need
is facilities for shipment, not special favours in
countries of destination. Nor does sugar require
such treatment because it is West Indian; it is
the controversy between cane and beet, and provided both are produced and sold under equal
conditions the former has nothing to fear in ordinary competition. The final act of the Brussels
Conference is supposed to have ensured this:
should it after all fail to do so, equality must be
secured by other methods. At least two British
possessions, Australia and South Africa, have shown
the way by levying a higher duty, not on foreign
as distinct from British-grown sugar, but on beet
as distinct from cane.

Having no manufacturing industries requiring
equipment or raw material, the wants of the
population of the West Indies are confined to
the necessaries, and such of the luxuries of life as
they can afford, which in their impoverished state
are extremely few. Nor do the necessaries go far
beyond cheap, if not the cheapest, food and clothing; the warmth of the climate renders anything
in the nature of artificial heat superfluous, and most
of the fuel imported that is not for cooking purposes,
is for the use of ocean steamships or the smaller
craft navigating local waters. Tools and implements, generally of the simplest kind, hardware
and building material, pretty well exhaust the

primitive requirements of one of the most backward portions of the earth that lays claim to civilisation. Books and literature must rank among the higher luxuries, and even the ordinary newspaper of diminutive size and contents has often to maintain a desperate struggle for existence.

As far as food is concerned the natural source of supply lies close at hand, and regularity is facilitated, for a considerable part of the year at anyrate, by the return trade that is available in the form of sugar and fruit. The United States provide most of the breadstuffs and meat, the latter pickled or otherwise preserved, a few of the islands furnishing fresh meat in limited quantities. Salted fish also enters largely into the consumption of the labouring class which constitutes the vast majority of the populace, and is of British North American, or more strictly of Newfoundland, origin.

Of the trade in more expensive foodstuffs Great Britain is able to claim a larger share, and regularly ships by each outgoing steamer a miscellaneous assortment of dairy produce and provisions, mostly tinned. But in breadstuffs it cannot hope to compete.

In clothing, on the other hand, it enjoys and maintains by far the largest proportion of the trade. This condition of things is what the United States have attempted to break down in their various negotiations for treaties of reciprocity.

They do not need any guarantee for a continuance
of the demand for flour, Indian meal, pork, and
pressed beef ; their only serious competitor for any
of these is Canada, and under present conditions
none of the sugar or fruit producing islands dare
offend the United States by affording a preference
to any other country, inside or outside the British
Empire, that would prejudice them ; it would be
foolish even to contemplate such a move.   But
American manufacturers would like to sell more of
their cotton piece goods, and boots and shoes, and
such like everyday requirements, and urge their
special claims at every available opportunity.   So
far therefore as any recent changes have been
contemplated, they have been in a direction that
would prove detrimental rather than otherwise to
British trade.

It is only under extraordinary circumstances that
a preference outside the Empire could be tolerated,
and there is nothing in the West Indian situation
to call for this.   They are far too poor and helpless
a community to be exploited by any group of traders
on the lookout to extend their connections, to whatever nationality they belong.   Unfortunately the
fiscal system everywhere prevalent throughout the
islands offers an invitation to deals of this character,
as there is hardly anything that is not subject to an
import duty, and in many instances export duties are
levied as well.   In Dominica the latter are carried
to so absurd an extent, that a list containing no

fewer than 39 items paying the impost, contributed in 1899 the insignificant sum of £1458 to the island revenue. What is really wanted to stimulate trade and encourage local prosperity, is not concessions and trading privileges to one country or another, but the striking away of the fetters that shackle every petty movement of produce or merchandise. And the first step in this direction is free inter island and colonial trade in place of the present ridiculous system that prevents one possession purchasing in another because the duty would have to be paid in both.

Trinidad has already two branches of trade—the regular, and another dealing with transhipments, principally with Venezuela. With a little friendly assistance on both sides the latter is capable of considerable extension. Venezuela is noted for its recurring revolutions more than anything else, and British merchants even before the latest troubles fought somewhat shy of the connection; the Germans tried it, more apparently to their sorrow than their profit, unless the advantage of the right of political interference is thrown into the scale. But Trinidad lies directly off its shores and enjoys regular and constant intercourse with the United Kingdom as well as the United States, and so affords an excellent entrepot. Venezuela, however, wants the rest of the world to trade with it direct, and by its tariff arrangements threw obstacles in the way of intercourse through Trinidad. Nor is the island government much more liberal. It imposes an export duty on cocoa, for instance, a commodity that is also largely produced in Venezuela, which when it is shipped *viâ* Trinidad has likewise to pay the duty. Were it otherwise, foreign cocoa would be more favourably treated than the native product; the proper remedy is to abolish the duty altogether. Notwithstanding all obstacles this trade has averaged in the past about £500,000 per annum each way; what recent events have done for it remains to be seen.

Such statistics as are of any value in appreciating the situation will be found in the Appendix. It must be borne in mind that without exception these possessions are debtor colonies; they may owe very little in the shape of Government loans, but so much private capital has been sunk by non-resident proprietors and investors, that the interest upon it amounts annually to a considerable sum, and ought to be discharged by the export of produce. Where year after year there is an adverse balance, that is, an excess of imports over exports, it may be surmised that the economic condition is thoroughly unsound. There are, no doubt, mitigating circumstances, such as tourist expenditure—nowhere yet, however, more than a trifling sum; the provisioning and coaling of ships, the materials for which are included in imports but not necessarily returned as exports; and the maintenance of naval and military stations at the expense of the Home

Government. But when all this is taken into account there is in many instances a serious deficit which can only be covered by expenditure of further capital, and in this respect the West Indies have long been a bottomless pit. Surely after so doleful an experience, the experiment is worth making of trade untrammelled, except in a few special cases, by customs imposts, and by raising the revenue required more in accordance with the equitable system in vogue in Great Britain, where until recently at anyrate no man was compelled to contribute to the revenue until he had made provision for at least the barest necessaries of life.

II.—WEST AFRICA.

The West Indies belong to the first class of Crown colonies, that is, possessions that are owned as well as controlled. West Africa comes under the second, where no permanent colonisation has been attempted, and the territory never alienated from its original owners or their lawful successors. It differs in another respect from nearly all other British possessions, inasmuch as the areas actually under British jurisdiction or falling within British spheres of influence are intermingled with those of other European powers which are often of far greater extent. Thus Gambia is only an enclave in the midst of a great French colony. Most of its trade is in the hands of Frenchmen, and practically the whole of its exports, consisting of earth nuts, go to France. Sierra Leone, also of restricted area, is similarly surrounded on every side by French territory, though its trade is principally British ; and alternating with the other colonies are French and German possessions of more or less magnitude and importance, while Spain and Portugal are well represented along the coast.

The activity of these various powers—with the exception of Germany one cannot say their incursions, because they have been there quite as long, if not longer than Great Britain—compelled the adoption somewhere about 1885 of a different policy to the one consistently pursued up to that period. It was no longer possible to confine occupation to mere strips of coast or the banks of navigable rivers, because the trade which ultimately found its way there nearly all originated in the interior, and if powers, hostile politically or commercially, secured possession or control of the interior, they were able to cut off and divert to their own outlets the regular trade of the districts. The word hinterland thus came to possess a very ominous meaning in West Africa, and has been the main cause of the interminable disputes that have sprung up there. The principal consequence, as far as Great Britain is concerned, is that colonies like the Gold Coast and Lagos are no longer confined to mere shipping ports, but run hundreds of miles into the interior and embrace kingdoms, while the most recent acquisition, Nigeria, is extensive enough to constitute an Empire.

Effective occupation is another term of fateful import in West African affairs, and no power was adjudged to have a claim to territory which at some time or other had not been visited and formally annexed by an accredited agent. Permanent occupation of course is out of the question: that would require armies on a continental scale, but each power is constantly exhibiting more or less military zeal in punitive expeditions, another expression West Africa has added to modern political phraseology. Collisions have been the not unnatural outcome of all this, and more than once have nearly ended in serious European war. Complications are of regular occurrence, and the capture by French soldiers on German territory of a rebel native king whose authority was supposed to be exercised within the British possessions has become far too trivial an incident to excite official, much less public, attention.

Some idea of the political situation is necessary before the trade can be rightly comprehended. A war of tariffs under conditions just narrated could only be carried on with the help of military operations, or at best with the connivance of interior traders. The circumstance that in West Africa the native chiefs are often among the most important of these has caused something of the sort to be attempted, and endless treaties exist supposed to confer special privileges on one nationality over another, but except in the Congo Free State, where means have been adopted for enforcing them which for brutality have rarely, if ever, been exceeded, these are seldom effective for any length of time, and as the African negro is as keen a trader as is to be found anywhere, he soon gravitates when left alone to the place where he can make the best bargains. Each nation represented has consequently to live in seeming amity with its neighbours, and as this results in a certain amount of mutual intercourse, it is very difficult to dissociate British West African trade from West African trade generally.

Nor is it advisable from a British point of view that such distinction should be made. The total value of the exports of the British possessions does not average much over £3,000,000 per annum, and looks a mere trifle for Great Britain to absorb. But West Africa does not produce foodstuffs suitable for European consumption, and thus the largest item of the import trade of the United Kingdom is barred from participation. What it does yield is limited almost entirely to raw materials of manufacturing industry, and it is not by any means the most important of these industries that the products are suited for. Several of them are absorbed in greater quantities than West Africa produces; the annual consumption of rubber and furniture woods, principally mahogany, being larger than the African supply of them. But for others, like palm oil and palm kernels, which until quite recent times constituted the backbone of the export trade of these possessions, there is nothing like a sufficient demand, and not only do foreign countries, principally France and Germany, import large quantities direct, but much of what is actually imported into the United Kingdom from foreign as well as British West African ports is eventually re-exported to the Continent.

It is interesting to compare the actual British requirements of these commodities with the British production as represented by the shipments from British West African ports. The year 1901 is taken to illustrate this, and though the figures naturally vary from year to year, it will always be found that production is in excess of consumption by a more or less important quantity.

United Kingdom.	Palm Oil.	Oil Nuts, principally Palm Kernels.
Imports . . .	60,606 tons.	50,090 tons.
Re-exports . .	34,443 ,,	17,675 ,,
Actual Consumption	26,163 ,,	32,415 ,,

Total Exports from		
Sierra Leone . .	548 tons.	16,175 tons.
Gold Coast . .	10,488 ,,	12,844 ,,
Lagos . . .	11,013 ,,	57,176 ,,
Nigeria . . .	41,968 ,,	56,871 ,,
	64,017	143,066

Without allowing for overlapping in time and differences in calculation (the African palm oil returns are given in gallons and have to be converted [1]) no less than 37,852 tons of oil, and 110,651 tons of kernels for expressing oil — not the same substance however as the other, which is obtained from the outer covering of the nut and not from the fruit of the palm tree—were disposed of to foreign consumers who presumably paid better prices than the British could afford. The latter, no doubt, could at a push substitute these products for others now obtained principally from foreign sources, such as linseed or cottonseed or copra, but only at considerable inconvenience and perhaps loss. Things are better as they are, inasmuch as British oil crushers and users get what they want on the most economical terms, and West African producers and shippers experience a far wider demand, and therefore get higher prices, than if they were entirely or mainly dependent on the British market.

The capabilities of West Africa have, it is true, scarcely yet been tested, and nearly everything it supplies to the outer world consists of natural products. Palm oil and kernels, timber and rubber, grow in wild profusion; no expense is entailed in cultivation and the cost depends almost entirely on the labour expended in collection and transport. Both soil and climate undoubtedly offer facilities for tropical products requiring skill and constant

---

[1] The rate here adopted is 300 gallons to the ton.

attention : the basin of the Niger for instance, should
be as suitable for the growth of cotton as the Nile or
the Mississippi. But that can only be undertaken in
competition with the rest of the world, and will
never reach a successful issue if it has to depend on
preferential treatment from any of the great consuming countries. There is abundance of land and
abundance of labour, both awaiting proper application and direction, and the real drawback to development is the execrable climate which renders life
intolerable to the ordinary European except for
brief periods, and enervates him even for these. If
medical skill and scientific investigation can overcome this obstacle, the future of the country as a
producer is well assured.

That means that it should become of equal
importance as a consumer, and of corresponding
value to the countries supplying it, among which
Great Britain has always hitherto been foremost.
The requirements, however, are of a varied nature,
and some of them at least, such as Great Britain is
not able to supply so well as its rivals. Among
them is spirits, a trade so many efforts have been
made unavailingly to suppress. Evils connected
with it there are sure to be wherever it is carried
on, but possibly as far as West Africa is concerned
they have been exaggerated. In any case two
difficulties stand in the way of abolition ; one the
reluctance, amounting to positive refusal, on the
part of the other European nations interested to give

15

it up ; the other and perhaps stronger one, a determination on the part of the natives to have it.
There are plenty of West African products from
which strong liquors can be distilled : happily few of
the natives have yet learned the art, but if put to it
by deprivation of what they are accustomed to get
they might easily do so, greatly to their detriment,
because however vile some of the compounds now
supplied them, they are probably superior to most of
what they would concoct at home.

It is at least satisfactory to know that the British
trade is not extensively involved, and that nearly all
the spirit supplied is of German and Dutch distillation, apart from rum, a good deal of which is shipped
from the West Indies *viâ* the United States. It is
cheap, if not bad, but in the latter respect at least,
agitation has resulted in a good deal of improvement. The traders on the coast whose interests are
in most cases identical with those of the merchants
at home, are fully alive to the evils of the traffic,
and do their best to curtail and not to stimulate it,
in which they are assisted by the Governments,
invariably led by that of Great Britain, which never
loses an opportunity of raising the duties, though
they are not always wisely regulated. Were the
liquor trade interested as well, it might be difficult
to prevent. efforts to increase consumption, consequently it is desirable from every point of view
that whatever the extent of this particular trade, it
should remain, as regards supply, in foreign hands,

and that nothing should be done to transfer it to British. Let the latter by all means control the distribution, as they are likely to do so more sparingly than any of the other nationalities interested.

The item is sometimes a considerable one in the colonial trade returns, in dealing with which the significance of it must not be overlooked. As far as other things are concerned, the supply by British manufacturers is as unobjectionable as it is desirable. Foremost among them, and by far the most important in the West African import trade, is cotton piece goods, and here, as in the case of most other British possessions except Canada, Lancashire enjoys something approaching monopoly and has scarcely anything to gain by capturing the trifle that falls to its competitors. Indeed it would have much to lose by recourse to preferential treatment, because the West African possessions of foreign countries are nearly as good customers as the British, and if the portion of the shipments to Gambia and Sierra Leone that are eventually destined for French territory be taken into account, in some years perhaps they are better ones. The goods are essentially of a cheap character, and other countries, Germany especially, have proved over and over again that where this is the chief element they can beat Great Britain. This does not apply, however, to cotton goods, at anyrate as far as neutral territory is concerned, and whether the demand is for the finest fabrics or the flimsiest prints,

Lancashire is equally able to supply them against all comers. In a country like West Africa, it is an immense advantage to be first established, as quality and pattern when once widely known are difficult to supplant, and the newcomer finds argument and persuasion alike of little avail in getting customers for what he has to offer.

In the third important branch of this trade, namely hardware, the question of cheapness does undoubtedly tell against the British manufacturer ; much of what the negro purchases both as tools of industry and for domestic use being of the rudest description, and in some things Germany and Austria enjoy as thorough a monopoly in the British possessions as Great Britain does for cotton fabrics. But for all that, of the many miscellaneous items classed under this head, which include the cheap and comparatively harmless firearms, the possession of which is so necessary to raise the negro to his proper standard of dignity, a large share falls to the English districts devoted so extensively to this branch of manufacture.

Though the European population to be found at any one time in West Africa is never con-siderable, does not in fact exceed a few thousand souls, nearly everything it wants requires to be imported. Thus a considerable sum included in the value of imports does not represent trade in its ordinary sense, but is rather for working expenses which in nearly every other country are defrayed as well as incurred on the spot. The cost of all this must be taken into account in the price paid for African produce, and necessarily places it at a disadvantage. To begin with, all provisions supplied require to be of the very best quality to keep during the voyage and withstand the climate on arrival; the freight charged on them is very high, and this is further enhanced by the customs duty which very few imports escape. Though the cost of living may be a good deal less than in South Africa—the opportunities for expenditure on anything else than food are severely limited,—it is excessively high in proportion to the value of the produce handled, and so counteracts much of the advantage enjoyed in other respects. This will have to be taken seriously into account in the promotion of fresh cultures, the two chief essentials to the success of which will be a much superior local food supply to anything that now exists, and a considerable cheapening of the cost of transport, not only from the interior, but oversea as well.

The Gold Coast Colony has assumed an added importance through the promised, rather than actual, development of its gold-bearing areas. This does not seem to have got very far beyond the floating of companies which has taken place to the extent of many millions sterling, to say nothing of what has been added by way of premium. A small portion of the money has gone to the maintenance of the various staffs sent out, which thus accounts for the considerable increase in the imports of the colony. Not much has yet been expended on machinery; since its value became of any consequence the figures which presumably include freight and landing charges, both heavy items, have been as follows :—

1897	£15,874
1898	16,863
1899	40,181
1900	29,197
1901	81,337
	£183,452

This was not all for mining purposes, but included what was wanted for the new railway to the mining districts. Neither can there be said to be any adequate return for the money that has so far been expended, the export of raw gold being actually less than in the days before activity prevailed, when there were always a few mines at work. The value of gold and gold-dust exported on one occasion at least, exceeded £100,000, and many times approached very close to that figure. For 1901 the value was only returned at £22,187, lower than anything recorded within the previous fifteen years. West Africa must, for the present at least, be treated from its actual commercial, and not from its prospective mining interest.

There is no part of the world where free trade conditions are so essential for everybody as West Africa. Free trade does not of course imply free imports, because revenue has to be raised to cover cost of administration, which of late years has very materially increased in consequence of the general unrest among the natives arising to a very large extent from the jealousies and rivalries of Europeans, and there is no means of effecting this except by customs duties or some other tax on trade which might prove still more objectionable. But these duties, whatever they are, should be uniform, not only throughout the British possessions, but the foreign ones as well. As it is, the tariff of no two of the British colonies is alike, and in framing them much more consideration is given to the rates prevailing in an adjoining French or German possession, than to anything in force in another under British control.

A striking illustration of this is to be found in the Gold Coast Colony, where two distinct tariffs are in operation, one west of the Volta, where British traders are in undisputed possession; the other, a much lower one, east of that river, where the competition of the German possession of Togoland enters the field. Perhaps it is too much to expect that either Portugal or Spain would willingly enter a general West African customs union; they fear, very likely with some reason, that without the protection at present in operation, their possessions would become commercially valueless to them. But France and Germany do not, nominally at least, impose any restrictions on foreign traders to which their own are not subject, and though France has recently been creating trouble with British traders, it has been by means of territorial concessions and not differential customs duties.

With the bulk of the revenue of these possessions raised from customs duties, anything approaching free trade seems a consummation a long way off. It is not so impossible after all, because most of the money actually obtained is from spirits and tobacco, and nobody would propose to eliminate these. The yield of the *ad valorem* duties on general merchandise is nowhere very considerable, and a little economy in administration would render them unnecessary. Perhaps it is too much to hope for anything of this sort, and a readjustment rather than a reduction of taxation would have to be resorted to. There is no reason whatever why moderate direct taxes, to take the form perhaps of licences for traders, should not be levied, provided care is taken to regulate them in accordance with extent of trade actually done, otherwise small men would be squeezed out and make it much easier for the bigger ones to establish monopolies. All taxation in West Africa is bound in the long run to fall on trade, and it matters very little whether it is direct or indirect. The main object of whatever system is established ought to be to impose as little hindrance to it as possible.

And were a union to be formed on some such lines it would certainly benefit British trade to a far greater extent than could be accomplished by any preferential tariff favourable to these colonies. That is doubtless one reason why both France and Germany might be chary of entering it, though it would benefit them relatively quite as much. In Indo-China, in Madagascar, in Northern Africa, wherever in fact France has founded colonies, it has aimed at securing the trade for its own merchants and manufacturers. West Africa has so far proved the exception; and there it is clearly recognised that development is only possible as long as trade is not harassed by higher duties than are prevalent in the adjoining territories of other Powers. Great Britain has consequently a good deal of say on the subject.

As matters now stand there can be no free exchange of products, other than native, which are generally specially provided for, even between the different British possessions, because the moment goods are entered at one they are liable to duty on which there is no drawback if ultimately moved to another where they again incur it, with the

exception that imports into Lagos are permitted
to enter Nigeria without further payment. But as
Lagos retains the money, it does not suit Nigeria
for trade to be conducted in this way.

The result is, the recurring petty wants of each
possession, and of nearly every trading station in
it, have to be supplied direct by the regular ocean
steamers instead of being distributed, as they might
be far more economically, from two or three localised
centres. An instance of how this can be done is
to be found in the West Indies, where one does
not usually look for anything particularly progressive.
But goods destined for the Windward and Leeward
Islands are transhipped at Barbados from the ocean
liners to smaller craft, which in their voyage pick
up whatever is to be shipped for corresponding
outward treatment. The system is incomplete,
because there too each group, indeed each separate
island, has its own tariff and custom-house which
know of no return on anything that has once passed
the portals. But were the tariffs of Barbados and
all the other islands assimilated, the former might
become an entrepot on a large scale where stocks
of most things could be kept and drawn upon as
wanted, instead of having to be ordered on each
occasion from Great Britain or the United States.
The Barbados custom-house, too, might be used
as a general clearing-house on all such goods, collecting the duties and periodically distributing them
according to ultimate destination, and the goods

once cleared would be absolutely free from further claims or restrictions.

A similar system in West Africa might require several distributing stations. But if adopted it would mean that ocean-going steamers would have only to call at three or four of the best and most suitable ports or harbours, while a fleet of small craft more fitted for the difficulties of local navigation would accomplish the rest, probably at far less cost than is now incurred.

Obstacles rather than facilities in this direction are what at present exist. Lagos, though itself a port requiring to be served by transhipment from ocean steamers, many of which cannot use it, has long been a distributing centre for the French possession of Dahomey through its principal port, Porto Novo, yet everything forwarded in this way has to pay transit duties, equivalent to one-fourth of the regular Lagos tariff. Could anything be more effective in stimulating direct trade with the French possessions ?

But another obstacle to this general intercourse has recently been created, and if not checked may assume formidable proportions. West Africa has no currency in the usual acceptation of the term. Formerly trade when it was not barter pure and simple, was conducted by the medium of cowrie shells, or brass rods, or some other form that would be looked at askance if tendered in Lombard Street. A great improvement has taken place in this respect, and it is said that in the course of seven or eight years about two millions sterling nominal value of British silver coin has been imported and distributed throughout the various possessions. This introduction of modern money has been accompanied recently by a prohibition of the import of brass rods and manilas, and is undoubtedly a step in the right direction, but in the way now adopted it is only a token coinage, and except for convenience, not much better than the others. The florins and shillings stamped with the King's head pass current throughout the British possessions at their face value, but no-where beyond except by special grace and favour. Neither France nor Germany are willing that the British revenue should annually profit from coinage circulated in their territories, and the former has imposed a duty of 25 per cent. on all such money seeking entrance to its possessions, wishing of course to circulate its own coinage in them.

Unless the trade of West Africa is to be seri-ously jeopardised and many of the native traders some day half ruined, the money introduced should be worth what it professes, and not as at present a good deal less than half. A genuine West African currency is calculated more than anything else to stimulate trade, but it must be one that will pass anywhere throughout the wide territories, or for that matter throughout the world. This can only be attained by a coin that is universal, irre-spective of where and by whom it is coined. It may bear on the obverse the head of the King of England, or of the Emperor of Germany, or the figure of the French Republic, so long as on the reverse it records the real value at which it will be universally current. It is not creditable to Great Britain that it should go on pouring in fictitious money at great profit to its own exchequer.

So far then from West Africa wanting any sort of preferential treatment to encourage trade expansion, what it stands most in need of is the breaking down of the barriers that still exist. This might be more easily accomplished were the whole of the territories under British dominion, and regret is sometimes expressed that other nations have intervened. At the best these are idle, because Great Britain is a long way from being the predominating power in that part of the world. It may have the best ports, the most available trade outlets and the largest commerce, but in point of territory France is immensely superior. With its many responsibilities, not the least of which are in West Africa, it could not hope for generations to come to develop the country in the way France with fewer other commitments is doing, and to that is largely due the very considerable expansion of trade that has occurred since both France and Germany became active in these regions.

West African produce is nowhere artificially handicapped as it would be the moment distinctions came to be made as to place of origin. It is free to pass wherever there is the greatest demand, and consequently where it is likely to command the best terms. Equally free should remain the return trade, and the nation that can do it cheapest is likely to come best off, not only in its own possessions but in those of its neighbours as well. And Great Britain has become sadly decadent if it cannot claim that advantage.

III.—THE FARTHER EAST.

Though the West India and West Africa possessions are scattered, there is, notwithstanding, a certain amount of cohesion among them; their produce is similar, their populations have much the same needs, and what affects one is calculated to influence the others in a similar manner. Not only are those in the Farther East more widely removed from one another, but there is no link between them unless it be that of trade, and when not self-contained, their economic condition is usually more dependent on the territories and peoples surrounding them than on connection with the British Empire.

CEYLON.

In some respects the most important is the island of Ceylon. The straits separating it from the continent of India are sufficiently narrow, that superficially it seems destined to be under the same government as the mainland, but there are several important causes that keep them apart. In the first place the Governor - General and Council of India have quite enough to do to govern the vast territories under their control, though experience proves that this is no real bar to expansion. But the interests are sometimes in conflict, and were they under the same direct rule one might be sacrificed to the other. As it is, their trade relations are considerable, and this is aided by the use of the same money, which at least obviates any risk attendant on exchange operations.

There is, moreover, another very important difference. In the chapter devoted to India we saw that the land and its cultivation were left almost entirely to the native community; the British element contenting itself with trade and industry in their various forms. But in Ceylon the ownership system has been more largely developed, and the greater part of the exportable produce of the island is actually cultivated by a body of planters, or their representatives, who own the land and furnish the necessary capital. They are, too, a particularly virile community and not easily daunted. Years ago the island was given up to the cultivation of coffee, but a disease broke out among the trees and caused wholesale destruction. Instead of relinquishing the plantations and allowing them to return to native jungle, or at best to be utilised for the growth of food by the natives, they were converted into tea-gardens, and so successful has been the result, that the Ceylon leaf has in recent years made far more rapid progress in public estimation than the Indian.

As the island is thickly populated the demand for so much land and labour for this purpose creates a scarcity of food, which is furnished by India in the form of rice. These two circumstances help to reverse entirely the trade connection with the United Kingdom, and instead of two-thirds of the imports being drawn from it, and less than one-third of the exports directed to it, as is the case with India, the opposite is the prevailing condition.

In 1900, for instance, exports from Ceylon to the United Kingdom were nearly 60 per cent. of the total, while imports therefrom were under 30 per cent. Imports from India on the other hand amounted to nearly 60, and the exports to only 10 per cent. Ceylon is making far more rapid progress than India in cultivating a taste for its tea in foreign countries, and whereas British takings account for no less than 87½ per cent. of the total export of India, fully one-fifth that of Ceylon is now shipped direct elsewhere, principally to Australia. There is in fact a small export duty levied, the proceeds of which are devoted to this extension. This is further accentuated by the very considerable re-export trade in tea done in the United Kingdom, a much larger proportion of it being of the Ceylon than of the Indian leaf.

Ceylon also possesses a valuable natural resource in its plumbago mines, the annual export of which averages about 20,000 tons. For 1899 the quantity increased to over 30,000 tons and the value was Rx.2,225,000. The United States are particularly good customers. Cocoa-nut oil, pulp, and fibre are also of consequence, while coffee is by no means an extinct industry, though a rapidly decaying one.

No textile or other manufacturing industries other than a small one in coir yarn and rope have sprung up like in India, and for everything of the sort the island is dependent on outside supplies. These are furnished principally by Great Britain, but in the cheaper textiles India is a strong competitor, and the extent to which each is drawn upon will be seen from the following figures, in tens of rupees :—

	1897.	1898.	1899.	1900.
Great Britain .	387,464	424,678	426,193	476,059
India . .	208,213	188,896	176,755	193,677
Other Countries	63,946	43,726	62,355	87,160
	Rx.659,623	Rx.657,300	Rx.665,303	Rx.756,896

In proportion to size and population the foreign trade of Ceylon is very extensive, and much the largest part of it is carried on within the British Empire.

16

MAURITIUS AND SEYCHELLES.

Mauritius, with its smaller chain of islands, with which may be included the Seychelles, formerly directly subject to the same Government, but now administered separately, is perhaps the least British of any of the possessions of the Empire, and there is only limited direct intercourse. Most of what exists with Europe is carried on by French steamers which include Mauritius in the circuit of their trade in those latitudes where the important possession of Madagascar is situated. As far as the principal island is concerned, it is devoted almost exclusively to one product, sugar, and nothing else worth speaking of is cultivated. Situated between India and the Cape of Good Hope, it finds markets in both, and distributes its annual yield between them. Like Ceylon, it was formerly in the hands of British planters, most of them of French extraction, who imported Indian coolies for the cultivation of their estates, but these have gradually ousted their former masters, and the island now contains many peasant proprietors who grow the canes and sell them to the factories which crush them and prepare the sugar for market.

The legislation against sugar bounties that has been adopted in recent years in India was ostensibly in the interests of Mauritius, whose cane sugar was being displaced in the Indian markets by beet. The falling off in the imports, however, was

only partially accounted for in this way : the great
demand that sprang up in South Africa afforded
a more attractive outlet, especially as the tariff
differentiated between cane and beet to the extent
of 1s. 6d. per cwt. That is all the countervailing
duty in India amounted to, for some time at least,
as regards German and Austrian sugars, which were
the ones to any great extent affected, but since the
cartels have been countervailed as well, this has
been considerably increased, and while the higher
rate prevails it may have the effect of attracting
Mauritius sugar that would otherwise have gone
to Cape Colony and the Transvaal, which may
thus have to look for their supplies elsewhere.

The smaller islands cannot grow sugar economically under modern conditions, which require larger
factories than would be possible in them. They
turn their attention principally to the cocoa nut,
the products of which, especially the oil, find ready
markets. The Seychelles pay particular attention
to vanilla which is their principal product, and is
distributed about equally between Great Britain
and France. The exports of this small group of
islands trebled in value within ten years. They
have also a manufacturing industry in the shape
of soap-boiling. Cocoa-nut oil is one of the
principal ingredients of this domestic necessity,
and countries which grow the cocoa-nut palm on
a large scale are thus peculiarly well situated for
the establishment of the industry, particularly as

abundance of labour is usually available. What is made in the Seychelles is largely exported to East Africa.

The import trade is carried on principally with India, and consists largely of rice, the natural food of the coolies, flour, and cotton goods for their clothing. Here we see the real cause of the anxiety of the Indian Government to maintain the connection, because if Mauritius ceased to supply India with sugar the return trade might not be forthcoming. The rice would have to be purchased in any case; but flour, cotton goods, and gunny bags might be obtained elsewhere if there were no regular and direct shipping communication such as is ensured by the consumption of large quantities of Mauritius sugar. India in this respect, therefore, is a competitor with British manufacturers, and enjoys not only the advantage of favourable location and natural flow of trade, but the additional one of the same currency, which like that of Ceylon is the rupee. Weights and measures, however, continue to be French.

HONG-KONG.

The other two British possessions in that part of the world are on a totally different footing. Hong-Kong is a small island where there is room for little beyond the town itself, and is in no sense naturally productive. It is a trade centre and nothing else, and its very existence depends on

China, which is the original source or ultimate destination of nearly everything that passes through it. To include its trade among that of British possessions is consequently indefensible, because in reality it is with a foreign country, and the British authorities so far recognise this, that while affording separate publication of the figures they are invariably placed in conjunction with those relating to China.

No doubt the existence of this colony has been a great assistance to British trade, and other countries have latterly been seeking to emulate the example by establishing similar stations of their own. Shanghai is a far more important centre for the commerce of the Celestial Empire, but it is also much more cosmopolitan. The Yang-tse region, of which it is the natural outlet, is the one that excites more envy than any other, and as all nations are supposed to enjoy equal facilities there, competition is likely to increase in intensity. The region tributary to Hong-Kong is likewise an important one, including as it does the great city of Canton, and the situation has hitherto assured for the British almost a monopoly of the trade. This is now threatened, first by the proximity of the French possession of Indo-China to the south, which has assumed so much importance since Hong-Kong was founded, and still more by the contemplated railway extensions which will place Canton and the valley of the West River in direct communication with other parts of the Empire. Hong-Kong may be destined, therefore, at no distant date to lose a good deal of its commercial importance, while at the same time it may increase in strategic value. The acquisition of Kowloon on the adjoining mainland is a recognition of this, and to some extent a preparation for the struggle that may be impending for supremacy in the Far East.

STRAITS SETTLEMENTS.

The Straits Settlements cover a more extensive area than Hong-Kong, but owe their importance, nevertheless, to much the same cause. The geographical situation enjoyed by the Malay Penmsula, which is on the direct trade route between east and west, has made Singapore the clearing-house of that part of the world, and its enormous trade figures bear no proportion to the productive capacity of the surrounding districts. This is by no means insignificant, and if it were for nothing else than the tin, would be worthy of note. Sago and tapioca are among its other special productions, and the cultivation of the sugar cane is being rapidly as well as profitably extended. Furthermore, it is the collecting-ground of the spice islands, which figure so prominently in the history and contests of the sixteenth and seventeenth centuries, and the appellation Singapore is given to a good deal that was never actually grown anywhere near it. No greater foresight has ever been shown by British adventurers than is to be attributed to the founders of Singapore, chief among whom was Sir Stamford Raffles.

A superficial examination of the details of the trade would lead one to imagine that for its size this possession was one of, if not the very greatest, producing and manufacturing centres on the face of the earth. In the latter capacity it can boast of very little ; the cotton goods, like nearly everything else, are merely in transit, and will be found on the import as well as the export side of the trading account. The former in this instance will always be the larger, because apart from the balance between the natural exports and the imports for distribution among the settled population, there is a trading profit which is partly used in the purchase of foreign commodities for those engaged in earning it, while by no means the least important branch of commerce is that in ships' stores, which figure in imports but not in exports.

They owe their position mainly to the absolute fiscal freedom they enjoy. No revenue whatever is raised from import or export duties; the only charges that fall on commerce are light dues and shipping fees, which on a total tonnage of upwards of $6\frac{1}{2}$ millions engaged in foreign trade alone that entered the three ports of Singapore, Penang, and Malacca in 1899, amounted to less than £20,000. The revenue amounting to about £500,000 altogether is obtained chiefly from licences for the sale of opium and spirits, with additions from land rents and stamps.

There are also moderate rates levied for municipal purposes in much the same manner as in English boroughs. The world might be scoured in vain for another similar instance of simplicity in national finance, or for the lightness of the burden it involves.

Another advantage they enjoy is the currency, though differing as it does from that of every other British possession, it might at first appear to be a drawback, especially as the fluctuations are sometimes very considerable. But to the enterprising that is often an additional source of profit, especially where the connections are world wide, inasmuch as changes are foreseen and acted upon, and the fixed currencies about which so much is said in praise nowadays have sometimes little else to recommend them than the additional ease they afford the indolent. This does not apply of course to fluctuations caused by manipulation such as are usual in countries possessed of inconvertible paper currencies, but this is not the case with the Mexican dollar or the British trade dollar coined as a substitute. These are based on silver and follow the good or ill fortunes of that metal, decided by policy rather than manipulation. The prosperity throughout the Straits Settlements and the Malay Peninsula generally, and the incentive that is being given to whatever production they are capable of, bear ample testimony to the virtues of a silver currency, and stand out in striking contrast to the results that have followed in India and other places that might be named from the attempted introduction and enforcement of a gold one.

But the possessions depend on something more than freedom in their own trade arrangements, and there can be no doubt whatever that they would be seriously injured by any attempted diversion of trade within the British Empire. That Empire cannot of course be run in the interests of Singapore or any other individual section of it; but before departures are taken, loss should be balanced against gain. The latter in the case of all the possessions we have so far dealt with is exceedingly problematical outside very narrow areas which would hardly benefit any of the others, and certainly not the Straits Settlements. But it is a serious thing to jeopardise any portion of a trade which annually reaches the sterling equivalent of some £50,000,000, less than one-fifth of which is done direct with the United Kingdom. Only part of it could in any case be affected at once, because a good deal is with countries lying outside the Empire altogether, some of it of an exclusively local character. But as soon as there is interference with the natural flow of the trade of India, or of Australia, or even of the more distant South Africa, the Straits Settlements are bound to suffer, and once started on a descending plane, the decline may be very rapid until they become well nigh worthless.

Few people think of possessions such as these in considering what it is the fashion to designate imperial trade. Trade is nothing if not cosmopolitan, and any endeavour to confine it within the bounds of an Empire, however vast, is sure to react unfairly on some portions of it. Singapore and the Straits Settlements may afford no opportunities for colonisation and vast internal development like Canada, or Australia, or South Africa, but they do act as a lubricant to prevent friction, and as such play far too important a part to be disregarded.

CHAPTER VII

MISCELLANEOUS POSSESSIONS AND PROTECTORATES

NEWFOUNDLAND

THERE are a number of isolated possessions in
different parts of the world, of varying importance
and sometimes of little trade value, actual or prospective. This is not the case, however, with the
oldest self-governing colony Great Britain has,
namely Newfoundland.   But its interests are too
small to demand any lengthy consideration, and it
cannot yet be included with any of the more
important ones, though in all probability it will ere
long constitute a part of the Dominion of Canada,
and so cease to have a separate existence.

This will almost certainly prove an advantage, as for a considerable time past its career at best has been a chequered one. Climate is permanently against it: in a country where during only two months of the twelve the thermometer does not fall below freezing-point, and in those two gets occasionally dangerously near it, agricultural prospects cannot be very inviting. Newfoundland, for quite different reasons, finds itself situated much the same as portions of the tropics, and has to import most of its foodstuffs. Its own surplus products are limited to two, fish and minerals. The former of these has hitherto held almost supreme sway, and it is only latterly that the mineral resources of the island have been systematically developed. But dried codfish has long been a commodity of almost world-wide consumption, and this harvest of the sea is distributed everywhere. Unfortunately for Newfoundland, France has made special efforts to encourage the industry, and by the payment of substantial bounties enables its fishermen who make their headquarters on the neighbouring small islands of St. Pierre and Miquelon to compete very seriously with the British, enjoying as they do equal privileges as far as deep-sea fishing is concerned, and having sufficient facilities for drying and curing.

Nor is there in any case a sufficient consumption of codfish within the British Empire to take off what Newfoundland annually catches, because wherever population is at all dense, and especially in the United Kingdom, home fisheries are adequate for most purposes. Religion, too, has almost as much to do with this particular industry as with the manufacture of ecclesiastical furniture, and Roman Catholic countries are far and away the best customers. In this instance Spain, Portugal, and Brazil figure most conspicuously, and render account for the greatest part of Newfoundland's export. Great Britain does import some, and re-exports a good deal of it, and the West Indies are also fair customers, but this particular trade is not likely to be helped by federation with any other part of the Empire, unless it speedily results in a settlement of the seemingly interminable disputes with France.

Fish oil is another branch of this industry, but finds its principal market in Great Britain, as does also cod liver oil, so well known for its medicinal properties. There is also the seal fishery with its resulting trade in skins and oil; nor must the lobster fisheries and canneries be overlooked, the product of which finds its way mostly to Europe. Salmon is likewise caught during the season, but instead of being canned as on the West Coast of America, is pickled and packed in tierces and exported in this way. But all these are insignificant alongside the staple industry of dried codfish, and if anything, they rather bring the island into competition with Canada.

On the other hand, internal association with the Dominion may do much for the mineral resources, which consist of iron and copper. So much attention is being given there to the iron and steel industries that anything in Newfoundland calculated to assist them is certain to be developed, though with an abundance of iron-ore on the mainland the island supplies may be destined for export, perhaps for the use of British furnaces, to which, if the quality proves at all suitable, they will be most welcome. Newfoundland may thus find itself the centre of an industrial activity it has never before experienced, and so help it to recover more rapidly from the crisis in its affairs which led it some little time ago to sell nearly the whole of its available assets to a wealthy contractor in the hope of weathering the storm.

The Dominion would certainly be a gainer by federation at the expense both of the United States and the United Kingdom. The first of these two countries now supplies a large share of the breadstuffs and provisions, a trade that would pass to Canada the moment the island became subject to the Dominion tariff. As it is, Canada figures more largely in the import trade than any other country, but this item of course would disappear, and one result of federation would be a considerable shrinkage in the figures. The United Kingdom stands next on the list, about one-half the imports from it consisting of textiles and wearing apparel. This would likewise be affected, because the duties, varying from 25 to 35 per cent., being much the same as in Canada, would still be applicable to British manufacturers, while Canadian cottons and woollens would be exempt just as they are now in Manitoba or the North-West Provinces.

Where, as in this instance, the interests of Canada and Newfoundland appear identical, neither has anything to lose and may have much to gain, it is difficult to understand why they have so long held aloof from one another. Until recent years, however, the future outlook in the Dominion was by no means assured, and it might naturally have objected to undertake the responsibility of another colony in serious financial and economic straits, to say nothing of the political complications in which it was involved. Now the prospect is everywhere of the brightest, and there need be no hesitation. Newfoundland, too, might have serious doubts as to whether it would have improved its condition by such a surrender of independence. It can have no reasonable ground for refusing to ally itself with a prosperous and progressive neighbour which will still leave it a constituent part of the Empire with which it has always declined to sever its connection, at the same time reducing the cost of most of the necessaries of life through the disappearance of the import duty on all Canadian products.

It was doubtless these considerations that induced

the United States Administration to endeavour recently to negotiate a reciprocity treaty with Newfoundland. The only obstacle to it from an American point of view is a slight competition that might arise in green fish as distinct from the cured varieties, but on the other hand America has much more to gain. The conclusion of this treaty would necessarily add to the difficulty of federation with Canada, though when the time is fully ripe it is hardly likely to prevent it.

BERMUDA AND BAHAMAS.

Situated in the Western Hemisphere are a number of other minor possessions, most of them islands, like the Bahamas, too small to be retained for any trade they afford. They are often included in the West Indies, but wrongly so, because not only are they under separate government, but the products they yield are altogether different. Bermuda is a military and naval station, and for that reason more objectionable to any great Power in that part of the world than ordinary colonies. Happily Great Britain and the United States are on the most amicable terms, and retention of this island implies no threat to the Great Republic of the West. British interests in that part of the world, however, are far too important to dream of relinquishing it, as was done with Heligoland years ago, and these are likely to be increased substantially when the Isthmian Canal opens another highway between east and west. It enjoys a more temperate climate than the West India Islands, which are within the tropics, and is consequently more suitable for maintaining a garrison. Its mild and equable climate indeed makes it a favourite health resort, and it is largely used as such by Americans.

The regular intercourse this necessitates tends to throw what ordinary trade there is into the hands of the United States, which supply most of the requirements of the civil population, whether permanent or temporary. The British troops, of course, are served as much as possible from home, but even their food is drawn from the other side of the Atlantic. In another respect than that of holiday resort, Bermuda stands to the United States much as the Channel Islands do to Great Britain, namely, as caterers of early market garden produce, and large supplies of potatoes and onions are shipped each spring for American consumption.

The Bahamas are too near the tropics to be suitable for this particular culture, and confine themselves to fruits like pineapples and oranges. But their chief industry is a sponge fishery, which is very productive, and yields America a fair proportion of its requirements of this useful article. The cultivation of a fibre similar to hemp was undertaken some years ago, but has not attained to any considerable proportions.

17

BRITISH HONDURAS.

British Honduras forms part of the isthmus of Central America, and is valuable solely for its timber, principally logwood and mahogany, the bulk of which is exported to the United Kingdom. This does not entail very frequent or regular communication, as these commodities are not perishable, but like other tropical countries it requires constant supplies of breadstuffs and provisions which North America is most conveniently situated for supplying. A considerable part of the import trade thus flows from that quarter, and is assisted by a return of fruit. Great Britain as usual gets a fair share in the supply of textiles, and hardware, and such like goods, and as Honduras lies in the zone where fashions are sometimes a year or two behind Paris, the London drapery houses are able now and again to move off a little old stock which might otherwise accumulate on their hands to an inconvenient extent.

In none of these instances is trade now, or ever likely to be in the future, of any considerable volume, and it would certainly be most inadvisable to check its flow in natural channels.

SOUTH SEA ISLANDS.

On the far side of America, in the Pacific Ocean, are several other scattered groups. The most important are the Fiji Islands, which, like Mauritius, are given up principally to the cultivation of sugar, to which is added on a considerable scale the cocoa nut. But as far as Great Britain is concerned these islands are rarely heard of, as nearly the whole of their intercourse is in the first place at least with Australasia. The bulk of the sugar is exported to New Zealand, which depends for its supply of that commodity on these islands. A little goes to Victoria and New South Wales, but has to compete with Queensland, which as a member of the Australian Commonwealth has now the advantage of free trade, though there is an excise tax which minimises the full benefit that would otherwise accrue from the import duty.

The other islands are devoted to the culture of the cocoa-nut palm. The fruit is dried into copra, and shipped at intervals to New South Wales, where the oil is extracted. Part of this is used in the local soap factories, and the remainder exported to the United Kingdom for the same purpose. Much of this development has been due to the enterprise of an English firm which some years ago extended its operations to the Australian continent.

On the other hand, the islands obtain nearly everything they want from New South Wales, and among the goods purchased are many of British manufacture : indeed the advantage New South Wales enjoyed over New Zealand and the Australian Colonies generally was its free trade policy, which has now been sacrificed through federation. That may possibly divert this branch of trade to New Zealand, and so simplify the political situation, that country being very desirous of transferring Fiji and the other islands from the direct control of the British Crown to its own jurisdiction, and an obstacle in the way has been the commercial connection with New South Wales. The exports of these islands regularly exceed the imports by very substantial sums, and so justify the conclusion that they are very profitable to their proprietors and cultivators.

FALKLAND ISLANDS.

In the South Atlantic near to Cape Horn are the Falkland Islands. They would be almost out of the world were it not that the steamers trading between the west coast of South America and Europe pass close by and are so able to make regular calls. The chief industry of the inhabitants beyond supplying their own requirements is pastoral, and they export to Great Britain sheepskins and wool. The volume of this trade is quite insignificant.

BRITISH NEW GUINEA.

A much more troublesome possession is British New Guinea, off the north-east coast of Australia, and likely therefore to be associated in its trade relations with that continent. These so far have been of very trifling extent, no inconsiderable part of the population of the island indeed consists of dangerous savages. Whatever the advantage of possession may ultimately prove to be, the risks are tolerably apparent, and arise mainly from the ambitions of Germany, which is an immediate neighbour.[1]

BRITISH NORTH BORNEO.

Travelling homeward by way of the East, we meet with several Protectorates as distinct from actual possessions. British North Borneo is an instance of territory administered and developed by a chartered company, though happily one without a political history. One of its exportable products is a peculiarity of the East, namely edible birds' nests, for which there is no demand in Great Britain, or indeed anywhere else in Europe. The great hopes of the territory are built on the discovery of minerals; the country is in too uncivilised a state to afford much prospect of agriculture on an extensive scale such as is practised in other islands of the Eastern Archipelago. Tobacco, however, is being cultivated, and a railway has been constructed mainly in the interests of this industry. The latest return of the export shows a value of not far short of £100,000.

Off the coast of Borneo is the island of Labuan, nominally a Crown colony, but the administration of which has of late years been under the Borneo Company, and for all practical purposes may be

[1] Since this paragraph was in print the administration of British New Guinea has been transferred from the British Colonial Office to the Australian Commonwealth.

included with it. Sarawak is also associated with it, and the history of this country, ruled by an English family who have become Oriental potentates, is something of a romance. It is in a more advanced stage of development and civilisation than any of the surrounding territories, and its trade consequently has assumed greater dimensions. With the United Kingdom, however, neither have any direct intercourse worth speaking of, practically the whole of their trade passing in the first instance through the Straits Settlements, while the local merchants are nearly all Chinese.

MALAY PROTECTED STATES.

Not far removed is the Malay Peninsula, covering the British possession of the Straits Settlements. As we have previously observed, these are of very limited area, but a number of native States of considerable extent are virtually under British protection and have British residents and officials, though little interference takes place with their internal government. The advantage of this state of things is that other countries are precluded from annexing them and diverting, or in any way interfering with their trade, which is very considerable. It is these States in fact where nearly all the so-called Straits tin comes from, and the large coolie population engaged in mining it requires to be fed and clothed. Rice and cotton goods are imported to supply the wants, but almost entirely by way of Singapore or Penang. Sago and tapioca, sugar and spices, and indiarubber also form part of their output, but almost everything, whether inward or outward, passes through the Straits Settlements, and helps to swell the already considerable volume of their trade.

AFRICAN PROTECTORATES.

The great Protectorates, however, are to be found in Africa. Those in the southern portion of the continent may be dismissed : everything connected with them in the way of trade has previously been discussed in the chapter on South Africa. The most important of all was, until recently, to be found in West Africa, and was under the administration of the Royal Niger Company. This chartered undertaking ceased to exist on the 1st January 1900, and its territories passed under direct control of the British Crown as Northern and Southern Nigeria, so that anything applicable to them is almost equally so to the rest of the West African possessions.

We must turn to East Africa, therefore, for this particular form of government. British East Africa and British Central Africa are something more than spheres of influence, but are never likely to become colonies in the real sense of the term. Like Nigeria, the development of East Africa was first undertaken by a chartered company, though it relinquished the task for quite different reasons to the Royal Niger

Company. It found it, in fact, impossible, and
nothing short of national effort was ever likely to
have achieved success. This has been made in the
form of the Uganda railway, by means of which it is
hoped to open out the heart of Africa to trade, and
some parts of it perhaps to settlement.

Trade has so far been very limited in extent, as
the country has very little to offer except rubber and
ivory, and cannot therefore absorb much in the way
of manufactured goods. The presence of the East
Indian coolie, who has been imported into these
regions as a labourer on the railway and other public
works, causes the gravitation of trade towards the
East rather than the West, and even the rupee
currency has been adopted. Rice and cotton piece
goods are already freely supplied from that quarter,
but India has no use for such things as ivory and
rubber, which find their natural market in Europe.
The value of these possessions lies in the future,
and the probabilities this offers are to be found
fully discussed in Sir Harry Johnston's work on
the Uganda Protectorate.

Meanwhile the real trade centre of that part of
the world is Zanzibar, the island of that name
together with the neighbouring one of Pemba being
also included in the British Protectorate. The
annual value of the turnover is estimated at something like £3,000,000, divided about equally between
imports and exports, though the real volume is
about half this figure, because nearly everything

appears on both sides of the account. Thus cloves, ivory, and indiarubber are collected and transported to Zanzibar, and thence distributed to the various places of consumption. Rice, cotton goods, hardware, and other merchandise of a more or less useful character are imported from Europe, India, and the United States — American sheetings form quite a feature of the piece goods trade—and sent for barter into the interior. Zanzibar is in fact the Singapore of East Africa, but without its freedom from political complications, as not only are Germany and Portugal in close proximity, but there is the problem of the slave trade which is an exceedingly knotty one, and causes friction with the dusky potentates of the land.

British Central Africa is really the extension of Rhodesia north of the Zambesi, but the mouth of that river being in Portuguese territory there is no direct outlet, and such trade as there is is afforded ample facilities through the port of Chinde. Along with that of British East Africa generally, it is mostly in the hands of East Indians.

GIBRALTAR AND MALTA.

Nearer home are two small possessions upon which a very high value is set, but purely for naval and military as well as strategic reasons. One of them, Gibraltar, is a barren rock which produces nothing, and everything wanted for its garrison and the very considerable civil population that always by some means finds subsistence in a garrison town, is dependent entirely on what is imported. Fresh food is supplied largely by Spain, or from the opposite shores of Northern Africa; less perishable commodities are shipped from the United Kingdom, but this cannot be described as trade.

Malta on the other hand is prolific, both as regards population and cultivation, and is also the chief naval station for the British fleet in the Mediterranean. For its size its trade is prodigious, but is for the most part merely a transit one. It has a customs revenue of something like £200,000, and the dutiable commodities upon which this is collected are valued at about £1,000,000. They consist almost entirely of food and drink, largely the latter, and are imported from Mediterranean countries to a greater extent than from the United Kingdom. There is some regular trade besides that is not dutiable, including food and wearing apparel, the latter probably to a large extent of British manufacture.

The land of the island is also put to the utmost possible use, and in addition to cereals, yields early potatoes, onions, and cumin seed which find their way mostly to British markets.

ST. HELENA.

Situated on the steamship route to South Africa is the island of St. Helena, not quite as barren as Gibraltar, but of no commercial value whatever. It

is important historically rather than in any other
way as having been the final place of detention of
the Great Napoleon, and at a later date the temporary home of many of the Boer prisoners taken
during the South African War. Happily their period
of incarceration was of much shorter duration.

CYPRUS AND EGYPT.

It is only with some diffidence that two other
countries with which Great Britain is intimately
associated, without having any claims to actual
ownership, can be introduced into this chapter.
They are Cyprus and Egypt. The former is an
island nominally belonging to Turkey, whose
suzerainty is recognised by the payment of annual
tribute. Part of this at least has hitherto come out
of the British Exchequer, though under ordinary circumstances the island is well able to pay its own
way. It enjoys an active trade in its own, as well
as foreign, products. Comparatively little of this,
however, is direct with the United Kingdom, though
a part of what is done with both Turkey and Egypt
may eventually filter through in that direction. If
not exactly a white elephant, it is a connection from
which Great Britain has derived no special benefit in
the past, and one which offers little in the future.
With the Cypriotes perhaps it is otherwise.

Egypt stands on an entirely different footing
both politically and commercially. Also a part of
the Turkish Empire, it has become something more

than a mere business connection of the British. But though it is to British administration, and particularly to the skill and energy of one man, Earl Cromer, that its wonderful prosperity is due, no advantage of this can be taken which is not equally open to every other nation in the world. It has never been sought; nor would there be any reason to allude to such a thing if the new born zeal of imperial federation did not from time to time cast covetous eyes towards the dominions of the Khedive. From that point of view they must be left absolutely alone. If other nations have benefited from the progress of the country, none have done so in quite the same degree as Great Britain, and that must continue to be the full extent of the commercial reward to be looked for.

Such is a brief summary of the outlying, and from a commercial point of view, less important portions of the British Empire. With the exception possibly of Newfoundland, they offer, as they are, no serious trade problems for solution, and had best be left out of any schemes of preferential trading, even assuming such are ever likely to become at all widespread. Any possible gain is utterly insignificant compared with the ill-feeling that might be aroused, and in the real interests of these possessions they must be left to form their own trade associations.

CHAPTER VIII.

The Colonial Trade of the United Kingdom.

ONE of the principal objects aimed at in the past
expansion, no less than the present consolidation,
of the British Empire, is the extension of oversea
commerce, more especially that portion of it
carried on within the Empire itself. As we
have seen in previous chapters, only a trifling
percentage is what may be termed oversea
colonial, that is between the various possessions
themselves when separated from one another,

except in the few instances where a number of smaller ones make use of a larger as a clearing-house or distributing centre. The United Kingdom is the real magnet, one pole attracting from all quarters of the world, while the other sends forth its own innumerable productions to them.

The United Kingdom too, though but a small portion of the Empire as regards both area and population, has immense capacity for absorbing the surplus products of all the rest, and it is this more than anything that constitutes the real bond of union. France, for instance, is extremely jealous of colonial competition with its own agricultural industry, and would not tolerate it at all in manufactures. It is still a sore point with the French farmer that wheat and wine are admitted free of duty from Algeria and Tunis, though as regards the latter possession there is a limit set to the quantities that can be so imported. The United States at the very beginning of their colonial career are exhibiting still stronger feelings of hostility where they feel any of their own industries may be adversely affected, and have so far refused to make trade concessions, much less grant entire freedom, when this is likely in any way to be the outcome. But British policy is to exclude nothing; whatever a colony has to dispose of that can be put to any use in the United Kingdom is always sure of a market there. The line might be drawn at the edible birds' nests of Borneo and one or two other things of that description, but there is not much that a British merchant will not buy on speculation on the off chance of finding a customer for it somewhere, and if birds' nests were at a big discount he would not be above banqueting his friends on them in order to cultivate a taste and a trade. They surely cannot be much more nauseous than caviare.

This of course is equally true as regards foreign produce, and has become rather a sore point. Why purchase 75 per cent. of the country's needs from foreign sources when colonial ones with a little stimulus might be able to supply a good deal more than the remaining 25 per cent., is the question constantly asked. But the colonies are hardly justified in putting it unless they can show they are accumulating surpluses they are unable to dispose of, while the United Kingdom is getting what it wants from foreign competitors. In reality it is the reverse of this that invariably happens, and colonial produce often finds a market when the foreign is diligently seeking one. A simple illustration of this is afforded by so important an article as wheat. The United Kingdom consumes more of this cereal each year, and as home production does not correspondingly keep pace, if indeed it is not actually going back, requires to import

constantly increasing quantities. The total in
1901 reached nearly 70 million cwts.; in 1897 it
was barely 63 millions. But 1897 was a year of
considerable scarcity owing to failure of the crops
over the greater part of Europe, and whatever
wheat British colonies had to sell would have found
a ready, not to say an eager, market. 1901 was a
year of fair abundance when colonial wheat might
not have been so much wanted. Yet what are
the facts revealed by the following figures?

Imports of Wheat into the United Kingdom.[1]

	1897.	1901.
Foreign Countries .	57,346,820 cwts.	52,854,520 cwts.
British Possessions .	5,393,360 ,,	16,854,010 ,,
	62,740,180 ,,	69,708,530 ,,

The former year, all the wheat British possessions had to sell, or cared to sell, was a little over
5 million cwts., though prices were comparatively
high, and British consumers had to eke out the
supply with more than 57 million cwts. of foreign
produce. But in 1901 the colonies apparently had
nearly 17 million cwts. to dispose of and the home
country took it, reducing its foreign purchases to
under 53 millions, though there was undoubtedly
more to be had if it had been wanted.

[1] All statistics in this chapter are taken from the Annual Board
of Trade Returns of the trade and commerce of the United Kingdom.
In most instances the figures for 1901 are used in preference to those
for 1902, as being available in fuller detail.

It may be said at once that this was business and not philanthropy. There are not many men who will pay their relations 5 per cent. more for what they want to purchase than they can get it for from a stranger, and there is no pretence that Canadian or Australian wheat was bought in 1901 at a relatively higher price than any other. But on the other hand it was not necessary to take anything less than current market values to dispose of it, and on equal terms the colonial had the advantage over the foreign grain where it was equally suitable. If Canada had had another five million cwts. to dispose of, it could probably have done so on the same terms, but if the United States had wanted to sell another five or ten millions, it is quite likely they might have had to cut the price, at anyrate to the extent of a cent or two a bushel.

Take another case, the reverse of the last. The demand for indiarubber has been growing even faster than that for wheat, and the British supplies of this commodity also are drawn both from colonial and foreign sources. For the same two years the figures were as follows :—

Imports of Indiarubber into the United Kingdom.

	1897.	1901.
From Foreign Countries .	272,872 cwts.	426,294 cwts.
From British Possessions .	124,057 ,,	40,180 ,,
	396,929 ,,	466,474 ,,

18

Actual requirements increased in the interval by nearly 20 per cent., yet the supply from British possessions fell to less than one-third. This did not arise from any preference for the foreign article, but from sheer inability on the part of the colonies to furnish it. With most of them, the West African possessions especially, it was a new industry, and so profitable that they set to work to kill the goose that laid the golden eggs, and in the haste to extract all the rubber they could and grow rich, the vines were destroyed and fresh ones had to be planted and allowed to mature. But British manufacturers, and especially British export merchants who handle more than half the total import, could not wait for this, and meanwhile obtained their supplies wherever they could get them. But there will be a market again for the colonial produce as soon as it is available, and the foreign import may undergo corresponding reduction in consequence.

Wheat and indiarubber are by no means isolated instances of this sort of thing. Ordinary trade returns may not exhibit similar movements in so marked a manner, but in five years out of six, if not the entire six, the same influences are at work in nearly all commodities which have a colonial as well as foreign origin, and everything else being equal, the former is almost certain to command an advantage, though it may not always be so distinctly visible.

Why this should be is not at first clearly apparent, especially if we have to eliminate sentiment as a regular factor in the equation; as an occasional one it does no doubt operate. The controlling influences have really to be looked for in those broad principles which in the long run govern all international trade and reduce it to barter. A nation that persists year after year in buying more than it can afford to pay for, finds itself eventually in a more or less serious condition of insolvency, while another which sells more than it can well spare in exchange for something that is for the moment more attractive, will equally suffer in its internal development. There are methods of striking a fair balance, some of them very intricate and difficult to manage, but the British Empire is, on the whole, a well-adjusted pair of scales, each side of which responds to whatever weight is added to, or removed from, the other, which makes the machine work smoothly.

This becomes more evident when we contrast the movements of the colonial with the total oversea commerce of the United Kingdom. The latter, as is well known, exhibits an enormous excess of imports which is variously accounted for, and about which a good deal of difference of opinion is supposed to exist. One thing, however, is quite clear; it has not yet seriously impaired the prosperity of Great Britain whatever it may be destined to do in the future; indeed the reverse appears to be the truer contention, namely that Great Britain

has thriven under it.   But when the colonial trade
is taken by itself, it will be found to be much more
evenly balanced, though there is good reason why it
too should exhibit a considerable excess of British
imports.   In the first place, all the colonies are
indebted to Great Britain for interest on loans,
in most cases for Government borrowing as well
as the investment of private capital in trading
and industrial undertakings.   Then the colonies own
very little shipping, and their commerce is carried
on mostly in British bottoms, which involves the
payment of freight outside the country, adding to
the indebtedness.   All colonies that are prosperous
meet these charges by shipment of their produce,
and this is generally the case with the British ones.
But that produce may not be, and is not always,
shipped to the United Kingdom, and the trade
balance sometimes makes it appear as though it
were really Great Britain that was indebted to
the colonies.

The best way of showing this is by the figures,
which for 1901 were as follows :—

	The Whole World.	Colonial Possessions only.[1]
Imports from .	£521,990,198	£104,970,865
Total Exports to .	347,864,268	110,320,386
Excess of Imports	£174,125,930	Exports £5,349,521

These figures represent merchandise only, all
movements of coin and bullion being eliminated.

[1] Exclusive of Hong-Kong.

But as regards two or three of the British possessions this is hardly fair, because they pay for a
considerable portion of their imports with the gold
they actually produce. South Africa, for instance,
discharges, or ought to discharge, its liabilities to
Great Britain in gold bullion, just as Canada does
in butter and cheese, and the one is as much a
merchandise commodity as the other.

The colonial import is subject to two other
considerable modifications, which happen, however,
to affect the figures in opposite directions, leaving
the total not much different to what it stands in
the table. The first of these arises from the trade
in diamonds, which are received in London under
registered letter post, and not recorded among the
official figures of imports. Their value is declared
at Cape Town on registration, when a fee of one-half
per cent. of their value is payable, and for the
year 1901 amounted to £4,877,042, which must
be added to British imports, with no doubt something more to represent actual selling value.

On the other hand, a portion of the recorded
import represents goods merely in transit. The
total value of merchandise actually declared as
passing through British ports on through bills of
lading in 1901 amounted to £8,274,437, most of
which was of colonial origin, destined for foreign
countries, principally the United States. That
country, in fact, receives a good deal of its
British colonial produce in this way, and a re-

capitulation of the larger items affords an idea of what it amounts to :—

Country of Origin.	Goods.	Value.
India	Jute Manufactures	£1,033,528
Do.	Skins and Furs	668,009
Do.	Undressed Leather	177,825
Do.	Dry Hides	147,438
Australasia	Unwrought Copper	791,178
Do.	Wool	224,626
Do.	Gum	59,962
Do.	Sheepskins	49,470
Do.	Furs	9,428
Straits Settlements	Tin	1,237,295
Do.	Pepper	13,556
South Africa	Wool	44,179
Ceylon	Plumbago	14,578
West Africa	Ginger	9,738

As this trade would mostly be negotiated direct, the only benefit derived from it as far as the United Kingdom is concerned is from the labour employed in the work of transhipment. Presumably too, the colonial trade returns included them in their exports to foreign countries, and not to the United Kingdom. The figures appear again in the British exports of foreign and colonial merchandise, so that the total turnover is swollen to this extent by trade that is really not British at all. The remainder of that large item does represent business that has passed *bonâ fide* through the hands of British merchants.

In the case of the gold-producing colonies, the imports of gold ought to be included in the figures to make them represent the true balance of trade. But this only applies to any appreciable extent in two instances, South Africa and Australasia, including New Zealand. Canada ships all its gold to the United States, and any movements of bullion that pass between it and the United Kingdom are only exchange operations.

India also produces and ships gold, but its bullion operations in recent years have been such a muddle, that it is impossible to say when they are in liquidation of indebtedness, and when they are not. By its gold standard law, fifteen rupees are always to be obtained from the Treasury in exchange for an English sovereign, and it was quite a common practice to ship sovereigns from London to Bombay or Calcutta, and tender them for rupees, the Treasury immediately shipping them back to London to buy silver to replenish the depleted stock of rupees. The absurdity, to say nothing of the wastefulness, of such a process is evident, and it was sought to obviate it by depositing the gold in the Bank of England, and ear-marking it. A more practical way was discovered by shipping Australian gold destined for London *viâ* Calcutta or Bombay, which though not quite so direct, was a good deal less circuitous than the method just explained. Gold imported from India, therefore, ought sometimes to be credited to Australia; this was especially the case during 1901. As for the

Indian import itself, it would frequently puzzle the combined brains of a financial magnate and a currency expert to decide how it should be classified.

In addition to being a gold-producing, India is a gold-hoarding, country, some of the wealthier natives adopting this method of investing their savings. Even when India possessed a silver standard unchallenged by anyone, it had enormous reserves of gold treasure which were being constantly added to, and occasionally drawn from, in cases of emergency. Whatever movements in gold occurred in those days were easily explainable, but since 1896 the most vigorous efforts have been made, with the assistance of the authorities at home, to confirm the gold standard, and the movements between the two countries have resulted in a game of battledore and shuttlecock, as the following figures conclusively show :—

	United Kingdom Gold Imports from India.	United Kingdom Gold Exports to India.
1896	£1,234,991	£1,939,915
1897	1,496,614	2,513,055
1898	1,656,135	2,650,484
1899	1,725,562	1,933,203
1900	3,778,331	2,637,539
1901	6,946,334	2,448,301
1902	3,212,843	2,023,028
	£20,050,810	£16,145,525
Total movement in seven years	.	£36,196,337
Net ,, ,, ,,	.	3,905,285

Truly the mountain laboured to bring forth a mouse, and the people who principally profited have been the carriers—sometimes the steamship companies, sometimes the Post Office—and the underwriters who insured the gold.

It is no more correct to say that British trade with each possession, or group of possessions, is nearly evenly balanced because the whole is, than that Great Britain shows an excess of imports from each foreign country with which it trades because that is the aggregate result. The colonies are to be found on both sides of the account as well as foreign countries, and to understand the position more thoroughly, it is necessary to divide them into two classes: the first, in which the United Kingdom shows an excess of imports; the second, of exports. The figures fluctuate considerably from year to year, but only those for 1901 are given, which convey a sufficiently general idea as to how the matter stands. The smaller possessions are omitted in detail, and Hong-Kong altogether, because its trade is really foreign. This applies likewise to some portion of that of the Straits Settlements, the collecting and distributing centre of the Dutch East Indies through which an important British trade is carried on with them. But in this instance there is no means of distinguishing, and the figures must be given intact and taken for what they are worth.

Possessions yielding an Excess of British Imports.

	Imports.	Merchandise. Exports.	Balance.	Gold. Net Import.
Canada . . .	£19,854,585	£9,250,526	£10,604,059	..
Australia . . .	24,217,669	23,513,662	704,007	£4,822,222
New Zealand . .	10,594,587	6,068,230	4,526,357	744,502
Ceylon . . .	4,476,552	1,594,544	2,882,008	..
Straits Settlements .	6,112,304	3,282,728	2,829,576	..
Newfoundland . .	532,725	437,873	94,852	..
	£65,788,422	£44,147,563	£21,640,859	£5,566,724

Possessions yielding an Excess of British Exports.

	Imports.	Merchandise. Exports.	Balance.	Gold. Net Import.
India	£27,391,734	£35,746,399	£8,354,665	..
South Africa . .	5,132,308	18,939,147	13,806,839	£1,662,058
West Indies . .	2,280,530	2,806,890	526,360	477,867 [1]
West Africa . .	1,954,580	2,716,499	761,919	19,731
	£36,759,152	£60,208,935	£23,449,783	£2,159,656

All British Possessions.

Imports . £104,970,865   Exports . £110,320,386

On balance, therefore, the United Kingdom exported in 1901 a greater value of merchandise to British possessions than it imported from them. This would in any case be surprising, and is all the more remarkable because it is of very rare occurrence. The last time it happened was in 1888, when the trade with Canada was comparatively small and imports nearly balanced exports,

---

[1] This exceeds the recorded export of British Guiana, the only gold-producing portion of the West Indies. The remainder must have been shipped in liquidation of indebtedness, the circulation or reserves being correspondingly reduced.

and when Australia was purchasing British goods at the fast and furious rate that resulted ultimately in disaster. Usually the difference has not been very great, but when the gold is added it has become considerable. Take the year 1898 for instance, when the output of gold in South Africa reached its maximum, and we get the following :—

Imports from all British possessions	.	£98,896,380
Exports to all British possessions	. .	87,763,047
Balance Imports	.	£11,133,333
Gold imported from South Africa .	.	16,768,997
Gold imported from Australia	.	7,231,386
Gold imported from New Zealand .	.	334,863
Gold imported from West Indies .	.	593,067
Net excess of Imports .	. .	£36,061,646

This, in the aggregate, was a perfectly natural result, and enabled the possessions to discharge their liabilities to Great Britain ; though individually there is so much variety that it by no means follows that each possession achieved the object in the orthodox fashion. But even in the aggregate, 1901 must have fallen a long way short, and this must be attributed mainly to the South African War, which in the first place diverted supplies of the produce of other colonies there, and in the next stopped, and for a time reversed, the flow of gold. The corresponding movement to that given above was as follows :—

Balance Exports, as given on page 276 .   .   . £5,349,521
Gold import from Australia   .   .   . £4,822,222
Gold import from New Zealand   .   .   744,502
Gold import from West Indies   .   .   477,867
Gold import from South Africa   .   . 1,662,058
                                        ——————— 7,706,649
                                                 ————————
            Net excess of Imports £2,357,128

To which would have to be added that portion of the gold from India which originated in Australia.

Apart altogether from the war, this is what is called developing the Empire : sinking great sums of money in military expeditions and experiments of all kinds which have yielded no adequate return as yet, whatever they may be destined to do in the future. It might have happened that increased production resulting from this expenditure showed itself in larger exports of colonial produce to foreign countries, which would have been quite satisfactory. But again in the aggregate there is no evidence of this, and to realise the position each must be examined in detail, more especially as it would be invidious to draw too fine distinctions as to the relative value to Great Britain of these respective possessions from the mere drift of their trade, and this is the best answer to give to people who maintain that trade with a foreign country is worth nothing, if it is not positively detrimental, because it is very one-sided. Canada is not less important than South Africa because it shows, what to the

United Kingdom is an adverse balance of its merchandise trade, whereas South Africa exhibits a highly favourable one. If value and importance were to be estimated by monetary outlay, then South Africa would be an easy first; but if Great Britain were compelled to relinquish one or the other, it would not be Canada.

Or again, there is no comparison from a British point of view between the West Indies and Ceylon, both tropical possessions. The former are a perpetual source of anxiety to the mother country as well as a drain on its exchequer; the latter costs it neither thought nor money. Yet theoretically at least, the West Indies ought to be the more valuable : they buy more from Great Britain than they sell to it, while Ceylon does exactly the opposite. The position is aggravated too, because the West Indies after all only buy from the country to which they sell most of their produce, while Ceylon effects its purchases from one with which it does very little return trade, namely India. India is within the Empire, it is true, but that fact is not in this particular instance likely to afford a great amount of consolation, say to Lancashire cotton manufacturers.

The forces at work in producing the results we are now dealing with have been fully gone into in preceding chapters, and it now only remains to consider them in so far as they affect the trade of the United Kingdom.

If South Africa has necessarily attracted in

recent years the closest attention, Canada has called forth what may be described as the greatest affection, and the interest evoked has not been without good cause. More lasting and solid progress has been made in the Dominion within the last five years than in all the other possessions of the Empire put together, and it is not without reason that Great Britain looks to it for a solution of its difficult food problem. From 1896, when Canada's awakening had hardly begun, to 1900, there was a steady increase in the value of Canadian produce imported into the United Kingdom, though part of it must be attributed to a rise in prices. In the first of these years the value was £16,047,263, in the last £21,764,021, an increase, that is, of £5,716,758, or more than 35 per cent. There was a smart setback in 1901, when the fall reached nearly £2,000,000, but it was quite temporary, and the figures for 1902, amounting to £23,142,009, again beat any previous record. The falling off did not arise from any backwardness on the part of British importers and consumers, but merely because, as must invariably occur in an onward march, Canada experienced a slight setback and had not quite the same surplus of its products to dispose of.

The table on page 282 shows that the Dominion ranks only third in imports with the United Kingdom; it is probably only a matter of two or three years before it heads the list, never again very likely to be displaced, because the rapid peopling of the Far West now going on, means that no inconsiderable portion of the immense food supplies obtained from the United States are destined to be furnished by Canada. It ranks a bad fourth in the list of exports, and may remain in that position a much longer period. British exports to Canada increased from 1896 to 1900, at a higher percentage rate than the imports, but on a much smaller total, which left the aggregate gain considerably less. The actual figures were £6,225,961 and £9,058,789, equivalent to 45 per cent. Nor was the setback in imports in 1901 accompanied by a corresponding movement in exports, which as a matter of fact increased to £9,250,526, and left a nearly equal gain over the figures of 1896 on both sides of the account.

But that will not last. British imports from the Dominion will eventually grow at a more rapid rate than exports to it, and the divergence between them will steadily enlarge. The present proportion of exports to imports may be taken as somewhere about 45 per cent., so that whereas the actual difference between them on an import of £20,000,000 is £11,000,000, on one of £50,000,000 it will increase to £27,500,000. Canada is sure to develop its own manufacturing industries along with its agriculture, and as far as iron and steel are concerned, may almost monopolise it, though the loss in that case will fall on the United States and not on Great Britain. But it is at least satisfactory to feel that for every sovereign's worth of produce bought by the United Kingdom from Canada, Canada will take eight to ten shillings' worth of British goods in return, which is a far higher proportion than its great rival the United States.

The Australian trade balance is much more evenly adjusted, but though it would take very little to move it to the other side, it invariably shows a slight excess of imports, swollen materially of course, when the gold is added. Even then the total is insufficient to liquidate the indebtedness for interest on the great sums borrowed in the United Kingdom, to say nothing of what is invested in Australian trade and industry. The balance is made good by the credits arising from sales of Australian produce direct to foreign consumers.

Australia is a much better customer to British manufacturers than Canada, because it has no important manufacturing industries of its own, and there is no near competition like that of the United States to contend against. From this point of view, if from no other, the development of the island continent is of the utmost importance; the greater the population it accommodates and the more they produce, the larger will be the demand for British goods. But there is a stricter limitation to what the United Kingdom can consume of Australian, than of Canadian produce, and it is essential that foreign customers for it should be encouraged, which means that something may have to be conceded them in return.

Were some portion of Australia's present exports to be diverted to the United Kingdom from countries where they are now destined, that would not in itself increase Australia's purchasing power for British goods, as the credits would not be increased, though it might transfer a few orders from other countries merely as an exchange of trade. On the other hand,. were Australian production to increase, and the greater portion of it sold to foreign countries, there would certainly be an increased demand for British manufactures; not perhaps to a corresponding extent, but to a more or less important one, nevertheless. Between Canada and Australia, therefore, there is this very distinct difference; in the former case, British manufacturers and exporters will benefit partially from an increase of the colonial produce imported into the United Kingdom, and only slightly from what is shipped elsewhere: in the latter, they will benefit materially from produce sold and exported direct to foreign consumers, and but little from a diversion of import from foreign countries to the United Kingdom.

New Zealand depends for its prosperity more than either of the others on its association with the United Kingdom. A much less extensive wool grower than Australia, it has not the same quality to offer either, and in this particular commodity is consequently open to wider competition. But there is an unlimited demand for its meat and dairy produce which it has learnt to market both high in quality and cheap in price, and as long as these conditions can be maintained there need be no restriction to its progress. About the real prosperity of the country there can be very little doubt ; the excess of exports over imports is annually more than sufficient to cover its external indebtedness, and thus invariably leaves a balance to the good. That does not seem to prevent continual borrowing, which causes from time to time a good deal of criticism. The money may not always be wisely spent, but New Zealand is in much the same position as a young millionaire who thinks he can afford to throw away a hundred thousand occasionally without being much worse off. Only there are limits to that sort of thing which New Zealand must be careful not to overstep, as days of adversity may again be in store.

While British exports to these islands steadily increase, they have not done so at the same pace as the imports, for the very reasons just given. There is another cause, however, and that is the competition of the United States, which makes more marked progress in New Zealand than in any other British possession. This is all the more remarkable in view of the intensely pro-British sentiment of the people, though as usual the trousers' pocket is pretty tightly buttoned against it. There is a good deal of explanation for it in the matter of relative distance. New Zealand is always referred to in the United

Kingdom as the Antipodes, and rightly so, because no spot on the earth's surface could be much farther removed from it. The Pacific coast of America is a good deal nearer, and Americans have taken full advantage of this. Canada, rather than Great Britain, is the country that ought to be able to turn the tables, because it possesses similar facilities through Vancouver. Not equal ones, because San Francisco is still considerably nearer; more so than it is to either Brisbane or Sydney on the Australian continent. It is a matter of cheap transport more than anything else, and that is why New Zealand is so greatly interested in the overland route across Canada, which if it cannot shorten the actual distance, will materially lessen the time of covering it, and what is of even more importance, create competition with the all-ocean route through the Suez Canal. Until this is rendered thoroughly effective, the United States may continue to take big bites out of the apple. There has been a Canadian, as well as a United States, steamship service for some years, but the former wants improving materially, though it is well subsidised.

India is prominent among possessions yielding an excess of British exports. A reference to the tables of percentages on pages 179 and 180 would inspire the belief that the divergence is much greater than is actually shown on page 282. And even those figures relating to 1901 are quite exceptional, as in most years the excess is considerably smaller, and does not often go beyond three or four millions sterling. The explanation of the apparent discrepancy is, that as Indian exports greatly exceed imports, a smaller percentage of them yields a relatively higher figure.

The great increase in British exports to India in 1901, £35,746,399 against £30,966,938 in 1900, largely accounts for the transfer of the balance of colonial trade from one side to the other, because it was not accompanied by any material gain in the imports. As we saw in the chapter dealing with India, the Indian exports for the year ending 31st March 1902 rose to the highest point on record, but they were not directed to the United Kingdom. The increase consisted principally of oil seeds and raw cotton, the former used only sparingly by British manufacturers, the latter scarcely at all, while a further substantial gain in cotton yarns and piece goods meant direct competition with them. All the same, India's purchasing power was materially increased, and of that the United Kingdom obtained the full benefit. It was not because India suddenly found itself in affluence and able to indulge in luxury ; rather the enforced economy of previous lean years had so worn out the materials of every-day use and swept away all surplus stocks of them, that a great replenishment was necessary, which may not have to be repeated again in a hurry. It shows, however, in a very marked manner, how India's trade with foreign countries reacts upon

British producers, and why there is every reason for the portion of it apart from foodstuffs to be encouraged and stimulated.

The real balance of trade to be liquidated between Great Britain and India is thus in ordinary years comparatively small; nothing like the amount drawn in council bills on the Indian treasuries. But India obtains credits from foreign countries for what it exports to them, which are transferred to Great Britain by means of these bills.

Ceylon, too, helps to reverse the balance whatever it may amount to, and though the trade is quite distinct, the finances of the two countries are more or less intermingled. Ceylon purchases rice in large quantities from Burma, and cotton piece goods from Bombay, and becomes correspondingly indebted to them. Means of payment are provided by sales of tea to the United Kingdom, which in turn discharges its indebtedness by shipping cotton and other goods to Burma and Bombay. Thus a prosperous year in Ceylon usually means increased British exports to India.

A far larger balance than is recorded by India is shown by the figures for South Africa, which in an ordinary year is simply redressed by the import of gold. But for obvious reasons that was not possible for the three years 1900 to 1902 inclusive, during the greater part of which the output was restricted, when not entirely suspended, by the operations of the war. The inhabitants of the country had to live just the same, in addition to which there was the enormous military contingent to be provided for. The populace which would have earned its living from the gold mines and kindred industries, were enlisted instead, voluntarily or compulsorily, in the service of the campaign, and so in place of the excess of South African merchandise imports being discharged in gold, the settlement came out of the pocket of the British taxpayer, who would have considered himself lucky had that been all he was called upon to disburse.

But some time before the end of the war peace was anticipated, and large stocks of non-perishable commodities began to be accumulated at the principal ports, ready for despatch to the interior. This helped to swell British exports to South Africa without any equivalent import of merchandise or gold, and the visible liquidation of this business looks a long way off. Indeed, in view of the depredations requiring to be made good, the immense cost involved in the army of occupation, expensive civil administration, and the much slower revival of the mining industry than was anticipated, it may be years before there is a return to normal conditions.

The exact value of South African trade before the war is difficult to establish, because there were inlets and outlets for it that were not under British control. One thing is certain, however, that for some years the United Kingdom stood on velvet regarding it. In 1898 when political agitation was already at work stimulating the war spirit, British traders at least had every reason to be satisfied with the solvency of their South African connections, for they came out handsomely on the right side as the following figures show :—

British exports of merchandise	£13,147,665
British imports of merchandise	6,206,383
	£6,941,282
Imports of Gold	16,768,997
Excess of imports over exports from South Africa	£9,827,715

to which must be added the value of diamonds, for that year declared at £4,523,815. This does not, of course, represent the net return to South Africa itself, which imported merchandise freely from other countries as well as the United Kingdom, but left it to be paid for with the gold sent there ; that is, Germany and the United States and others were reimbursed for their exports to South Africa by credits on London.

What a striking contrast to the figures for 1901 as they appear on page 282, and still more so for 1902 when they are available in final shape. Whatever South Africa was politically before the war, years must elapse before it is likely again to show anything so economically satisfactory as the above.

The conditions governing British trade with the

West Indies differ from those generally prevalent in the self-governing possessions and India. The law of gravitation operates in a totally different direction, and only the influence of political association keeps the flow from the East as large or as steady as it is. Though nearly all the sugar and fruit produced are exported to the United States, the planters and owners of the soil are mostly domiciled in Great Britain, where they finance their estates and find it most convenient to supply them. This necessitates regular communication of which the merchants and larger tradesmen avail themselves as well, so that the bulk of non-perishable commodities continue to be supplied from the source that has furnished them for more than a century. Possibly that is one more instance of the non-progressiveness of the West Indies, from the result of which they suffer.

The different islands too, along with British Guiana, all act much in the same way. Take Grenada, whose production is almost entirely restricted to cocoa, nearly all of which is exported to Europe. It might be supposed that the return trade would be supplied in a very different manner to that of Antigua, which ships the whole of its sugar, representing almost its entire production, to the United States. But both are very much alike in this respect, each importing the same classes of goods from the United States and from the United Kingdom respectively, either direct or through the medium of agents located elsewhere, principally in the island of Barbados.

This greatly accentuates the argument in favour of a trade clearing-house for the whole of these possessions, to be used more perhaps for imports than exports, because the latter can generally be made up with entire cargoes, and where they consist of fruit will not bear transhipment. But a great storehouse, say at Barbados, whose chief port, Bridgetown, can display a similar reversible sign to the well-known inn at Land's End, on one side of which the traveller reads the "first house in England," and on the other, the "last house," would facilitate transactions on a large scale both with the United States and Great Britain, and, by obviating the necessity of so expensive a subsidy as is at present paid, permit of a more extensive localised steamship service at very likely a good deal less cost. British manufacturers and merchants would certainly derive considerable advantage in being able to execute large orders, instead of the paltry distribution of which the trade now consists.

It is of very little consequence on which side the balance of trade lies between the United Kingdom and the West Indies, because it can be readily adjusted with the United States. But unfortunately the excess of British exports only too faithfully reflects the movement in the islands themselves, most of them regularly showing an excess of imports. This is not the case in each individual instance, but it is so on balance, and the exceptions only aggravate the cases that contribute to the rule. These islands can never be prosperous until their exports regularly exceed their imports, whether the trade is done with the United Kingdom or some other country. Jamaica has at length turned the corner in this respect, and it is to be hoped will in future keep on the right side, to be followed at no distant period by all the others. Never mind what country it is that buys the produce; Great Britain is certain to benefit by the change more than any other.

Each recurring year finds the balance of trade between these different possessions and the United Kingdom on the same side, with of course, more or less wide fluctuations in the amount. With West Africa it is different, and the excess may one year be on the side of imports, and next of exports. Where several countries are interested in the same neighbourhood this might arise from a larger or smaller portion of each year's trade being diverted to one or the other. The natural flow should leave British imports from West Africa in excess of exports to it, because fair exchange ought to show a profit to the merchants engaged, paid them in the form of produce. In this respect the year 1896 appears to have been a profitable one, because imports into the United Kingdom exceeded exports by a sum of £170,748. This has since been changed, and recent years show the balance on the other side; 1900 to the extent of £371,832, and 1901 of £761,919. As West Africa has no surplus income or accumulated capital to pay for what it buys, this is an unnatural result, unless the exports of the British possessions to foreign countries more than redress the balance, of which there is no evidence.[1]

Oversea possessions very often have other attractions than trade. But with West Africa it is different; trade was not only the original object of every European nation that has gone there, but nothing has ever supplanted, or is likely to supplant it. The country possesses few, if any, of the attractions that make life endurable, much less enjoyable, and the only motive that can draw men thither is the hope of material gain, with which is invariably associated the desire to get away as soon as possible. But one which offers no inducements as a place for permanent settlement may possess considerable strategic value. West Africa enjoys no such advantage either. It does not lie on the direct route to anywhere of importance, and even if it did, almost total absence of harbours or safe anchorages for ships of what are now regarded as of very moderate tonnage, while rendering means of local

---

[1] An article on "British Trade with West Africa," published in the first number of the *Journal of the African Society*, October 1901, deals in considerable detail with this matter. It is far too lengthy to reproduce here, but what follows is mainly extracted from it, and readers particularly interested in this branch of the subject are recommended to have recourse to the article itself.

defence easy, shut it out of any scheme of national offence or defence. The value of West Africa to a European nation depends absolutely and entirely on its trade; destroy that, and there is nothing left to make the territory worth retaining.

Nobody can be accused of mercenariness by applying this test to West African possessions and deciding to let them stand or fall by it. Great Britain would be inconvenienced rather than distressed were their products cut off to-morrow, and unless these colonies can be made a source of gain, they are valueless; indeed if destruction to life and injury to health were to be taken into account, retention under such circumstances would be positively detrimental to the national well-being.

How is the test to be applied? Trade nowadays possesses so many ramifications that it is an exceedingly difficult matter to assess its value. An oversea possession may be a source of fortune to a few favoured individuals, but only at the expense of a great many others, and possibly of the nation to which they belong. West Africa has experienced something of this sort in its past history. The iniquitous slave trade of the eighteenth and early part of the nineteenth centuries was immensely profitable to those engaged directly in it, as well as to others to whom the benefits eventually accrued; but it was at the expense of untold misery to millions of human beings, and at last involved Great Britain in an outlay of £20,000,000, when such a sum meant a great deal more than it does to-day, while the drag which the West Indies have never ceased to be on the national exchequer can be directly attributed to the evil results. Nothing of this kind is ever likely to occur again; but other trades, less reprehensible in themselves, may end in similar results, in which case they ought to be suppressed in the interests of the many, not encouraged for the benefit of the few.

In one respect West African trade does not differ from any other: it affects many interests besides those directly engaged. The mere exchange of products, whether it be, as is still largely the case in West Africa, by pure barter, or as is more usually prevalent elsewhere, through the medium of money, is only one element, and that not always the most important. The distribution of the products that are received on the one hand, and the manufacture of those delivered in exchange on the other, may and often do employ more capital, disburse more wages, and yield a greater profit than the actual trade in them, and it is necessary to investigate far beyond the volume as expressed by figures to gauge real value. This must nevertheless be the first step, because the merchants' and traders' profit or loss necessarily exercises a very decisive influence in expanding or retarding business in any given direction. The consumer, the manufacturer, and the wage-earner may all be achieving satisfactory results, but unless they are prepared to share them with the merchant their opportunities for doing so will soon be curtailed, unless, as sometimes happens nowadays, they deliberately displace him. In this particular branch of commerce that is an unusually difficult undertaking, and the West African merchant is more than likely to hold his own against such incursions.

Formerly it was by no means a difficult matter to estimate the profits of this trade taken as a whole, though not of course of the individual trader; that secret was securely locked up in his bosom or his books. He took his supply of beads and calicoes, hardware and gin, and bartered them on the coast or along the rivers for palm oil and ivory and gold-dust, which he brought home and realised, and the aggregate of all these transactions as recorded in the published figures of imports and exports presented a fair idea of the result. There was no complicated distribution between capital and revenue, and the extent to which the value of the African produce imported exceeded that of the goods exported in payment, making due allowance for the incidental expenses at both ends, might always be regarded as the profit. Now there are many cross currents; the produce shipped to one country is frequently paid for in the goods received from another, and the merchants have become cosmopolitan in their dealings. But this has merely extended the area over which the principle has to be applied without materially weakening the principle itself, because

the employment of fixed capital in West Africa
has hardly yet commenced on an extensive scale.
Unless, therefore, the average annual export of the
whole of the West African possessions exceeds in
value the corresponding average annual import, the
result of the trading is disastrous ; not necessarily to
everybody concerned, but intensified to those who
are unfortunate in proportion to the success of
others.

This state of things in time will be modified,
as it has been in other countries, by the process of
development of which there now seems good prospect. The influx of capital in the form of railway
material, mining machinery, and anything calculated
to give permanent increased value to the industries
and productions of the country, may raise imports
for the time being considerably above exports and
yet leave the economic conditions perfectly sound.
A movement of that sort invariably goes to extremes : the United States, Canada, Australia, every
South American Republic, have in the course of their
history been deluged with material, the liability for
which has for a time proved a millstone round their
necks, and retarded rather than hastened their
progress. West Africa has to travel a long way
before it reaches that stage, but there is an intervening one. Interest must be provided on whatever
capital is employed, and its payment, to be economical, must be in the increased yield of the produce
of the country itself, which in time will swell

exports, and once more cause their volume to exceed that of imports, particularly at periods when development becomes stagnant.

There are one or two points in this connection that must not be overlooked. Perhaps the most important is that West Africa is by no means entirely British, and that future success, from a commercial aspect, depends on continued friendly relationship, not only with European neighbours established there, but with the inhabitants of the territories recognised as within the British spheres of influence. France is doing a great work in Africa, and accomplishing it most successfully. A superior base of operations affords it natural advantages Great Britain hardly enjoys, but as Englishmen participate handsomely in the results of all civilising enterprise, they should be the last to cavil at it.

Unpleasant, and perhaps unavoidable, political and territorial disputes have arisen in the past, but happily these now seem disposed of, and a spirit of amity prevails, as evinced a short time ago by the concessions made on the Gambia River with the full concurrence of France. British traders on the West Coast have necessarily to look after themselves first of all, and it must be galling, say in Sierra Leone, to see business diverted from them by French activity in the hinterland. But there are other interests to be considered as well, and if that activity results in demands upon British manufacturers far in excess of any loss that accrues to the colony, it is a distinct national advantage, though it may involve unpleasant consequences to individuals.

Again, important dealings in many articles of produce can now be protected by means of hedging with futures. This advantage is denied the West African trade, which has to take all market risks. It may be weeks, and even months, before produce purchased can be disposed of, and if prices decline heavily meanwhile, losses may be serious. This naturally has its compensation in rising markets, when profits will be so much larger. Such fluctuations render official trade figures unsafe to dogmatise upon : they may appear favourable when actually losses are being incurred, or disastrous when profits are being realised. But over a series of years they undoubtedly tell the truth.

There is ample room for a greater extension of West African commerce than has yet occurred, and it is, moreover, a section that is for many reasons desirable to cultivate. British manufacturers may not be able to consume all the products of the country, though if these were sufficiently cheapened there is no adequate reason why they should not utilise a far greater proportion of them than they do. Palm oil and oil nuts, for instance, could the enormous cost of interior transport be sufficiently reduced, might be landed eventually at prices that would enable them to displace other products, now imported from foreign countries.

20

Were British manufactures cheapened correspondingly to the African consumer, demand for them
would be so much larger, and as profits are cut so
fine and depend so largely on the volume of business, increased turnover would benefit alike the
merchant, the shipowner and the manufacturer.

The excess shown in the imports from the Straits
Settlements is to a large extent fictitious on account
of the transit trade already alluded to, and when
this is deducted there is not a very great difference
between the two sides of the account. There is a
considerable transit export to Singapore as well, in
which Colombo, the principal port of Ceylon, is
becoming a keen competitor, but in each case, the
actual destinations being known are entered in the
original returns. Thus the extensive trade with
Java, the Philippines, and other countries in the Far
East, is directed in the first place to one or other of
these British possessions, though returned officially
as foreign, and not colonial, exports. This is as it
should be, but inasmuch as the opposite course is
adopted with imports, the figures are misleading.
In any event, the fluctuations with a possession like
the Straits Settlements are of no moment, because
most of the trade is eventually of a transit nature,
and as the goods purchased outright by Singapore
houses and shipped to them, are distributed throughout the whole of the Eastern Archipelago, the bulk
eventually goes to consumers who owe not the
slightest allegiance to the British Crown.

Newfoundland, in 1901, changed sides, that is, it had previously almost invariably shown an excess of British exports. The cause of this is easily traced ; in the first place the import into the United Kingdom of fish, fish oil, and iron ore, showed a material increase, while one of the usual items of export, new ships, was not on this occasion represented at all, the fishermen of the island having presumably maintained their fleet with second-hand vessels, which is not to be wondered at when the very high cost of construction in British yards during the greater part of the years 1900 and 1901 is taken into account. The year 1902 will show this change still more accentuated, otherwise there is nothing to call for remark as regards this particular possession.

A reference once more to the table on page 282 shows that after deduction of the trade of the various British possessions enumerated, there is not a great deal left to be accounted for. And when further deduction is made of the figures for the Channel Islands, the inclusion of which, any more than of the Isle of Man or the Orkneys and Shetlands, in the returns of foreign commerce is open to question : of Gibraltar and Malta, the exports to which are due to other than trade reasons, what remains amounts to a mere bagatelle. Exports for 1901, however, were swollen to the extent of nearly £1,300,000 by materials for a new cable in the East, which were distributed between Aden and the islands of Ascension and

Mauritius, as the most convenient depôts, but by no stretch of the imagination can this be credited to the trade of these particular dependencies. And with regard to the others, there is scarcely anything to be added to what has been written in the previous chapter, as in most cases the trade that does eventually find its way to the United Kingdom passes in the first instance through one or other of the larger possessions.

An exception must be made of East Africa, less on account of the extent of its trade than of the circumstances attending it. These possessions or Protectorates are essentially claims for posterity, and as far as the present generation is concerned are proving somewhat costly ones. What their ultimate value may prove to be is matter of pure conjecture; meanwhile we must console ourselves upon being engaged in the work of civilisation.

Not that there is an inconsiderable turnover of trade in these regions. We saw that Zanzibar accounted for something like £3,000,000 annually. But only a mere trifle of it is done with the United Kingdom, whose imports for 1901 amounted to £95,420 and the exports to £82,320, which included £11,683, the value of coal destined for the adjoining island of Pemba, an important coaling station for steamers engaged in the Eastern trade. And as regards the East African mainland, the showing is still more wretched, imports having been valued at only £7186, though exports attained the more considerable dimensions of £92,502; exactly how these are paid for is perhaps best explained by the annual vote in the House of Commons for this particular Protectorate. Nor are the figures improving; the imports from Zanzibar are just about half what they were in 1897 as well as being lower than for several previous years, while exports are also smaller, though nothing like to the same extent. The import from East Africa in 1901 was certainly the highest recorded, though that is not saying very much. That the exports fell in the same five years to less than half is perhaps a matter for congratulation.

But it must be borne in mind that there has been no direct intercourse between the United Kingdom and these dependencies, and trade must perhaps be looked for by some other route. The most likely is Aden, at which most of the steamers regularly engaged with India and the Far East periodically call. Aden is termed a British possession, though under the jurisdiction of the Government of the Bombay Presidency and not of either the Colonial or Foreign Offices. There is some trade with it, though it certainly is not all African, as Aden is a distributing centre for Arabia, and to some extent for the Persian Gulf as well. British imports from it were valued in 1901 at £154,632, and exports to it, after deducting £212,106 for telegraph material, at £260,404, which included £141,009 for coal for other than local use. The addition as far as East Africa is concerned cannot, therefore, be very great.

The fact is, the trade of that part of the world so far as it is done with Europe at all, is falling more and more into the hands of Germany, quite a material percentage of the Zanzibar turnover being with German East Africa. That country is laying itself out for the development of these territories more than of any it possesses. Among other means adopted is the subsidising of a line of steamers, but it is hardly correct to maintain that this is for purely East African purposes. South Africa is very likely after all the principal objective; the steamship service is a comprehensive one and embraces a great part of the entire African continent. It is an alternate one also, one voyage being through the Suez Canal along the East Coast of Africa, round the Cape and back home by the West Coast; the other reversing the route, so that whatever advantages each offers may be secured.

The subsidy is substantial, amounting altogether to £67,500 a year, and there is nothing sufficiently attractive to induce Great Britain to compete against it on anything like such terms, or for that matter with France either, which has also a much more effective service in that part of Africa. But what is practicable is an alternative route to South Africa through the Mediterranean and Red Seas, which shall include these territories in its itinerary. With the Transvaal British

territory, intercourse with it through Lorenzo
Marques will no longer have the same drawbacks
as formerly, and will probably increase, while it
is an open question whether Durban cannot be
more economically served by the Suez Canal route
than *viâ* the Cape. In that event a rearrange-
ment of the old, and not the creation of an
entirely new service is all that is needed.

In any case it is a matter of some doubt
whether the future of East Africa is not more
intimately bound up with India than with the
United Kingdom. Already its trade is largely
in the hands of native Indians, who naturally
look eastward rather than westward for such
oversea connections as they desire, and this
tendency is on the whole to be encouraged.
Possibly the ultimate advantages of these territories will reach Great Britain through its Indian
Empire.

There are many inferences to be drawn from
the points that have been under review in this
chapter, but the colonial trade of the United
Kingdom is so closely interwoven with the
foreign, that it is necessary to consider that in
something like the same detail before it will be
safe to arrive at any conclusions.

CHAPTER IX

The Foreign Trade of the United Kingdom

It is frequently pointed out that the colonial
trade of the United Kingdom constitutes only
about one-fourth of the total, and that consequently it demands at best but secondary consideration. But like most generalised statements,

this is apt to be misleading unless the respective one-fourth and three-fourths are more closely scrutinised and compared. We find, for instance, that colonial imports are only about one-fifth of the total, and this proportion does not improve; indeed the tendency is distinctly in the opposite direction. On the other hand, colonial exports in 1901 amounted to one-third of the total, or nearly half the foreign ones, and this proportion is becoming steadily larger. Of British and Irish produce and manufactures indeed it is considerably more than half, because the re-exports of foreign and colonial merchandise are chiefly to foreign countries. Exactly how the position stands is best shown by the following figures :—

	The Whole World.	Foreign Countries Only.[1]
Imports from .	£521,990,198	£417,019,333
Exports to .	347,864,268	237,543,882
Excess of Imports	£174,125,930	£179,475,451

The exports were constituted as follows :—

	To Foreign Countries.	To Colonial Possessions.
British and Irish .	£177,846,700	£102,175,676
Colonial and Foreign	59,697,182	8,144,710
	£237,543,882	£110,320,386

From the point of view of the British manufacturer and producer, therefore, colonial is relatively of far

---

[1] Including Hong-Kong. All statistics are again taken from the Board of Trade returns and abstracts.

more importance than foreign trade. In 1901, British possessions absorbed a sovereign's worth of goods for every sovereign's worth they furnished of their own commodities, whereas foreign countries took only a trifle over eight shillings. Further, the proportion is steadily dwindling, as a summary of recent years will show :—

	Imports from Foreign Countries.	Exports of British and Irish Produce.	Percentage of Exports to Imports.
1890	£325,755,857	£178,688,414	55
1895	321,918,889	157,839,765	50
1896	349,398,033	157,830,651	45
1897	357,607,500	155,520,019	43
1898	371,648,322	152,157,594	41
1899	379,089,414	179,583,352	47
1900	414,610,576	199,575,282	48
1901	417,019,333	177,846,700	43
1902	422,307,361	176,692,299	42

The exports and percentages from 1899 onwards have been improved by the inclusion of new ships, of which previously no official record was entered; in other words the figures before that year ought really to be somewhat larger. Colonial as well as foreign returns would be further increased by the sale of old ships which are still excluded, though in some recent years the amount involved must have been considerable. But colonial trade alone cannot have been materially affected, as these items are not important as far as it is concerned. But when everything is taken into account, the percentage of exports to imports as regards foreign countries was in 1902 the lowest on record.

The explanation of this state of things is extremely simple. Foreign countries have not dumped their commodities on the United Kingdom in order to get rid of them on the best terms obtainable, but rather have been stimulated to produce them because the United Kingdom had need of them, and was willing to pay substantial prices. They consist principally of foodstuffs and raw materials, and whenever manufacturing industry is active, the demand for both is correspondingly increased. Everything the colonies and India had to offer was greedily taken, but the deficiency was still so large that constantly increasing quantities had to be drawn from purely foreign sources.

British imports may be divided into three comprehensive groups : foodstuffs, raw materials of manufacture, and manufactured articles. The first two are easy to identify, the third more difficult, and the classification adopted by the Board of Trade is open to criticism, as indeed any other they introduced would sure to be. Many so-called manufactured articles enter largely into British manufacturing industry and have merely undergone some preliminary process that has reduced them from the state of crude material. Leather is a notable instance of this.

The foreign countries furnishing them may be divided into four groups : the first supplying all, of which the United States afford a typical illustration ; the second two, invariably food and raw

material, of which the Argentine Republic among
foreign countries is perhaps the most prominent,
while nearly all British possessions come within
the same category ; the third supplying food
alone like Denmark; and the last sending little
else than raw materials, of which Brazil and other
South American Republics are examples.

With the first it may be taken for granted that
if they can supply the United Kingdom with everything, they can do so equally for themselves, and
consequently need little in return, and it is the
countries of this group that make up most of the
excess of British imports. The second assist in
the same direction, though not to the same extent,
as most of them are considerable purchasers of
British manufactures; while the third and fourth
are very much mixed, some having their own
manufacturing industries, which, if they cannot
compete with foreign ones, are at least paramount
at home, while others depend for almost everything
of the sort on outside sources, and in such cases
it not infrequently happens that their trade with
the United Kingdom yields it an excess of
exports.

The grouping might almost be extended to
include continents, but here exceptions would
become more numerous, because all, except the
newest as far as discovery to modern civilisation
is concerned, include countries in every stage of
development. North America, if not monopolised,

is at least dominated by the Anglo-Saxon race, and the only two countries it embraces, one foreign, the other British, are both on the same side of the United Kingdom trading account.

Continental Europe offers the most complex problem of all. It is the vortex of civilisation and competition alike, and the interchanges between the different countries, especially those of the western half, become positively confusing. Nowhere is this likely to be more apparent than in a great free trade centre like the United Kingdom, where nearly everything can come and go without let or hindrance. In the woollen industry, for instance, large quantities of yarn are exported each year to Germany, France, and elsewhere, while an almost equal weight is imported from several of the same countries. This seems a wasteful process; really it is an economical one, British spinners having attained to great proficiency in one branch of the industry, their continental rivals asserting their equality, if not their superiority, in another, though inferior, branch of it. The trade in manufactured goods appears still more perplexing to anyone but an expert: why should Germany supply the United Kingdom with so much cloth, generally of the cheapest qualities, and France with more, this time of the very best, while British looms manufacture both, not only for British wear, but for German and French as well? Fashion and price are the controlling forces, and where the former operates, tariff arrangements are often set at nought.

On the whole, however, the United Kingdom imports a great deal more from Western Europe than it exports to it. According to the Board of Trade returns there is one exception, namely Germany, which invariably shows an excess of British exports, and this circumstance is frequently advanced in contention that German competition is much overrated, and that Germany is really a better customer to Great Britain than Great Britain to Germany. But this is not actually the case, and only appears so on account of the way the trade is distributed. Both Rotterdam and Antwerp are great highways of German commerce, and when the trade returns of Holland and Belgium are examined they are found to yield an enormous excess of British imports. For a great deal of it these two countries are only indirectly responsible, nor is Germany entirely so for what they are not, as we shall see presently.

But if Germany's trade with the entire British Empire be taken into account, then the balance, actually as well as nominally, is on the other side. Provisional figures for 1902 have been issued showing that German imports from British territory were valued at the equivalent of 58½ millions sterling, while exports amounted to only 53½ millions, proving how immensely the import trade from outlying possessions preponderates over the export. The

former was valued at nearly £23,000,000 ; the latter
at slightly over £10,000,000, so that India, Australia, and other dependencies were able to discharge
indebtedness to the mother country to the extent
of £13,000,000 by credits on Germany. The net
trade balance in favour of the British Empire as
a whole, was about £5,000,000, and while it has
in recent years been somewhat reduced by the
growing excess of German exports to the United
Kingdom, there has been more than a corresponding
increase through the rapid gain in German imports
from outlying territories. However much Germany's
competition may be resented by British producers
and manufacturers, its custom is of untold value
to other portions of the Empire.

France, on the other hand, yields an overwhelming excess of British imports ; far greater according
to the Board of Trade returns than is actually the
case. Switzerland, Northern Italy, and Austria ship
their goods across French territory and through
French ports, and help to swell the total. These
three countries also find outlets through Germany,
and to some extent eventually through Holland,
which controls the greatest of European navigable
waterways, the Rhine. The Baltic ports of Russia
are closed to navigation a considerable portion of
the year, and as the foreign trade of that country
flows principally through the north, it has to make
use of German or other outlets for it during that
period at least.

Thus the trade relations between the United Kingdom and the greater part of Europe are extremely complicated, and, for most of the countries named at anyrate, must be examined in their entirety. The figures over a series of years are given in Table B of the Appendix, but for 1901 they are here reproduced separately, and comparison made with the returns of the countries themselves which are likely to be more correct as to distribution, though by no means absolutely so as regards totals, because complete particulars of origin and destination are not forthcoming.

Trade with United Kingdom according to British Returns.

	Imports from	Exports to
Germany	£32,207,214	£34,221,080
Holland	32,871,843	13,744,021
Belgium	24,666,081	12,624.691
France	51,213,424	23,700,820
Austria-Hungary	1,191,294	2,838.904
	£142,149,856	£87,129,516

Trade with United Kingdom according to Foreign Returns.[1]

	Exports to United Kingdom.	Imports from United Kingdom.
Germany	£45,337,450	£27,634,300
Holland[2]	35,472,250	20,690,750
Belgium	13,681,000	10,772,220
France	47,929,480	24,074,080
Switzerland[2]	7,614,160	1,880,960
Austria-Hungary	7,787,080	5,689,125
	£157,821,420	£90,741,435

[1] 20 marks, 25 francs, 24 kronen, and 12 gulden to £1 sterling.
[2] Includes bullion and specie.

The difference between the two sets of figures is rather considerable and is to be accounted for in several ways. Two of the countries include bullion and specie in their returns, and diamonds also amount to something, but in addition a good deal of foreign produce passing through Dutch and Belgian ports, especially the former, in transit to the United Kingdom, is probably included in the trade returns, while the Board of Trade figures assign it to the actual countries of origin. The higher value of imports from the United Kingdom compared with British exports is partly due to freight and charges.

Switzerland does not appear at all in the first table, no British returns being published regarding it. Russia and Italy are not included, because only a small portion of their trade passes through the others, most of it being carried on direct. But the six countries enumerated in the second list pass nearly everything either direct or through each other, and the totals consequently afford a fairly correct idea of the actual volume. It will be observed, moreover, that not one of them actually imports more from the United Kingdom than it exports to it.

With the Scandinavian countries and Denmark, dealings are much more straightforward, as no transhipment or use of foreign territory is involved. Sweden and Norway furnish primarily raw material, principally timber and its products, which include a great deal of wood pulp for papermaking, and metalliferous, mainly iron ore, as well as iron in a more finished state. Denmark depends for its British connection on farm products, and shipments of butter, eggs, and bacon, especially the first, have attained to very large proportions. All three export to the United Kingdom far more liberally than they import from it, but it cannot be said that they do so in discharge of any recurring liability; they are clearly instances where the balance of indebtedness requires regularly to be settled, and in the case of Norway, part of the adjustment is through the medium of second-hand shipping. None of them are large consumers of British manufactured goods, and coal, in bulk at least, accounts for the greater part of the return trade. In that and everything else there is German competition, and though Germany is by no means so good a customer to them, its favourable situation affords it a material advantage.

The Empire of Russia, spread over so extensive a portion of both Europe and Asia, affords, relatively to its size, but a small amount of commerce with the United Kingdom. There is no record yet of any trade with the Asiatic dominions; its arrival and establishment on the eastern seaboard has been too recent to permit of anything of the sort, and everything recorded passes through the ports of the Baltic or the Black Sea. From the latter, imports consist almost entirely of grain, and petroleum from the famous oilfields of the Caspian; a miscellaneous assortment of other commodities aggregating as a rule but a small total. With the north the trade is far more diversified, though agricultural produce is its most prominent feature. Raw materials, like timber, flax, hemp, and linseed, figure extensively, and so render Russia an appreciable factor in the industry as well as the food supply of the United Kingdom.

The highly protectionist policy adopted over a considerable period greatly restricts that return trade for which Russia should really afford excellent opportunities, and coal and machinery constitute the two leading items in it. As the country has been passing through a severe industrial crisis, attributable to the extravagance of its fiscal policy more than anything else, it is not surprising that this side of the account has recently undergone considerable shrinkage.

Southern Europe presents altogether different features. Spain is one of the most richly mineralised countries in the world, and were its treasures properly developed, ought to be one of the wealthiest. As it is, it allows them to be exploited by others and removed in an almost natural state for employment in industry elsewhere. Great Britain is principally concerned, and derives immense supplies of iron and copper ore and pig lead from the Spanish mines.

Spain is also a land of the orange and the grape,

and its southern ports are mainly occupied with the trade these create. The United Kingdom is again the objective of most of it, so that taking everything into account, imports from the Spanish territory far exceed exports to it. The latter are again curtailed by the intensely protectionist policy of Spain, which in Catalonia has a seat of manufacturing industry that has never yet been able to hold its own against the open competition of the rest of the world. With the West Indies entirely lost, the struggle to monopolise the home markets is keener than ever, and naturally tends to restrict British export trade in whatever directions it is affected by it.

The other portion of the Iberian peninsula, Portugal, is much more limited in resources as well as area and population, and has consequently a less extensive commerce. Like its neighbour, however, it gives more than it gets from the United Kingdom, though in this instance the result is natural, inasmuch as the balance is in discharge of indebtedness, whereas Spain's external liabilities are mostly incurred with France.

Italy is an exclusively Mediterranean country, and the only one so far dealt with that actually, as well as nominally, preponderates in its imports from the United Kingdom. British exports to it in 1901 were valued at £8,293,484, and imports from it at £3,383,858, the difference being reduced to some extent, but by no means obliterated, by the overland shipments from the northern part of the peninsula. What is left is fully and easily accounted for. Italy also aspires to be a manufacturing country on a large scale, but is deficient in supplies of fuel, and as a consequence is, after France, the best individual customer the British coalowner possesses. For 1901 the value of this item alone was £3,964,622. Were it eliminated, Italy would probably rank on the same side of the account as the others.

The United States long since cast a covetous eye on this particular trade, and hoped eventually to capture it. From the point of view of one section at least of British politicians and economists, they ought to be welcome to it, and a certain measure of assistance was afforded by the imposition of the coal tax. They enjoy some natural advantages as well, inasmuch as America regularly needs considerable supplies of Mediterranean produce, and might load the ships with coal as a return cargo. Possibly a still better way may be found, as it looks as though the coal transport of the future will, like the tank steamer for mineral oil, be specially constructed, and unsuited for general cargo. Even then distance ought to tell in favour of Great Britain unless the trade is wilfully destroyed. But for the time being the prolonged strike and the demoralisation that ensued completely turned the tables, and from being competitors with British coalowners, the United States developed into important customers.

In the case of Scandinavia, of Denmark, of the Iberian Peninsula and Italy, trade with the United Kingdom may be described as natural. All the countries provide commodities that are only to a limited extent produced in the British Islands, and could not be obtained more economically elsewhere. Even Denmark cannot be described as a supplanter, and only in a moderate degree as a competitor, with the producers either of the United Kingdom or of British possessions, because it supplies a deficiency which none of the others are competent for the present to make good. They take a fair assortment of British goods in return, and though it might be somewhat larger, it could not materially affect existing relations.

But with Western and Central Europe, the group that is represented in the table on page 320, it is altogether different. They too yield much that the United Kingdom cannot do without, or obtain on more favourable terms elsewhere. On the other hand, there is a great deal that does not fulfil the second at least of these conditions. The most important single item of trade is sugar, supplied by all these countries except Switzerland. That it is purchased and imported because it is the cheapest in the market goes without saying, but it does not follow that it is on that account the most economical. It is frequently asserted that if Great Britain purchases sugar from Germany or France, these countries take British goods in payment. This is not the case necessarily, and it certainly is not actually, as a reference to Table B in the Appendix will show, because British imports from this group have been growing at a more rapid rate than exports to it. If Great Britain wants an additional million pounds' worth of sugar, France, or Germany, or Austria are ready to supply it, but will not, if they can help it, take a single additional article of British production in return, preferring to liquidate the credit in some other way.

Another item of scarcely less magnitude than sugar is for silk manufactures purchased from France, Switzerland, and Germany. Precisely the same argument is applicable here ; these countries endeavour to sell all they can without encouraging a return. Other articles aggregating a considerable sum fall within the same category, and though present conditions may favour the trade, it does not by any means follow that serious efforts should not be made to divert it in directions where, as far as the United Kingdom is concerned, it might prove more lucrative.

Because at its best the British export trade with Western and Central Europe confers relatively little benefit on British industry. The figures look large, but when they come to be analysed they are found to be productive of scant return to the manufacturing industries of the Kingdom. A very considerable percentage is re-export or transhipment business, which yields no return except to the merchant and shipowner, and though this is by no means to be despised, it would be more satisfactory were the profits larger and more widely distributed. This actual division is best shown by the following tables in which the exports are distributed between British and foreign commodities :—

British Exports to North-Western and Central Europe, 1901.

	British and Irish Produce.	Foreign and Colonial Merchandise.
Russia . . .	£8,673,334	£5,537,619
Germany . . .	23,573,785	10,647,295
Holland . . .	9,089,149	4,654,872
Belgium . . .	8,156,203	4,468,488
France . . .	16,472,068	7,228,752
Austria-Hungary . .	2,141,185	697,719
	£68,105,724	£33,234,745

British Exports to Scandinavia and Southern Europe, 1901.

	British and Irish Produce.	Foreign and Colonial Merchandise.
Sweden . . .	£4,456,959	£982,165
Norway . . .	3,243,026	598,137
Denmark . . .	3,615,223	548,255
Portugal . . .	1,710,829	383;163
Spain	4,827,110	628,413
Italy	7,612,562	680,922
	£25,465,709	£3,821,055

Nearly 35 per cent. of the exports to the first group are thus of a nature that afford no employment to British industry, beyond the mere handling of the merchandise, while some of it yields no profit to British merchants either, inasmuch as the goods have been purchased abroad in their respective countries of origin and shipped *viâ* London or Liverpool as a mere matter of convenience, sometimes, perhaps, at cheaper rates of freight than goods actually destined for those ports. There is a reverse movement, that is, a percentage of the import from these countries also consists of transit goods, forwarded in the same manner through continental ports, though it is comparatively insignificant.

The proportion of the second group is only some 13 per cent., and the countries constituting it are thus of more relative value as customers. The two together, along with the United States to which allusion will be made later, account annually for about seven-eighths of this particular branch of commerce, and to all but a small fraction of it as far as countries outside the British Empire are concerned.

A corner of Europe that occupies a prominent position in British commerce is usually associated with a corresponding portion of Asia, and designated the Levant. Manchester possesses few, if any, more important customers, for though shipments of cotton goods to India are greatly in excess, and to China generally so to a less extent, in both instances much of the trade is done by great mercantile firms who are either themselves manufacturers, or have manufacturers constantly producing standard qualities of goods for them. The Levant is in the hands of a multitude of shippers, many, if not most of them, of Greek or Armenian origin, and the diversity of their requirements furnishes employment for a similar diversity of manufacturers. As already observed, this trade as regards the cotton industry of Great Britain ranks a good third, and in some years even occupies second place, outstripping China, though if affairs in the Far East should become fairly settled this is hardly likely to occur in the future. It is scarcely to be wondered at that Germany makes such strenuous efforts to gain a firm footing in this part of the world which offers so promising a field for its textile industries; and for others too, if only the procrastination of the Turk could be replaced by some of the energy of Western civilisation.

This particular branch of commerce is of such dimensions that it annually throws the balance in favour of the United Kingdom. Turkey is one of the most hopelessly indebted countries on the face of the earth, but Great Britain is now only to a very moderate extent its creditor, France occupying the chief position in that respect. It is a marvel how the Empire manages to pay its way and provide at the same time for the enormous demands of its rulers, and it is only by the most prodigious exactions that this is accomplished. The territories it embraces, how-

ever, are so rich, that under anything like decent
government they would yield an ample surplus of
produce to meet all foreign liabilities, and at the
same time very likely increase the inward trade.
Asiatic Turkey grows some of the finest barley in
the world and finds a ready market for it for
malting purposes in the United Kingdom. It also
produces the choicest fruits, which are in universal
demand throughout Europe and America, but inasmuch as the United Kingdom is its best customer
it is only natural that the return trade should flow
from it. The good government of what constitutes
the Turkish Empire is thus of far more than
political interest to Great Britain, for on it its
most important manufacturing industry is largely
dependent.

Greece stands by itself, and as a rule shows an
evenly adjusted account in its relations with the
United Kingdom, which is the chief buyer of its
leading export commodity, namely currants, as well
as of minor ones like olive oil and tanning materials.
Generally the balance is in favour of Greece ; for
1901 it was the other way, owing to exceptionally
large purchases of cotton goods following somewhat
restricted ones in previous years. Another limb
entirely severed from the Turkish Empire, Roumania,
exhibits a greater volume of trade than Greece, but
not nearly so equally divided. It is a keen competitor with the United States and the Argentine
Republic in the growth of maize, and its shipments

of this cereal alone are generally in excess of its imports of British goods. Wheat and barley are items of varying importance, but except corn it has little to offer to foreign buyers. The semi-independent States still under the suzerainty of the Sultan have little direct trade, but pass most of what is destined oversea through the Turkish or Danubian ports to which it is attributed.

It would be difficult to discover a more striking contrast than that afforded by the Turkish Empire and what is still at least its nominal dependency, namely Egypt. For nearly a quarter of a century the progress of the latter has been uninterrupted, and the result is nowhere more clearly evidenced than in its trade returns. It is generally a mistake to turn the undivided energies of any country into one particular groove, as sooner or later the industry is almost sure to fail. This has not occurred yet as regards Egypt, which devotes constantly increasing attention to the culture of cotton, and with its by - products constitutes something like seven-eighths of the total exports of that country. An even larger proportion than this figures in the returns of trade with the United Kingdom, though a fair quantity of the raw cotton regularly entered is merely in transit for the United States, which are every year becoming more important customers for it. Great Britain is still the best, however, and enjoys in return an overwhelming preponderance in the supply of the leading Egyptian requirement, cotton goods. British exports fall a good deal short of imports, and trade with the United Kingdom thus helps to furnish the wherewithal for paying interest on the Egyptian debt, as well as contributes largely to those reserves which have been so wisely and efficaciously employed in the development of the country under its present administrators.

Other countries of northern Africa bordering on the Mediterranean have likewise passed more or less under the domination of European nations, and their commercial intercourse with the United Kingdom has been affected in consequence. Algeria, for all practical business purposes is a part of France, and subject both to its tariff and its laws, with the result that the bulk of the trade is almost as much internal as between any two ordinary French provinces. Tunis will eventually occupy the same position, but for the time being treaty rights protect British cotton manufacturers, or rather place them on much the same footing as their French competitors, and reserve that portion at least of a formerly lucrative connection. But inasmuch as Tunisian products are more and more diverted to France, where they enjoy special tariff privileges, the balance of trade as regards the United Kingdom falls on the export side.

Tripoli and Morocco, respectively at the

eastern and western confines of what is virtually
French territory, are both in a political sense still
free countries, though how long they will remain
so is an open question. Their trade is on nothing
like the scale of the others, though it may be
more valuable to the United Kingdom, because
unrestricted; but the loss of a portion of it would
not be so serious a matter as has frequently
resulted from other political and economic changes
of modern times.

Nowhere are such opportunities afforded for
the expansion and development so much craved
by the industrial powers of the world, as in the
vast continent of Asia. This is frankly and fully
recognised, and accounts for international political
interest having in recent years shifted to the Far
East. Recently they have been transferred somewhat nearer home again, and Persia, shorn of its
former glory, and of comparatively little value in
itself either politically or commercially, has become
the scene of negotiation and intrigue. This is
explained, as far as Russia is concerned, by the
persistent and not unnatural desire to reach open
water; though access to the Persian Gulf will not
attain the result unless the narrow outlet is controlled as well, otherwise the position will be little
superior to that emanating from the virtual
control of the Black Sea.

Germany's ambitions are of a different order,
the desire being to make of Persia and the

Persian Gulf a back-door entrance to the rich provinces of Asiatic Turkey on the one hand, and possibly to India on the other. As is the case with nearly all neutral territory, the United Kingdom has hitherto controlled the bulk of the trade, which, nominally Persian, is really distributed over the greater part of Western Asia, except possibly that portion of it, at one time not insignificant, devoted to arms and ammunition, destined for the hill tribes to the north of India.

The steady encroachment Russia is making on this particular trade is not by reason of open competition through the regular channels. By building good roads in the northern parts of the country it is making the overland approaches to the principal consuming centres in the interior both easier and less· costly than from the southern ports, and as these new arteries are really under Russian administration and control, the trade that passes over them drifts almost entirely into Russian hands. It is further assisted by the grip that is being obtained over the finances of the kingdom through the well-known extravagance and increasing impecuniosity of its ruler, as well as the system of bounties that Russia knows so well how to manipulate when there is any chance of making them really effective. Persia bids fair at no very distant date to become little more than a dependency of the Russian Empire, if, indeed, the greater portion is not actually incorporated in it, and under such conditions both British and Indian trade, as regards exports at anyrate, are sure to be curtailed.

It is not Persia, however, on which the future hopes of British merchants and manufacturers are centred. Nor is it the enormous area of Northern Asia which is already incorporated in the Russian Empire, and from which they are likely to be as rigorously excluded as from the European section of it. What has hitherto been the most prolific portion of the continent, both as regards trade and wealth, belongs to them already, but inasmuch as it is British energy and capital that have made India in these respects what it is, there is ground for believing that if applied elsewhere similar results might ensue.

But to achieve entire ·success, a free hand is necessary, and that is what Great Britain is not destined to secure in China. Political domination the same as in India is not desirable, even if it were possible, and the monopoly formerly enjoyed without it has passed away for good. Germany and Russia have shown themselves politically powerful, but without as yet exercising any important influence as regards their own trade; their efforts having been restricted to railway and similar concessions which have involved the expenditure of large amounts of capital without any return, or the immediate prospect of it. Eschewing politics and political intrigue, the United States have made serious inroads upon trade, and in some instances have succeeded in almost entirely displacing what was once exclusively British.

Still, there is room for both, and very likely for all, could all agree among themselves to give and take fair play. The notion prevails, that wherever free trade exists it means British preponderance, if not monopoly, and in this respect the ideas of British and foreign protectionists are at utter variance. What the former are now clamorous for is protection within the Empire, and free trade or equal opportunities outside it, though how far the first would neutralise the second is a matter that would have to be tested by experience that might prove costly. But as far as China is concerned, no preference of any sort has been wished, much less asked for.

Nor has the incursion of the United States prevented a rapid growth of British exports in the staple article of trade, cotton goods. It might have been more satisfactory had the former monopoly been maintained, but it is an open question whether competition did not inspire the enterprise which resulted in such substantial development, checked for a time by the civil outbreaks, but resumed since with undiminished vigour. It is not the problem of division that has to be faced by the nations interested in the trade of China so much as reimbursement. China has never been a creditor nation, and has lately become distinctly a debtor one, yet goes on adding

22

materially to its liabilities by the regular excess of imports over exports. That this, along with the indebtedness incurred for the so-called indemnity, is being discharged out of capital resources is amply demonstrated by the position of the silver market, which for a time became utterly demoralised by the sales that were effected for Chinese account, whereas under ordinary conditions the country should be, and actually is, a buyer and importer of the metal. The rapid exhaustion, too, of the available supplies as a means of payment does not improve the situation.

This adds materially to the difficulties of British trade with China, the future of which is enveloped in a good deal of obscurity. That country figures more prominently than any other, with the exception of its neighbour Japan, in excess of British exports over imports. How is the difference liquidated? No doubt by drafts drawn by the China branches of the principal banking houses on their head offices in London. But where does the money come from to purchase them? That again may not be troubled about so long as it is actually forthcoming.

If China had gold mines the mystery would be solved, but in their absence it remains one. There is no apparent addition to the resources of the people, no creation of productive public works, no accumulation of capital value in any form to justify the annual outpouring of what elsewhere represents wealth. The only natural conclusion to be drawn is that the country is being impoverished, and if this really be the case, another crisis is impending, financial and economic, which may or may not end in further political disturbance.

The country most involved in such an upset would undoubtedly be Great Britain, because it is most prominent in creating the drain. It is no answer to say that value is given for the money. A man may keep himself supplied with shirts for a good many years by selling the furniture of his dwelling, or even the tiles off its roof, but if he is not replacing them the crash must come sooner or later. And what one wants to know is, how is China making good this, and other similar outlays?

Other interested countries are more favourably situated. Russia, for instance, was regularly, until the Boxer outbreak, debtor to China, taking far more of its commodities, principally tea, than it supplied of its own. In this respect there has been no change, only Russia now takes the tea in discharge of its share of the indemnity, and so wipes out the foreign credit China previously had at its disposal. Neither France nor Germany had much interest either way, but the same event must have turned them into creditor nations whose demands have also to be satisfied. The United States were for a long time debtors, and discharged their obligations principally in silver, of which China was then able to make good use. This was gradually displaced by cotton goods, a more profitable method of settlement for the United States, and an equally efficient one as regards China. Only Great Britain was left to demand money rather than money's worth.

The position is aggravated further by China's relationship with other parts of the Empire, which might possibly have helped to redress the balance. We saw in the chapter on Australasia, that in that case also exports to China somewhat exceeded imports from it, though this was mainly due to silver. Canada is invariably on the right side, though only to a trivial extent; the import balance rarely, if ever, exceeding £100,000. But India throws it further askew by the large shipments of opium, cotton yarn, jute manufactures, and other goods it annually ships to China, and a reference to pages 179 and 180 shows that whereas China ranks a good second in the countries to which India exports, giving an average of over 12 per cent. of the total, the imports are nowhere, and rarely exceed 3 per cent. The balance added to that incurred with Great Britain renders the total quite a formidable one, which should, if it does not actually, cause anxiety regarding the future.

The obvious way of overcoming the difficulty is for China to increase its exports; it would not much matter what country they were to, only the United Kingdom would be preferable. This can only be done by depriving the Chinese population of a portion at least of their already scant supply of the necessaries of life, or by increasing whatever surplus production already exists. In the latter respect India is a formidable competitor, which Great Britain can have no desire, nor any object, in displacing. It does not, for instance, want China to cultivate opium to the serious detriment of the Indian Exchequer, nor does it wish to reverse the process of supplanting China by Indian tea. China, unfortunately, has nothing else that the United Kingdom stands very much in need of, and this way leads merely to a blind alley. Coal and iron are supposed to abound, and the development of these minerals is the avowed object of the capitalists seeking concessions. But why? Great Britain and the United States and Germany do not want Chinese iron and steel; they want to supply China with their own. Gold, as already hinted, would, theoretically at least, solve the problem; it might actually intensify it by leading to a scramble among the Powers for the territory yielding it.

Meanwhile there is nothing to do but watch and wait. Optimists who regard China as another India will have occasion to pause and readjust, if they cannot reconcile, the conflicting features. The worst thing that Great Britain can do, either for itself or China, is to plunge into a morass from which no outlet is visible, and trade and investment in the Far East had better be restricted to certainties, and not stretched out to embrace the vaguest possibilities.

The British connection with Japan does not

improve the situation. From a British point of view it has so far proved eminently satisfactory, for not only has custom been good, but payment has been prompt. About where the latter came from there can be no secret. Japan went to war with China, beat it in open fight, exacted an indemnity, fair and reasonable, received the money, lodged it in the Bank of England, and generously disbursed it to British shipbuilders and manufacturers. But China had to pay for it all, which makes the situation still worse for China. Japan having eaten its cake has no longer got it; has, indeed, taken a big bite out of another in the shape of a substantial foreign loan.

To avoid travelling the same road as its big but infirm neighbour, Japan must alter its course and retrench its foreign expenditure. It may not be altogether satisfactory to see British exports to Britain's latest ally shrink by millions at a time, but that will undoubtedly afford the best guarantee for future stability. Periods of expansion cannot go on without an occasional halt, and one is already overdue as regards Japan. The Chinese bank has closed its doors, and Japan cannot afford to go on purchasing annually from the United Kingdom, or for that matter from any other country, five or six millions sterling more than it sells to it. And it is very much in the same position as China regarding European wants. It furnishes the same commodities, tea and silk, with the addition of rice, which again

compete with India and Burma, and are not therefore to be unduly encouraged. Development of
trade with the Far East is not quite the simple
thing it looks.

Only a short time ago it was regarded a far cry
from the extremities of the old world to what is
still, in point of discovery, the new, located in the
Western Hemisphere. But many things have happened in the interval, and there has been an
emphatic illustration of the old adage that too
far east is west. The inhabitant of San Francisco
who formerly wished to get to Japan, or China, or
Australia, had to cross the continent to New York,
traverse the Atlantic Ocean, and from some part
of England or the continent of Europe pursue his
journey eastward. Now it not infrequently happens
that the inhabitant of Western Europe, with the
same ultimate destination in view, reverses the
route, and travels through New York and San
Francisco, or perhaps Vancouver, to reach it. This
has naturally established intimate trade relationships between America and the East, and introduced
to Germany, and especially to Great Britain, a
new and formidable competitor in these regions
of the world.

This does not affect those already existing
between America and Europe, and it is with them
we come now more particularly to deal. As far
as the United Kingdom is concerned, there has
been a great and rapid expansion, one way at least,

though it cannot be attributed to anything that has occurred in the East, or only to the extent that the greater demand for British manufactures there has increased the requirements for the food and raw material which the United States are specially competent to produce. Even that does not account for the prodigious total of upwards of 141 millions sterling which the value of the imports from the United States reached in the year 1901, that is, more than one-fourth the total from the whole world, and materially in excess of what was received from all British possessions added together.

This constituted a record, and though it would be unwise to predict that it will remain one, there are reasons for thinking that such may actually prove to be the case. The world had been passing through a long period of commercial and industrial depression, with only short spells of occasional relief, when the great change came over it somewhere about 1896, and found it totally unprepared. The immense area and boundless resources of the United States, added to the untiring energy of the people, afforded that country an opportunity such as had not been presented before, even to it, and it was taken the fullest advantage of. But others have been creeping ahead; more slowly perhaps, but still surely, and the first decided lull will find plenty of competitors to dispute the ground won by the great Republic of the West. Canada, for

instance, has taken a step forward in the production
of cereals which may materially reduce the demands
on the United States surplus ; and in other things,
notably metals, supply has once more caught up
with demand, and made it no longer possible for
American producers to dictate prices and conditions
as they did for a time. Both in quantity and value,
therefore, the huge total already mentioned may
prove very hard to repeat, and the year 1902
already exhibits a decline to under 127 millions,
a loss of 14 millions.

The whole sum, moreover, does not represent
actual United States produce or manufactures. As
with the United Kingdom and other European
countries, a certain quantity of merchandise passes
through each year in transit from elsewhere. When
one finds indiarubber, coffee, cocoa, rum, and other
tropical produce in the list of British imports, it
becomes clear that some discrimination is necessary,
and that other countries must be contributory.
This is actually the case, as Central and South
America and the West Indies export part of their
produce to Europe *viâ* New York or other North
American Atlantic ports. The Havana cigar trade,
for instance, is done principally in this way, and
represents a considerable sum annually credited to
the United States, for which there is perhaps more
reason now than formerly. Most of the lead is of
Mexican origin, though perhaps smelted in the
United States, and a great deal of silver likewise,

though that is not included in merchandise returns. Still, when everything of this nature is accounted for, it only amounts to a moderate percentage of the total, and the vast bulk of the £141,015,465 represented legitimate United States products, the proceeds of which went intact into the pockets of the citizens of that country.

What is the set-off against this? The total exports from the United Kingdom to the United States during the same period amounted to £37,651,150, or little over 25 per cent. of the imports. But to state merely the total is misleading, because it was made up as follows:—

British and Irish Produce and Manufactures .	£18,393,883
Foreign and Colonial Merchandise . .	19,257,267
	£37,651,150

In other words, for every £7 or £8 sold by the United States to the United Kingdom in 1901, they only took £1 of British goods in return. Not the whole of the foreign and colonial merchandise was a set-off or credit, because part of it was merely in transit and never handled at all by British merchants. We had occasion to note the colonial portion of this trade on page 278, and there was in addition a similar foreign movement. Part of the item represents merchandise actually imported into the United Kingdom for sale, and therefore carried merchants' and brokers' profits, but these cannot have amounted to any considerable sum.

The balance of over £100,000,000 had to be liquidated in other ways. Part of it was due for interest on American investments, still largely held throughout the United Kingdom, particularly of the better class, and for other indebtedness, but to nothing like the extent named. The sale of securities accounted for a good deal, and there were other means employed for adjusting the balance.

Central and South America afford a great contrast to the United States, inasmuch as many of the countries situated there exhibit an excess of British exports. In this case it is by no means always a desirable feature, because Spanish republics are not ordinarily the sort of countries to have in one's debt, as recent experience with Venezuela amply demonstrated. In the case of the smaller States this is largely, if not entirely, rectified by the process already alluded to, namely the shipment of their produce *viâ* United States ports. In the case of Mexico, the discrepancy is very considerable, but it is set right by silver, the most valuable product of the country as far as export is concerned. Besides, Mexico stands in better credit than most of its neighbours, and there is less risk even if the balance does happen temporarily to be on the wrong side.

The most striking instance of this was formerly the Brazils, and a reference to Table B in the Appendix shows that for the quinquennial period 1891–95, British exports exceeded imports by upwards of £20,000,000, or over £4,000,000 a year. This has gradually narrowed, until in 1901, for the first time, the balance was on the other side, and though the total volume of trade in 1902 considerably increased, the same thing occurred again. The causes that have led to this are far from satisfactory, as they have been accompanied by a more serious shrinkage in exports than any particular growth of imports.

The staple product of Brazil is coffee, and the United Kingdom happens to be a tea, not a coffee drinking country, in which respect it is almost unique, having only Russia to keep it company among the great nations of the world. Of the coffee that is actually drunk, moreover, very little comes from Brazil, the sources of the British supply being the West Indies, the Central American States, and to some extent India, all of which yield on an average a somewhat higher grade. But Brazil is also the greatest producer of indiarubber, and has extended this portion at least of its trade with Great Britain, the high prices which ruled for a time materially adding to import value. On the other hand, the intense depression in the coffee market due to over-production seriously crippled the country, and the import trade was further injured by depreciation of the currency, which for a time stood at only about one-fourth its nominal metallic value. And to add to all this, the competition of the United States and Germany has been particularly keen, and has been helped by the circumstance of their being much more extensive customers for Brazilian produce, principally coffee, than the United Kingdom, which affords a distinct advantage when the rate of exchange is liable to such wide and violent fluctuations.

Brazil was long the most important customer British merchants and manufacturers had in South America, but that position promises in future to be permanently occupied by the Argentine Republic. In this instance, too, the relationship is more natural, inasmuch as Argentine products are in greater demand in the United Kingdom than Brazilian, consisting as they do principally of food. In cereals and fresh meat, it has become a serious rival, not only of the United States, but of some of the British possessions, and as far as the former at least are concerned, the rivalry is to be encouraged, because relatively, Argentina buys so much more largely of British goods in return. There is, it is true, a strong protectionist sentiment prevalent throughout the country which has resulted in some very unwise fiscal legislation, but it is not sufficiently far advanced, nor likely to be so for a long time to come, to attempt to displace the standard manufactures of Europe and North America. Development must therefore redound to the advantage of those who have been accustomed hitherto to supply its needs. The financial crisis through which it passed, the disturbance of its currency and other attendant features, are not confined to Spanish American

republics, but accompany more or less the early
progress of all countries.   The era of revolution
appears to have closed, and nothing more alarming
is now threatened than aggression on neighbours,
which must be regarded as a symptom of modern
progress, if not of Western civilisation.

The West Coast of South America has been
pretty much a British preserve ever since ownership was relinquished by Spain, if not indeed
before that event happened, as the rich trade it
had to offer was the principal inducement of the
Elizabethan adventurers who first made England's
influence felt in that quarter of the globe.   Chili
and Peru, which monopolise most of the commerce,
represent an average of upwards of £10,000,000
annually of the trade of the United Kingdom,
and it is very often a particularly lucrative one,
as it is in the hands of a comparatively limited
number of houses.   The division, too, is not unequal ;
British imports regularly exceed the exports, but
by no such astonishing proportions as is the case
with the United States.   There are increasing
opportunities for competition in the export branch,
because foreign countries purchase so largely of
Chilian commodities, particularly nitrate of soda,
the principal fertiliser employed in the agriculture
of Western Europe.   The gold and silver mines
are no longer a source of wealth, but copper
figures largely in the output, and Chilian wheat
and Peruvian sugar help to supply the world's

demands for these foodstuffs. Confined as both countries are for the greater part of their length to the narrow strip of land west of the Andes, their opportunities for expansion are not considerable, but they may be none the worse for being restricted to the steady development which has been the feature of modern times, if the short-lived nitrate boom be excepted.

This survey pretty well exhausts the list of independent foreign countries with which the United Kingdom has any intimate trade relationship. There remain, however, the oversea possessions of some of them, which in several instances are not unimportant. Most countries, unfortunately, draw a ring fence round their colonies the same as they do round themselves; often with very effective results as far as the outside world is concerned. France notoriously adopts this policy, and when, as in the case of Madagascar, the trade has from time immemorial been in British hands, the change is disastrous to those whom it affects, though they may be few in number.

France, however, has not yet followed this course as regards West Africa, though there are not wanting signs of restlessness pointing in that direction. Germany is equally free in its treatment of its more limited possessions there, and if Spain and Portugal are more exclusive, they are not entirely prohibitive. British trade with foreign West Africa is consequently an item of consideration,

and for some time past has averaged over £2,000,000
per annum.   It is growing, and consequently worthy
of all encouragement, as that section of the world
is likely to be destined ultimately to play a more
important part in commerce than it has yet done.

For the very same reason that the particular
products of British West Africa find more consumers outside the United Kingdom than within
it, the foreign territories ship theirs elsewhere.   As
far as Great Britain is concerned, the trade is thus
mainly an export one, and consists to a large extent
of cotton goods, for which there is practically an
unlimited demand with the opening up of the
continent.   Though it preponderates so considerably on one side, that is not in this instance any
disadvantage, because the balance is presumably
accounted for by the European countries responsible.
That does not mean that they make good the losses
of reckless trading—British traders require to be
more cautious in such cases than in their own
territory—but merely that payments will be forthcoming provided the business is done on sound
principles.

One or two of the groups of small islands lying
off the West African coast have recently come into
prominence.   They belong to Spain and Portugal,
but have been exploited by British capital and
energy.   The Canaries are the most noteworthy,
and in their case it was misfortune that proved
their ultimate salvation.   They relied almost

entirely on the cochineal industry, but German
chemists found a substitute for the dye yielded
by the little insect long before they succeeded in
displacing the vegetable indigo of India.   With
ruin staring them in the face, resort was had to
the cultivation of the banana, which has brought
more prosperity than was ever before enjoyed.
Imports into the United Kingdom have now
reached upwards of a million sterling against less
than one-fourth that figure a decade ago.   But
this does not represent value received by the
islanders, as it includes freight and shipping
charges calculated at a fairly high rate, and
they consequently cannot take anything like a
corresponding value of British goods in return.
As a matter of fact, the exports are materially
swollen by coal for sale to passing steamers.   As
the islands are very circumscribed in area, there
is naturally a limit also to their production, which
is perhaps not far from being reached.

It is not every country that adopts the narrow
policy of France as regards oversea possessions.
Holland is as liberal as Great Britain, with the
result that British trade with the Dutch East
Indies is of considerable magnitude.   It ought
to be far greater ; but inasmuch as the principal
production of Java is cane sugar, it is practically
debarred from entrance into the United Kingdom
under existing conditions.   Imports have dwindled
to very small dimensions, but this has not checked

a steady growth in exports, which reach in annual value nearly £2,500,000, exclusive of British goods bought from Singapore merchants which at times must represent a considerable item. Java grows sugar so cheap that adversity has not overtaken it to the same extent as other cane-producing countries, but what it yields goes elsewhere than to the United Kingdom, principally to the United States.

The United States themselves must now be reckoned with as a colonial power. Where the territories acquired have become actually incorporated in the Republic, its tariff has been extended to them, and they are placed outside the range of international competition. But this has not happened yet with regard to Cuba and the Philippines, which remain open to British enterprise. The war sadly curtailed trade in both instances, though there has been some subsequent revival. Official imports from Cuba have fallen to very small figures, for the reason previously stated that cigars are shipped *vià* New York. Exports are still substantial, though merchants interested are in constant dread of curtailment. While the world regards sympathetically the demand for reciprocity between Cuba and the United States, its conversion would cripple, if it did not kill outright, most of the island's foreign trade which would be speedily transferred to American manufacturers.

Curiously enough British trade relations with the Philippines are entirely reversed, and further, the

United States have been accustomed to import a portion of their produce by way of the United Kingdom. This is not destined to last, but as hemp, which is the commodity chiefly concerned, is manufactured in the Eastern States, it has the entire breadth of the American continent, as well as the Pacific Ocean to traverse before reaching its destination, and the opposite route has proved the more economical. The centre of this trade, moreover, has always been in England, which is the largest individual consumer of the fibre.

The Philippines also grow sugar, excluded from British markets by European bounties. With an extension of the cultivation of the cane, they, too, would be likely to become better customers to British manufacturers, because whatever happens in Cuba, no similar policy of restriction is likely to be extended to them. The United States value too highly the open door in China to close one under their own control right on its threshold.

For a summary of the whole we must return once more to the opening of the chapter. It is sometimes contended that the annual excess of imports into the United Kingdom represents nothing more than the world's indebtedness to it. But granting that were the case as regards the 174 millions surplus imported from the whole world, no stretch of the imagination can make the world outside the British Empire, indebted to Great Britain to the extent of upwards of 179½ millions sterling, the figure reached for the year 1901. This may have been altogether exceptional and due to some extent to war expenditure, defrayed out of the tax-payer's pocket or from borrowed resources, but the fact nevertheless remains, that the normal imports from foreign countries annually exceed the exports by a sum considerably more than any actual or imaginary indebtedness amounts to.

There is another school which maintains that this excess is paid for out of national capital, and sometimes goes so far as to assert that it is defrayed in gold. There is more truth in the latter conten-tion than appears on the surface, though not perhaps in the sense in which it is intended. But it is certain that a portion of the annual imports into the United Kingdom from foreign countries is paid for in gold. It may not exactly be British gold in the sense that it is taken out of the national reserves. It is colonial gold, sent to London in discharge of colonial indebtedness, and used to pay for foreign produce. This is best illustrated in tabulated form over a period of six years, to go no further back—

	Net Imports of Gold from British Possessions.	Net Exports of Gold to Foreign Countries.	Net Imports into United Kingdom.
1896	£12,236,647	£17,891,992	£5,655,345 [1]
1897	24,152,624	24,152,337	287
1898	24,150,293	17,017,383	7,132,910
1899	16,168,475	5,171,030	10,997,445
1900	6,744,817	1,048,597 [2]	7,793,414
1901	12,407,950	5,657,587	6,750,263

[1] Export.   [2] Import

One lesson inculcated by these figures is, that the South African War had a far more extensive influence on British trade generally than appeared on the surface. In 1898, for instance, the United Kingdom had upwards of £24,000,000 of colonial gold wherewith to help to pay for its total imports amounting to £470,544,702. In 1900, it had less than £7,000,000 to disburse against £523,075,163. For the time being Great Britain became a debtor country, more especially to France, the United States, and Germany, which lent money freely on bills and other securities, because the liquid national assets were insufficient to meet current liabilities. It is the first time in history such a thing has occurred; all previous wars, whatever their magnitude or duration, were financed and paid for by British investors and taxpayers. How serious a commercial crisis might have resulted had not the rest of the world been both able and willing to afford accommodation was not realised, and neither, much less both, these contingencies can be counted on in the future.

It does not necessarily follow that the gold is shipped to countries to which Great Britain is indebted; its distribution is governed more by financial and exchange, than trade, reasons. But as long as Great Britain loses the gold, it does not matter whether it goes to Paris or Timbuctoo in the French Sahara; to Berlin or to Samoa in the Southern Pacific; to the United States or some

country designated by them : the fact remains that
it has disappeared. Nor is it necessary to cavil
at the result. There is nothing so useless as an
unemployed hoard of gold. Whether the reserves
of the metal in the United Kingdom are adequate
or not to the enormous financial and commercial
interests at stake is another matter : most countries
would regard them as totally inadequate. Still,
they answer the purpose, and hitherto it has always
been possible to increase them with a slight effort,
and until the highest authorities decide that they
must be permanently added to, payment in gold
answers the purpose as well as in any other way.

It may not be so satisfactory, because it carries
no profit beyond the fractional percentage that may
be derived from an exchange operation. It might
be better, for instance, if some of the commodities
supplied by foreign countries were furnished by
British possessions, and their gold sent elsewhere
without passing through London at all. But this
is only theory, more fitted for a discussion on international trade distribution.

Broadly speaking, the United Kingdom is a
much bigger and better customer to the world
outside the British Empire than that same world
is to the United Kingdom. Trade between them
is something more than barter, and has to be
liquidated by other means than the simple exchange
of commodities.

CHAPTER X

GENERAL CONCLUSIONS

Is the British Empire to be regarded as a unit, or as a number of separate and more or less independent countries? Politically there can be no doubt whatever as to the answer : any attempt of one part to dictate to another regarding its internal constitutional arrangements would not only be resented, but if pressed too far might lead to actual disruption. No common political system for the self - governing possessions has proved feasible, and for those under the direct control of the Crown corresponding deviations in method are equally essential to meet the conditions they present.

If political unity is impossible, what prospect can there be of commercial union which will affect many more interests, both as regards numbers and diversity? A study of the preceding chapters must have convinced the reader that the circumstances of no two of the countries are alike, and very often the greatest differences are found to exist where they are closest together, as for instance between India and Ceylon, or Australia and New Zealand. Each one in turn is just as anxious to extend its relations with countries outside the Empire—as far at least as the supply of its own particular products is concerned—as are the United States, and Germany, and France, and every other commercial and industrial nation. But as a matter of fact there are yet very few natural commodities produced within the Empire in sufficient quantity to supply its internal demand, while there are still fewer manufactured articles that are not turned out far in excess of what it requires. As it is the outlying portions that are responsible for the first, and Great Britain for the second, there is thus from the very start this radical distinction to be observed.

Of commodities that may be classed as of first-rate importance in the world's industries, there is but one upon which the Empire is anywhere near self-reliant, and that is wool. Of it, there is always a substantial surplus, and Australasia, South Africa, and India have to look to foreign consumers to take it. There is also a certain quantity of foreign wool imported annually into the United Kingdom, and some of it consumed; but a portion at least consists of qualities that are not produced in any British possession, and does not, therefore, enter into competition. On the other hand, it is maintained that by some fiscal arrangement the need for foreign wool could be entirely obviated, and consumption restricted to that of British growth, using the adjective in its wider sense.

But there is something beyond the wool-growing or manufacturing industries to be considered in this case, though neither could be materially affected by such a change, because there would still be a sufficiently large surplus of the British staple above all requirements to ensure competition and maintain the natural price, unless regulated by combination. The trade in wool, however, is of considerable importance, and nothing must be done calculated in any way to jeopardise it. As values have fluctuated very widely in recent years, a mere recapitulation of them may prove misleading, and a statement of quantities will show better how the position stands.

Wool Trade of United Kingdom.

Imports.	Average of 5 Years.	1901 only.
From British Posses-sions . .	577,073,989 lbs.	583,934,611 lbs.
Foreign Countries .	121,000,171 ,,	128,337,166 ,,
Total . . .	698,074,160 ,,	712,271,777 ,,
Re-exports . .	296,514,718 ,,	294,830,461 ,,
Retained for Home Use . .	401,559,442 ,,	417,441,316 ,,

In each case it will be noted that the quantity retained for home use is materially less than imported from British possessions, so that if the re-exports had included the whole of the foreign import, there would still have been an excess of the British-grown staple. To interfere with the free movement of such a commodity would merely play into the hands of foreign trade rivals, and give Antwerp and Havre, already keen competitors with London and Liverpool, an advantage in the international wool market they do not at present possess.

Among commodities of minor importance there is another fibre used in textile industry, jute, that is virtually a British, or to be more exact an Indian, monopoly. It is the cheapest that is grown, and used for the roughest fabrics which can at the same time be woven of great strength, but of late other uses have been discovered which is bringing it into competition with the more costly fibres. But inasmuch as it is not produced in merchantable quantities anywhere outside India, not only the United Kingdom but the whole world is dependent for supplies, either in the raw state or in some stage of manufacture, on that source. Monopoly in this instance is not exactly the road to fortune, because any attempt to establish a high basis of prices at once brings in the competition, not of other countries, but of other materials. Cheapness is its one and only safeguard.

An important article of food can be placed in the same category as wool and jute. But unlike them, the tea of India and Ceylon has displaced in quite modern times the growth of China, which for a long period enjoyed almost as complete monopoly as jute does to-day. There was at least one serious obstacle to be overcome in the process of displacement. The flavour was different to what tea-drinkers had become accustomed to, and the taste for the invading leaf had to be cultivated. This has been so successfully accomplished throughout the United Kingdom that China tea has been

almost driven out of the market, and now constitutes but a mere fraction of the total import. The
result has been attained by persevering effort, and
not from any change of whim, amply demonstrated
by the fact that China has so far managed to hold
its own among the other tea-drinking peoples of
the world, as outside the British Empire neither the
India nor Ceylon leaf is much in vogue. That it
has been accomplished, too, without any artificial
aid from tariffs—the high duty levied almost everywhere on tea is a distinct hindrance to consumption
—is the best evidence that when conditions are
natural no forced measures are necessary to achieve
ultimate success; when they are unnatural, no
amount of forcing will ensure it.

This by no means exhausts the list of commodities which either are, or with very little effort
might be, produced in sufficient quantities within
the British Empire to supply the Empire's needs.
But none of the rest are of much consequence
relatively, though some of them may be to individual industries. Allusion has been made in a
previous chapter to palm oil and palm kernels, both
produced in British West Africa far in excess of
the requirements of the United Kingdom. Something similar is true of other soap-making materials,
such as cocoanut oil, so that the soap industry may
be regarded as essentially a British one. Outside
these, there are a few spices, one or two farinaceous
foods like sago and tapioca, and some dyestuffs,

notably indigo, but it is not always quite so easy
to say that they are products of the British Empire,
because where the chief import is from the Straits
Settlements, much may be in reality of foreign
origin.   The great bulk of the world's tin comes
from the same place, but is actually mined in the
Malay Peninsula.   Most of the States comprising it
are under British protection, and this particular
item may be said therefore to be much in the
traditionary position of Mahomet's coffin, suspended
midway between earth and heaven.

The situation of this small group, representing
at the very utmost 10 per cent. of the value of the
total imports into the United Kingdom, may be
easily summed up.   Where British supplies are
regularly in excess of British requirements, no tariff
differentiation can affect values under normal conditions ; that is, there will always be sufficient
competition to prevent the duty on the foreign
commodity becoming effective, and if the latter
continued to be imported, it would be the producer,
not the consumer, who would bear the burden.
That would rarely happen, because the foreign
article would seek markets where it was not so
penalised, and in finding them, very likely displace
the British product to the detriment of the British
producer, who might experience no equivalent gain
at home.

At quite the other end of the list is the most
important raw material used in British industry

which has to be procured from oversea. India grows considerable quantities of cotton, but the particular qualities have ceased, except under very exceptional circumstances, to be of any value to the British manufacturer, who confines himself almost exclusively to other staples. No other part of the Empire produces raw cotton in fair merchantable quantities, and such consignments as do from time to time come forward, afford a bare day's meal for a modern spinning mill.

This has come to be recognised, if not exactly a disgrace, at least a serious reflection, on the resources of the British dominions, and efforts are being put forth to see if the state of things cannot be remedied. With this object the British Cotton Growing Association has been constituted, which, though not strictly speaking a commercial body, aims indirectly, if not directly, at the advancement of the interests of its members. Through agents and correspondents it is making diligent inquiries wherever conditions of cotton culture appear in any way favourable, with the view to ensure a greater amount of independence of the Southern States of America. The only country which can be said at present to enter into the faintest competition with it is Brazil, but the attention devoted there to coffee has excluded almost everything else, and while the world's demand for cotton has been increasing at a very rapid rate, Brazil has done next to nothing to meet it. The steppes of Central Asia

have assisted slightly, but only under conditions
that preclude competition outside the Russian Empire, which imposes a heavy duty on the American
staple to protect the native growth.

Egypt is doing all that can be expected, and
with the latest barrage of the Nile will, in the
course of a few years, have reached the limits of
economic production, which is entirely dependent
on the waters of that river. The question arises,
however, whether by some similar process the cultivation in India can not only be very considerably
extended, but possibly at the same time a material
improvement effected in the quality, the best of
which at present only competes with the medium
grades of American. There is the necessary heat,
and generally sufficient moisture, if only it were
more equally distributed. The cotton plant requires
the latter in abundance and at frequent intervals,
the result being, that where, as in India, the dry
seasons are prolonged the staple of the fibre is
seriously injured, both as regards length and
strength.

Still this is no drawback in Egypt, a rainless
country dependent altogether on the surface drain-
age of its mighty river, which is so effective that
the staple of the cotton is superior to almost
anything obtainable elsewhere. Irrigation, then,
if properly directed, may accomplish this in India
also, and it is irrigation that is looked to. Hitherto
its object has been mainly directed to ensuring food

supplies, and how inadequate the result yet obtained is testified by the succession of disastrous famines that have overtaken the land in quite recent times.

To divert irrigation to cotton planting from food cultivation will require a great amount of justification under existing conditions, for whatever money and labour are available for the purpose ought certainly to be used in combating the famine spectre. It is just another illustration of what was made so prominent in the chapter dealing with India. With the best of intentions no doubt, it is desired to extend the cultivation of cotton, possibly at the expense of foodstuffs, which are far more needed. An increasing export of the fibre would be pointed to as another evidence of India's increasing prosperity, though in reality the population might have less to eat than before. To stimulate the production of cotton, or of any other exportable product, consequently requires the utmost consideration before being undertaken, for while under proper safeguards the result may add to the wealth of the country, if the process is undertaken mainly with the object of supplying other parts of the Empire with something they stand in need of, India may be subjected to considerable injustice.

This argument does not necessarily apply to similar experiments elsewhere. West Africa is another area favourably commented upon. There, cotton growing will not only be a new industry, but will not displace any more important existing one, as the land that would be devoted to it is at present either waste or covered with jungle yielding but a scant supply of products. Climatic conditions too should be favourable, for not only are there great rivers like the Niger and the Congo, with their tributaries, corresponding to the Mississippi and the Nile, but there is an abundance, sometimes indeed a superabundance, of atmospheric moisture as well, in the latter case likely to prove a distinct hindrance.

Assuming both cost of cultivation and quality of fibre to be suitable, the drawbacks are of a different nature, and relate chiefly to transport. Cotton is carried quite as a regular thing from New York and other North Atlantic ports to Liverpool at 12s. 6d. a ton, while the charges from any West African port would ordinarily be three or four times this figure. True, cotton is not grown in New York, and has to be conveyed there over great distances; but again the facilities are such that the cost is certainly less than will be incurred in transporting from a West African plantation to place of ship-ment. It is no use growing cotton in West Africa or anywhere else on as economical conditions as in the United States, if cost of transport to the mill is ultimately to be several times as great.

A strong incentive has been afforded to cotton cultivation in West Africa by the offer of free internal transport for two years over the Government railways, where these can be utilised, as well

24

as free ocean conveyance for a considerable quantity. While there is a certain amount of generosity, combined with commercial sagacity, in this procedure, it is a dangerous precedent to establish. It amounts, in fact, to a bounty, against which the United States or some other country may one day have occasion to protest, and possibly counteract in inconvenient ways. It would be much more to the point were the interests concerned to arrive at the lowest estimate at which cotton can be economically transported, and guarantee that the figure shall not be exceeded for a period of at least ten years. The cotton planter marketing his crop under free conditions for two years, may find himself very awkwardly situated if he has to deal with a monopoly to afford him the necessary facilities afterwards.

There are other places suitable for the culture, particularly in the South Seas. Some of the Pacific islands grow a little cotton already, but their area is very restricted at the best; New Guinea may some day afford greater opportunities, while Northern Queensland might also prove suitable were coloured labour available, which it is at present sought entirely to exclude from the Australian continent. But here another problem presents itself, for with cotton grown at home or within a few hundred, or at most, one or two thousand miles, of its own shores, Australia would certainly want to establish a cotton manufacturing industry of its own, and would probably not hesitate to resort to a very stiff measure of protection to accomplish such a purpose. The Lancashire manufacturer at present enjoys almost a monopoly of the trade, and does not wish to do anything calculated to jeopardise it.

Such are a few of the difficulties that crop up the moment an effort is made seriously to divert trade from one country to another. Russia, as already observed, settled them in this particular instance by a high tariff, but nobody has yet suggested that a duty should be levied on raw cotton imported into the United Kingdom in order to see what India or West Africa is really capable of accomplishing. There is no prospect of displacing the American staple for generations to come, if ever, and whatever production is undertaken within the British Empire will have to be in competition with it. The industry is of far too much consequence to Great Britain to play tricks with, or indulge in any sentiment over; when British territory can grow cotton economically, and railways and shipowners will transport it cheaply, it is sure of finding a market, but it must be in these directions, and these only, in which effort can prove successful, or be deserving of recognition.

If this be true of a raw material like cotton, how much more applicable to the food of the country ? The capabilities of production are not certainly a matter of such doubt; the British Empire already grows most of the food it requires for ordinary consumption, and it is only one portion of it, the United Kingdom, that experiences any regularly recurring deficiency of magnitude.

But when it comes to distribution, some of the points at least are the same as are confronted in the case of cotton. Wheat may be grown just as cheap in India, in Australia, or in Canada, as in the United States, the Argentine Republic, or the Black Sea territories; but if, as sometimes happens in the first two cases, they can raise barely enough for their own requirements, it is useless placing permanent reliance on their assistance. None of them can show such results as Great Britain, which averages of this particular cereal about thirty bushels to the acre. Canada comes nearest; India in a favourable season yields about twelve bushels, and then there is invariably a surplus for export. Australia is at the bottom with an average of about eight bushels only, reduced still further in years of drought; indeed in one of the principal wheat-growing districts, the Mallee in the north-west of Victoria, the outturn has not been exceeding four bushels, or little more than one-eighth what is looked for in a fair English season.

To place dependence on such sources of supply is to invite disaster sooner or later, and until conditions have materially and permanently changed they must be placed outside the category of the surplus-yielding portions of the Empire, and ranked rather with those foreign countries that are spasmodic. Besides, South Africa experiences a deficiency of cereals, likely to become more, not less pronounced, if industrial activity proceeds at anything like the pace anticipated, and Australia more than any other country affords it a natural base of supply, so that future surpluses are likely to be diverted to that part of the world, especially if a concession were made in the import duty. There is an enormous area in Australia awaiting cultivation, but population does not flow to it, and if the existing tendency should continue much longer, the combined wheat supply of Australia and South Africa will not, in the most favourable season, afford sufficient food for their combined populations. Both countries it should be remembered are essentially pastoral, as distinct from agricultural, and it is development in that direction that is calculated to prove most profitable in the long run.

But Canada claims, and promises to make good the claim, to be the granary of the Empire. There much the same conditions exist that prevail over a great part of the United States, which have hitherto been regarded as the world's granary. That the cultivation is far less intense than in the United Kingdom may best be judged from the fact that the average yield is only about one-half; thirteen to fourteen bushels in a fair season, something between fifteen and twenty in a good one. Further, the risks incurred are more considerable, though they affect quality and price rather than quantity. The high latitudes in which the Canadian wheat lands are mostly situated, while they shorten the crop period, render it liable both after it has begun and before it is over to visitation of frost, though this may be eventually eliminated as the extension of settlement abates somewhat the rigour of the climate. At anyrate, it is not pleasant to have to contemplate dependence on frost-bitten food when it might easily be obtained free from any blight.

All the same, Canada threatens at no distant period to displace the United States in the wheat markets of the United Kingdom, if not of Europe. The stimulus has at length been afforded which it never proved possible before to apply. What is now to be prayed for is the avoidance of any such disaster as will drive immigrants away again. But granting Canada's ultimate ability as regards quantity, there is still something missing. Its wheat can undoubtedly be used alone for bread, though it is not desirable. It is exceptionally hard, arising from the conditions under which it must necessarily be grown, and requires free admixture with softer grain such as Canada only produces in the eastern States in limited quantities. As the small amount of British grain now produced is mostly soft, the Canadian serves a useful purpose for admixture, but a great deal of soft wheat has nevertheless to be imported in addition, and much of it is from the Pacific coast of the United States, where climate is milder, conditions of growth more prolonged, and in other ways more generally favourable.

Quantity, therefore, is not the only point to be considered. It is quite conceivable that within a comparatively short period the wheat surplus of the Dominion may be ample to make good the deficiencies throughout the rest of the Empire, and still, where these exist, foreign imports may continue to be large while Canada has to dispose of considerable quantities outside. Egyptian cotton will no more answer the purpose of the spinner who is accustomed to spin American counts of yarn, than red Canadian wheat will do for the miller who wants Californian, and for this reason alone similarity of treatment is essential for all the growths of the world alike.

This is one reason against a differential duty on foreign corn as against colonial, such as is advocated by many people nowadays. A still better one is that it really is not wanted, because wherever conditions of wheat growing are naturally suitable, it can be done without, and where they are not so, it had better not be attempted. Canadians looked for many weary years at the vast belts of fertile wheat lands in the north-west, absolutely uncultivated, and regarded them as so much material running to waste. The fact is they were not wanted; the edge of civilisation had barely reached that far, and any attempt to develop them prematurely would have ended disastrously to those who undertook it.

The energies of the human race, or at anyrate the white portion of it, were being concentrated elsewhere, and it would have been neither wise nor profitable to dissipate them until the purpose was accomplished.

Preparation for such an eventuality is a necessity if the opportune moment is to be seized, and possibly Canada may have missed one for want of it. The finest lands in the world were useless as long as they remained untapped, and railroads in the United States always preceded, not followed, the onward march of population. Until the Canadian Pacific Railroad was carried across the continent, therefore, the incentive did not exist: with it, the first great outburst of American expansion has swept across Canadian as well as United States territory; without it, the former would still have been slumbering on in solitude. What is now wanted is extension, rapid enough to keep pace with, or even move a little ahead of, population, otherwise stagnation will assert its sway once more.

As a rule development of this character is premature, and it is only in the course of booms that it is temporarily caught up with. This was the case in the United States; it is so now over a considerable portion of Australia as well as of other countries. It never occurred before on any extensive scale in the Dominion of Canada, but having once been inaugurated, there is no reason

why the tide should again be turned back. That
there will be stoppages and occasional breakdowns
may be taken for granted; but the machinery
having been got into efficient working order,
Canada on the one hand, and Australia and New
Zealand equally on the other, should be able to
maintain, and gradually extend, their hold over
the trades for which they have proved themselves
admirably adapted. It is when they try to branch
out into others for which they are not, that the
pinch will be felt.

The greater part of the foodstuffs and raw
materials annually required by the United Kingdom may be subjected to these broad principles.
It is not because foreign countries enjoy advantages
over British possessions that they have established
pre-eminence, but only that hitherto many of them
have had the greater impetus. The need of room
for the overflow of population is often assigned as
the motive and necessity for the foundation and
extension of a British Colonial Empire, but Great
Britain itself has stood less in need of such an outlet than many other European countries. Towards
the steady stream of emigration that flowed from
them in the latter half of the nineteenth century
Great Britain contributed but a fraction; Germans,
Scandinavians, Russians, Slavs, Italians, have in the
aggregate, and sometimes in individual instances,
far outstepped the British race, and have had no
special motive, certainly no patriotic one, to settle

on British soil. The Irish has been the chief of
the emigrating races, and unhappily it has had
good reason to shun it. As expatriation was a
necessity, if indeed it was not often the motive,
of emigration, it mattered little under what flag
the new home was established as long as it was
a free one, with the result that the United States
and the South American Republics became the
principal centres of attraction.

Nor is it surprising that large numbers of British
emigrants preferred to join the main streams rather
than embark on the less swiftly flowing tributaries.
Canada, and Australia, and New Zealand, offered a
competency to everybody who chose to make a home
there, but not, in recent times, many opportunities
for accumulating immense fortunes : New Zealand
is said to boast of no millionaires whatever. The
United States, and to some extent South America,
always afforded the greater attraction, and though
few could hope to draw the biggest prizes, their
existence acted as a loadstone. Had all the British
emigrants of the last quarter of a century wended
their way to British possessions, their population
would certainly have been larger than it is ; but
against this must be set the emigrants of foreign
nationalities who have done so, but might have
gone elsewhere, who have contributed a very full
share of the increase, notably to Canada. But
even supposing the whole of the British—always
excluding Irish—emigrants of the last half century

had gone to territories under the flag, it may be doubted whether their and their descendants' united efforts, however wisely and carefully distributed, would have been anywhere near sufficient to supply the needs of the United Kingdom. Germans, Scandinavians, and almost every other nationality on the face of the earth, would still have to contribute, though they might be doing so to a far more considerable extent on British, instead of foreign, soil.

Let us see how this works out in practice. In 1901, the United States furnished the United Kingdom with upwards of £140,000,000 worth of commodities as compared with £105,000,000 from the whole of the British possessions. Most of them are, or might be, common productions of both—raw cotton and mineral oils are about the only important existing exceptions. What is it has given the United States the advantage? Not certainly any special favours shown them by Great Britain. They have had at their disposal, it is true, enormous sums of British capital. So have the colonies, and on the whole on better terms. They possess unbounded areas of agricultural and mineralised lands; the colonies have more of both. They enjoy an invigorating and healthy climate; in that respect they are behind, rather than ahead of, some at least of the colonies. They contain natural waterways, but have largely discarded them in favour of artificial overland routes of transport;

if the colonies are not always so favourably situated with the former, they are not thereby handicapped so long as they have equal recourse to the latter. There is hardly a point possessed by one which is not shared by the others, yet in one instance nearly seventy millions of white people have been attracted to participate, and in the other not much more than ten.

Yet as far as external aids are concerned, more has been done for the ten than for the seventy millions. It has always been the legitimate boast of Great Britain that its mercantile marine is the growth of natural conditions, and not forced by any system of bounties. If a challenge can be offered to such a statement at all, it is only in connection with colonial trade, and if it be true that subsidies do benefit trade in any way, then it is the British possessions that should have profited, for there are scarcely any that are not more or less liberally treated. Let us see what is paid in this respect each year—

Australia and New Zealand *viâ* Suez Canal .	£170,000
India, Ceylon, and Straits Settlements .	150,000 [1]
South Africa	135,000
Canada, including Pacific route to the East .	60,000
West Indies	120,000
West Africa	16,000
Aden and Zanzibar	9,000
	£660,000

[1] This contract includes a fortnightly service to China and Japan, and the total amounts to £245,000, of which the above sum has been proportionately allotted.

As the total colonial trade for 1901, imports and exports, exclusive of Hong-Kong included in the China portion of the subvention, amounted to £215,291,251, this is equal to a subsidy of upwards of 6s. per cent. It is not perhaps the proper way to regard it, because the money is mostly paid for conveyance of mails, which are in somewhat larger proportion to volume of trade than with foreign countries, but it is only the trade portion of the mails for which exceptional expedition is usually needed.

The corresponding sum paid for the conveyance of United States mails was slightly under £120,000, which on a total turnover for the year of £178,666,615 works out at about 1s. 4d. per cent. only, and this includes the bulk of the correspondence sent from the United Kingdom to Canada. Of the vast fleet engaged in this particular branch, moreover, only eight steamships, owned by two companies, are regularly subsidised, whereas a much larger number of those employed in the others—in the case of the West Indies and West Africa nearly all—get a share. If the whole foreign trade of the United Kingdom be taken into account, it will be found that the subsidies, inclusive of the balance of £95,000 allocated to China and Japan, amount to less than £300,000, which on a total turnover of £650,000,000 is barely 1s. per cent., against 6s. on the purely colonial. To put it another way, the shipping engaged in colonial trade receives Government assistance against foreign competition to the extent of a quarter of one per cent. of the value.

There is a more general outcry for a stimulus to be afforded to colonial trade by means of steamship subsidising than exists even in favour of preferential tariffs. Shipowners would not be business men did they not try to take advantage of it to their own profit, but inasmuch as it is only a limited number that can be admitted within the favoured circle, there is bound to be much opposition offered by those left outside. And before committing the country to further outlays in this respect, it will be well to realise what the existing ones are accomplishing, and whether sometimes they are not hindrances, rather than helps, to the expansion of trade.

It is notorious that on several of the subsidised routes shipping rings have dominated the traffic and exacted unduly high freights, while in one or two instances something like complete monopoly has been established. To some extent, undoubtedly, this has resulted from the help afforded by Government subventions, which have enabled companies to maintain a service at temporary loss in order to ruin or run off intruders.

Where trade is active, as was the case in South Africa for several years before the war, the hardship may not be clearly in evidence, though it certainly had the result of letting in foreign competition to an extent that might not otherwise have been possible, but where there is stagnation and depression, as in the West Indies, the outcome is simply ruinous. For many years the £80,000 paid annually to the Royal Mail Company enabled it to do what it liked there, and as economy, not enterprise, became the order of the day, everything was neglected, and for the slightest additional service extravagant terms were demanded, which had generally to be conceded, because the company held the connections and was thus master of the situation. While the total volume of the trade of these possessions dwindled, it was the heavily subventioned British portion upon which the loss fell; the entirely unsubsidised share with the United States was well maintained, and in some instances steadily increased. Reduction, not increase, of this particular subsidy would have been in consonance with ascertained facts, and when an entirely new service was established this treatment of the old one should have been enforced.

Instead, it was renewed under the old conditions, with perhaps just one or two added safeguards against abuse. As an experiment, the payment of £40,000 for a direct service with the island of Jamaica may be justified, but the indirect one then ceased to be of any further value, and a local service, with Barbados as its headquarters, was all that was necessary, and this could have been carried on for a much more moderate sum.

At the same time, it must be distinctly realised

that the Jamaica subsidy is an entirely fresh departure. There is no pretence about it being simply a mail contract, as all the others are nominally supposed to be, because it includes a guarantee of regular fruit shipments, the maintenance of local hotels, and other items quite outside the cognisance of the post-office. The development of the fruit trade ought to benefit the whole island, and is a legitimate object for levying taxation on it in moderation. But a tourist traffic will be to the advantage of very few of the inhabitants, and it will be quite inexcusable to pay a subsidy, raised from taxation either in Great Britain or Jamaica— in this instance it is from both—with the object of affording wealthy holiday seekers a cheap outing. That may not be done ; but it should be made quite clear that anything of this sort is worked at a profit apart from any State assistance whatever, or at least that the people who directly benefit shall be the contributaries, and not the general taxpayer.

Yet this is what any extensive policy of subventioning is bound to result in, and on such grounds is not to be encouraged. There may be other reasons why an extension of it will become necessary. If combinations of foreign-owned steamships and foreign-controlled railroads seek to exclude the British shipowner from participation in trade on equal terms, especially as regards facilities afforded and rapidity of handling cargo, something must be done in the way of counteraction. But it will not help American trade in general, or Canadian in particular, to place any steamship company or companies in the position now occupied by the subsidised lines running to Australia and the East, to South Africa or the West Indies. The question is, whether some form of national control ought not to be exacted in return for any subsidies that are in excess of bare payment for services rendered. It would be intolerable to interfere with the management of great steamship lines merely for what is given them for carriage of mails, which in the case of the North Atlantic service at least has hitherto generally left a profit to the post-office, whatever may have been the result to the steamship companies. But such payments as are made to the Peninsular and Oriental, the two West Indian and other lines, and especially the recent subsidy agreed upon with the Cunard Company, go beyond this, and a distinction ought to be established and care taken that the trading public is not handicapped. When the German Government pays a substantial mail subsidy it ensures at the same time that German manufacturers and traders shall be accorded terms that will enable them to compete with those of other nationalities. Hitherto, British payments have had exactly the opposite tendency.

It must be obvious that an increase in the imports of colonial, at the expense of foreign merchandise, cannot be looked for as the result of the

25

extension of the system of subsidies. From the transport point of view there is a distinct natural advantage as it is. It is clear that when the two sides of a trading account are nearly equal, there must be very much the same quantities to move on both, and consequently, regular and fairly equally balanced tonnage requirements. With British colonial trade, it is true, this works better in theory than practice, because when we come to split it into its component parts, there is much irregularity ; an excess of imports in the case of Canada, of exports with India. But on the whole there is a much better division than with the majority of foreign countries. A vessel chartered to carry home, or regularly employed in doing so, a cargo of colonial produce has the chance of earning a more or less full freight on the outward voyage. To secure a foreign cargo, it must frequently either go out in ballast, or make an indirect voyage hundreds, perhaps thousands, of miles out of its direct course, and incur at least one additional set of port charges. Without any extraneous help whatever, therefore, colonial freights should average somewhat lower than foreign ones. Yet it is notorious they do not, because there is not the same unrestricted competition.

The fact is, anything approaching monopoly of a distinct trade by a regular line of steamships is detrimental to it. The owner of the tramp steamer is watching every foreign port in the world where

there is a freight to be picked up, and moves round
to it as soon as he sees a chance. A dozen others
have done the same, and brisk competition ensues.
He pays far less attention to British colonial ports,
knowing that unless there is something approaching
a glut, the regular lines will have picked up what
there is before he gets there, and if they have not,
the shippers dare not patronise him, because they
would lose their rebates. The best he can often hope
for is to charter his boat to one of the ring as a
relief, when he must of course be content to take
less money than they are able to get, and which is
for the time being the fair market rate.

There are political, apart altogether from commercial, reasons why these regular lines of communication must be maintained. But there is no
need to extend them, and the best hope for British
colonial trade is that when it reaches dimensions
beyond the power of existing subsidised lines to
cope with, the strength of irregular competition
will be sufficient to break down all attempts to
maintain the permanent control of shipping facilities.

It is maintained, however, that the steady
growth of trade between some of these possessions
and certain foreign countries is to be attributed
to the policy of subsidising. France and Germany
notably, pay large sums for their respective services
with Australia, but the principal result has been to
open up important markets for Australian products
without having to import anything like the

equivalent in value of French and German goods, though British official figures as regards German trade seem to belie this statement. Both, in more recent times, have pursued the same policy as regards South Africa, though the results achieved have not by any means attained the Australian level, partly because South African produce, other than gold, which in the first place is nearly all shipped to London, is not wanted by them in such considerable quantities, even if it were available.

Perhaps it is in West Africa where European competition is keener than anywhere else, one result of which is that within ten years German imports of British West African produce have nearly doubled, and for the last recorded year equal more than three-fourths the corresponding imports into the United Kingdom. This must be directly attributed to the cheaper and altogether more satisfactory facilities afforded by the German shipping companies, which as far as the continental trade is concerned, have compelled the only British one to fall into line with them.

On the other hand, German exports to that part of the world have not grown to anything like a similar extent, whereas British exports have gained enormously. But this is owing to capital expenditure—the greater part of it on Government account—in the construction of railroads and other public works, and far too much of it on military expeditions of which there have been a constant succession,

and it is only to be expected that such orders will
be placed with home, in preference to foreign,
manufacturers. Were this portion deducted, it
would be found that the ordinary merchant trade
has increased but slightly in recent years, and that
Germany has secured a full share. It would probably have had more if an agreement between the
British and German steamship lines did not prevent
too much severity in the competition that would
otherwise have broken out, and helped to assure
the former the monopoly it enjoys in the purely
British portion of the trade.

But what is to be said of the growth of United
States trade with some of these possessions, which
has gone on uninterruptedly without the assistance
of any subventions whatever? Within the last
decade of the nineteenth century, German exports
to Australasia, helped by subsidies, rather more than
doubled in value; American exports without them,
more than trebled. Under exactly similar conditions
German exports to South Africa also rather more
than doubled, while the American quadrupled, and
are now in both instances far in excess of the
German. United States manufacturers and shippers
enjoy the advantage of unrestricted competition in
the freight market, and as a result are nearly always
able to command lower rates than British and
German lines, secure from similar competition by
their subsidies, are willing to concede. Canada has
long had a subsidised line belonging to the Canadian

Pacific Railroad, running to the Far East, but succeeds in doing much less trade than its unsubsidised rival, though some allowance should perhaps be made for the respective resources of the two countries.

The Dominion is now anxious to extend its connections with South Africa, and has begun by committing the error of again subsidising a service, which will establish monopoly instead of leaving the trade open. It might not have been conducted with quite such clockwork regularity, but whenever a sufficient quantity of freight offered, there would have been abundance of tonnage forthcoming to claim it at market rates. It looks rather like an admission on the part of the Dominion that without some sort of permanent assistance it cannot hope to compete successfully against its neighbour.

New Zealand is trying to follow the same course, but recently rejected tenders for a service with South Africa as altogether too extravagant, and is said to intend to invite new ones. If eventually carried through, the result will be to place trade between the two countries at the mercy of the contractors, who will be able to beat off all intruders. There do not appear to have been any difficulties regarding freight while the war lasted, and there is far greater abundance of tonnage available since it is over.

It is indeed a remarkable circumstance, and one that should be carefully noted, that the United States with only one important shipping subsidy,

and that a practical failure, and without any foreign
mercantile marine worth speaking of, should have
increased its foreign trade at a more rapid rate
than any other country in the world. Is it not
perhaps largely owing to the circumstance that it
can make cheaper freight arrangements than any
of its rivals, having the tonnage of the whole
world to rely upon? Yet not satisfied, they wish
to subject themselves to the same thraldom as the
rest.

As the success of American competition in the
markets of the world, and especially of the British
Empire, cannot be attributed to any artificial advantages the shipping engaged in it enjoy, it appears
idle to endeavour to check it by shipping legislation designed to confer special privileges on favoured
interests. Where this is recognised, another remedy
is often suggested in the shape of preferential
tariffs. A good deal has been said about them in
preceding chapters, but the broad question now
presents itself, whether such a policy is likely to
be any more successful than a reckless subsidising
of the mercantile marine.

At least no harm can be done by granting concessions on already existing duties, as in the case
of the Canadian preferential tariff, and of other
changes advocated in these pages; always provided
they do not lead to conflict with valuable customers. The result may not be in every case
what is anticipated, but the consumer is bound

ultimately to derive an advantage somewhere, which should help to ease the costs of home production. It is difficult, if not impossible, to intercept such rebates, because they are at once participated in by everybody engaged in the trades affected, and only widespread combination can prevent them reaching the consumer.

On the other hand, the imposition of non-existing duties is advocated with the primary object of benefiting the producer and stimulating him to increased production. But there is not by any means the same certainty that they will reach him. Perhaps the simplest illustration of this is afforded by the most typical of all possible applications of it.

It is contended that were a duty imposed on foreign wheat imported into the United Kingdom, from which colonial grain was exempt, the result would be a great increase in the production of the latter, more especially perhaps in Canada. Now it is quite certain that as long as the supply of home grown and of freely imported colonial wheat fell short of the demand, and had to be supplemented by duty-paid foreign grain, the market price would be ruled by the latter. British wheat would be protected to the extent of the duty; whether the farmer or the landowner benefited in the end is not a question that need at present be discussed. The wheat would be sold on the basis of the higher price created by the duty.

Colonial wheat would likewise be sold in the

British markets on the same basis. But would it bring any more in the north-west territories of Canada than the basis on which it was selling in the north-west of the United States? The English duty might be equivalent say to five cents a bushel, but it is quite certain that in the height of the season, when the vast bulk of the crop is marketed, the price of Manitoba wheat would be regulated by the quotation of Chicago, rather than of London or Liverpool. The Canadian farmer does not, like the English one, sell direct to the English miller; his wheat goes through several intermediate hands, and he is generally ignorant of the exact charges incurred. What is absolutely certain however is, that these intermediates are far more capable of combination, and it is they who would ultimately divide at least four of the five cents between them. Most of it would probably go to the railroad and steamship companies, who, few in number, would be able to play off the competition of the multitude of sellers on one side and buyers on the other. Their gain might not be any actual increase in rates of carriage, but rather the retention of the natural decrease that always follows development and the handling of larger quantities, and would not be any less real on that account, though not apparent to the public gaze.

It is hardly necessary to say that such a scheme receives enthusiastic support from almost everybody interested in Canadian transport. The greatest admiration may be entertained for the enterprise of the men who carried the Canadian Pacific Railroad across the American continent at a time when its success was regarded as doubtful at the best. But surely they have been amply rewarded without recourse to the pockets of the British taxpayer, and they will find the best and surest road to continued success in sharing it with their Canadian customers, upon whose patronage they are so largely dependent.

Hitherto, cost of Canadian transport has compared unfavourably with the United States; with the rapid expansion of the north-west there is no reason for a continuance of this, any more than for higher shipping charges from Canadian, as against United States ports, at anyrate beyond a small additional charge for insurance. A combination of land and ocean transport such as is threatened in the United States may prove fatal to Canada, and the utmost care will have to be taken, not only to prevent both falling entirely into the same hands, but to prohibit any close alliance between subsidised ocean lines and continental railroads beyond what is necessary for the economical working of traffic.

Legislation of any character whatever, calculated to confer special trade privileges, whether on individuals, on corporations, or on countries, ought to be regarded with suspicion and adopted only with the greatest caution by the Parliaments, either of the United Kingdom or the colonies. It is not that colonial trade is less important, or less worthy of encouragement, than what is purely foreign ; rather the reverse. It is of the utmost consequence that British possessions, wherever they are situated throughout the world, should be stimulated to produce whatever the Empire needs, less for political or sentimental reasons, than because there is in the long run far more liberal exchange of trade between them.

Nor is this trade to be estimated merely by its volume, at anyrate as far as the exports of the United Kingdom are concerned. Much the same expense is incurred in raising a hundred, or a thousand, or a million bushels of wheat in Canada as in the United States, and under normal conditions the same is true as regards the sugar of the West Indies and of continental Europe. Of the eventual selling prices received in a British market, much the same proportion is in each case distributed between labour and other incidental costs.

But it is in the outlay of this distribution that the great difference arises. Germany may take an even larger proportion of merchandise in payment for what it sells to the United Kingdom than Canada, and yet in the real value of the two there is no comparison. Most of what Germany gets of British production, exclusive of coal, is of crude, or at the best partially manu-factured material : pig-iron, cotton and woollen yarns, and a miscellaneous assortment of articles for further use in manufacturing industry, of which a great part of the value is represented by the material they contain, originally of foreign import. On the other hand, Canada purchases the iron in its more finished stages, and fully manufactured cotton and woollen fabrics, in the value of which the wages paid to British labour figure much more extensively. As far as actual benefit to the United Kingdom is concerned, therefore, more is derived relatively from exports to Canada than from shipments to Germany.

This feature is far more conspicuous when colonial and foreign trade are taken in their broadest aspects, apart altogether from distribution between separate countries, and is well illustrated by Tables D and E to be found in the Appendix. In highly finished manufactures such as clothing and wearing apparel of all kinds, of which the wages of labour constitute the principal element, there is almost invariably an overwhelming preponderance in favour of colonial markets, and in some of the more highly finished forms of iron and steel, as well as of other manufactures, the same remark applies, only not perhaps to quite a similar extent. On the other side the only highly finished manufactured goods in which foreign countries exhibit a great preponderance are various kinds of machinery, destined eventually to intensify the competition with British manufacturers. On the whole, it is perhaps no exaggeration to say that there was more money left to circulate within the United Kingdom as the result of the export of £102,000,000 of British and Irish goods to colonial possessions, than of £178,000,000 to foreign countries, and were the item of coal eliminated this assertion might be made without a moment's hesitation.

Just here another difficulty presents itself; there are countries included under the general term foreign, which are in this respect equally or even more valuable than many British possessions. British exports to what may be termed Spanish and Portuguese America, that is the whole of the Central and Southern portions of that continent, and the island of Cuba, are equal to, if not in excess of, imports therefrom, and are, moreover, of a highly finished character. The total is greater than to any British possession except India, and the same care requires to be observed to conserve and extend it.

The Far East, again, is a customer for British manufactured goods altogether out of proportion to what it supplies the United Kingdom of its own products; the Turkish Empire is usually on the same side. Fiscal legislation to encourage colonial trade should really be equally extended to include countries like these ; legislation aimed against foreign countries could hardly help but embrace them, and so prove extremely inimical to British interests : to one, more perhaps than any other. Cotton piece goods are to be found in Table E; that is, the bulk of the export is to foreign countries. But it is the countries alluded to that are concerned, and if anything were done to jeopardise and destroy this trade, what was left with foreign countries would, as far as Lancashire is concerned, scarcely be worth having.

A fiercer conflict has raged for years round sugar than any other commodity that is produced, naturally or artificially. The opponents in Great Britain of the bounty system based their arguments, primarily at anyrate, on the injustice done to the West Indies and the British refining industry. But it is really a far wider question than that. It may be doubted whether the most stimulating fiscal legislation that could be devised would succeed for some years in leading to the production in British possessions of one-fourth the annual sugar consumption of the United Kingdom, after provision for the wants of other portions of the Empire at present supplied. It is quite certain, however, that within three or four years at the outside, sufficient cane sugar could be grown throughout the world to supply British consumption without recourse to a single ton of beet. It would be grown in Cuba, Java, Brazil, Peru, and other tropical and semi-tropical countries, the very ones, that is, whose custom is of most value to the British manufacturer. Thus £15,000,000 or so annually expended in continental countries in the purchase of sugar results in a return trade of problematic volume and value; were the one cut off the other might be curtailed to some extent, though the net loss would not be great. Were the whole of this £15,000,000 transferred to tropical countries, it would almost certainly bring an equivalent of the most desirable kind of trade, because in finished, instead of partially manufactured goods.

The sugar question is thus not a colonial one, or only so in a very limited degree. It affords an excellent example of the main issue as it affects Great Britain under existing trade and industrial conditions, inasmuch as it points to the expediency of diverting trade, wherever possible, from highly advanced to more backward countries, whether they happen to be inside or outside the British Empire. But certainly not by forced or artificial methods. Cane sugar growing countries will require no favours when the economic conditions controlling the trade are sound, and where any industry does want such treatment it had better be left alone as far as neutrals are concerned, and those interested allowed to fight the battle.

Circumstances have changed a good deal, however, since the imposition of a duty on sugar for purely revenue purposes. Any previous attempt to deal with the bounties must have resulted in duties that did not exist; now it only requires their modification. And whether the Brussels convention is

consummated or not, there is no reason why the
British tariff should not, in the near future, be
altered to discriminate between the two kinds of
sugar, not colonial and foreign, but cane and beet,
with the result that while the consumer will lose
little or nothing directly, he will gain materially
as a unit in a nation of manufacturers.

The use of such an argument is admittedly
risky, because it can be pushed to dangerous
extremes.   If a policy of this character is justifiable
as regards sugar, why should other colonial products
be excluded ?   Of the three indirect taxes imposed
in consequence of the South African War, that on
sugar is universally recognised as the least objectionable, and its continuance will cause less protest
than either of the others.   It may, some day when
the price advances, tend to curtail consumption, but
there are few people who will be much worse off
in having to forego the quantity of sugar represented
by the duty, and there are some who may be
better, because there are many cases of excessive
use.

This cannot be said of either coal or bread.
Nor as to who pays these taxes can there be very
much doubt.   When the export duty on coal was
enacted, it was confidently asserted that it would
be incurred by the foreign buyer, and under the
peculiar circumstances then existing that might
have been the case.   It was, however, of short
duration, and inasmuch as the price of coal

represents to a greater extent than anything else that can be named, other than similar mineral ores, the wages of getting it, that wages are regulated by prices, and that the duty is deducted in estimating price for the regulation of wages, it follows that as a general rule the bulk of the duty must be paid by the working miner.

Further, on a reduced wage he will pay more for bread. Threepence a hundredweight on wheat may be an indivisible sum on the loaf; nevertheless it is bound to be added to it in the course of the year. It means that on an advancing wheat market the price of the loaf will be raised sooner than it would be without the duty; in a declining one the drop will be deferred, so that for a certain number of weeks during each recurring movement the consumer will make good the tax. It may be no great hardship to pay a trifle more for sugar, or to use a little less; the same does not apply to an enforced reduction in wages or the outlay incurred on the chief necessary of life.

The real safety of the principle lies in its fundamental application. As long as a duty can be reasonably justified, manipulation of it is not of any great consequence, and the wrangling as to whether or not it is protective is straining at the gnat while swallowing the camel. The tobacco duty has always been outrageously protective, yet the consumer has never felt it burdensome. But if the duty is not fundamentally sound, no manipu-

26

lation will justify either its imposition or continuance. On this basis, whatever happens to the sugar tax, provided it is not made unduly burdensome, is of little consequence, while a ceaseless agitation should be waged against the others until they are repealed.[1]   From a British point of view there are very few such duties that can be justified, either for revenue purposes or the more doubtful uses of fiscal preference.

On the whole, it is difficult to see what legitimate action on any considerable scale is practicable by imperial or colonial legislatures in the promotion of closer trade relationship.   In the future, as in the past, the work will best be accomplished and most securely established by individual effort, assisted by such judicious advice and administration as Government can often afford.   Two incidents help to illustrate this.

Some years ago, a Dominion Government in Canada determined to encourage the export of butter to the United Kingdom, and guaranteed shippers a minimum price based on current market values. It was rarely realised, and the difference had to be made up out of the exchequer.   Packers and shippers, secure of their price, thought anything good enough, and made Canadian butter disagree-

---

[1] The circumstance of this paragraph appearing in the closing pages of the book permits note to be made after it is already in type of the abolition of the corn duty, announced by the Chancellor of the Exchequer in his Budget speech.   This is satisfactory, and would have been still more so had the coal tax gone along with it.

able to the nostrils and palate of the British consumer.

This was Government assistance. Another administration succeeded which guaranteed nothing, but tried interference. It appointed inspectors to examine every parcel of butter for shipment, and to prohibit the export of everything found to fall below a certain standard of excellence. Canadian butter as a result has gained a high reputation, and it is hardly necessary to say which policy has paid the farmer best. The Government, it is true, provides cold storage and other facilities at its own initial expense, but makes an adequate charge for their use.

While this may be taken as how to do it, an English Government department more recently afforded an instance of how not to do it. A small deputation representing one or two important business interests waited on the President of the Board of Trade with the request that he would standardise weights of 100 pounds and multiples thereof, as well as 112 pounds. This was virtually the recognition of the metric system without in any way discrediting or discarding the old one, and by so very simple a process the two would have existed side by side and resulted in the survival of the fittest. The reply was blank refusal, with the suggestion that the purpose could be accomplished by the use of nests of standard weights; that is 100 pounds could be obtained by screwing together 56,

28, 14 and 2 ; or 25 pounds with 14, 7 and 4, and so on.

It is by attention to details such as these that governments can render real assistance. But they are far too petty for ambitious politicians who want something heroic, and are content with nothing less than subsidies involving the expenditure of hundreds of thousands of pounds, and of far-reaching schemes embracing empires.

It is possible to go even further, and maintain that individual effort in Great Britain is not capable of doing a great deal; the initiative must come from the colonies themselves. Great mercantile houses have always their established connections which they are loth to disturb, and where these work satisfactorily a good deal of inducement is required to effect a change. A grain or provision merchant, for instance, accustomed to satisfy his requirements with United States produce, will not try experiments with Canadian until it has established some reputation in the market, and it is for packers and shippers to see that this is done ; very likely at first with the help of young and enterprising firms who have no such connections, and run no risk of sacrificing trade they have long enjoyed.

As a rule, such enterprise gives the best promise of success where the same interests are at stake on both sides. A shipper is less anxious to force trade for the sake of a small profit or commission if it be likely to result eventually in a loss in which he will be involved, and will exercise greater care in maintaining the standard of quality if a reputation for such has been gained. In most trades this is coming to be generally recognised, and even where houses are not actually established at the opposite end, accredited representatives are appointed to watch the purchases or sales as the case may be. There may not be the faintest suspicion of fraud, yet at the same time there is often much to be gained by making every party to a transaction responsible for its result from beginning to end.

On the other hand, the benefit to be derived from this close association is more doubtful when the trade is an all-round one, that is, not confined to imports or exports alone, but a combination of both, such as is frequently to be found in the case of Australian and Indian trade within the British Empire, and also with most South American among countries outside it. This contrasts strikingly with United States, and even Canadian methods. The American merchant invariably devotes himself to one special branch of commerce. He deals in grain, or provisions, or cotton, and confines himself practically to that one market. Every transaction must stand on its own merits; the relative values between buying and selling markets are calculated to the smallest fraction, and include every item likely in any way to affect them. Each is settled by means of bills of exchange as it is entered into, and the result is that profits are cut very fine, and often amount to nothing more than a small commission, the frequency and magnitude of them being relied upon for adequate return in the long run. The establishment and extension of what are known as future markets have reduced this branch of business almost to an exact science.

Many other points require to be taken into consideration where transactions are entirely or partially settled by reverse ones. The trade of the West African merchant is often pure barter, and he must simply weigh the value of one class of goods against another. In all other British possessions, and with almost every foreign country, the money standard is the basis, but it is impossible to know what other considerations are passing through and actuating the mind of the merchant at the same time. His transactions are not necessarily settled on the instant by bills of exchange, or only nominally so, unless the currency happens to be of such a fluctuating nature that risks cannot be lightly run, and then there is generally the inclination to speculate on it. But inability to close out and realise a consignment of goods may militate against the purchase of others which afford excellent prospect of profit, and the chance rejected, which if offered entirely by itself would be eagerly availed of.

While, therefore, in theory the combination should have a stimulating effect, in practice it must frequently exercise a restraining one, though in the case of very large establishments it is usually guarded against by the departmental system, which makes of each branch a separate concern, worked irrespective of any of the others. That is perhaps the reason why business with these countries is so largely in the hands of great and wealthy houses, the small merchant not being able so easily to dissociate one part from another. And as such firms are invariably conservative in their traditions and tendencies, the system is bound to impose a certain restraint on new development which partakes at all largely of the nature of experiment or speculation.

These are essentially matters against which no legislation can provide, or for that matter would be justified if it could. The less governments interfere as a rule the better, but the idea prevails, and it is generally a mistaken one, that when one does so, another must follow suit to counteract it. Such a course may undoubtedly at times be necessary, but something like a principle can be established where this is the case. A nation is entitled to adopt pretty much whatever legislation it likes for its own internal regulation. If it decides that it will eat black bread instead of white; abstain altogether from flesh food; or import every foreign article it requires for its own consumption in ships built and owned by its own citizens,—who shall interfere? But when it attempts to dictate what the internal regulations of other countries shall be, or how their requirements are to be supplied, the nation affected has a right of say, and is not true to itself unless it exercises it.

Were this principle broadly applied it would help to simplify many difficult points. The competition of the United States in many British possessions is keenly felt, and at times deeply resented, but so far it has never received any direct State support, and in most instances has been perfectly straightforward. Goods may be sold abroad at much below the current rates at home, but that is legitimate enough, unless the prices charged are persistently below cost of production, of which there is little or no proof. The British manufacturer, without any assistance afforded him by protection, not infrequently exacts more from the home consumer than he does from the colonial or foreign buyer. But the matter would assume an entirely different aspect were the United States Government to grant substantial sums of money to those engaged in this occupation, or, what amounts to the same thing, if combinations of highly protected interests availed themselves of the advantages afforded to sell persistently in other markets below legitimate values.

Canada has tried to check this competition and has signally failed; once more imports of dutiable merchandise from the United States have increased by more than double the corresponding movement from the United Kingdom. New Zealand has been the latest colony to cry aloud against the invasion, and to express through its accredited representatives a determination by some means or other to check it.

But from a British point of view is this desirable in either instance? Natural situation must always afford the United States material advantage as regards Canada, which no fiscal legislation can overcome. But if for every six million dollars the United States add to their exports to the Dominion, the United Kingdom contributes another three, is it not to the interests of the latter that the former shall extend their trade by leaps and bounds? It may also be perfectly true that the United States have quadrupled their exports to New Zealand while the United Kingdom has added but fifty per cent. to its own figures. But when one represents £1,000,000, and the other £2,000,000, it is not difficult to understand which has gained the most, and if for every further million added by one, two can be gained by the other, the best wishes of every British citizen should be extended to the development of the trade relationship between the United States and New Zealand.

That there is some connection between the two circumstances there can be little doubt; exactly how much, or where it begins and where it ends, cannot be signified. But development is undoubtedly stimulated, not only in New Zealand, but in many other countries, by cheap and good agricultural implements and other machinery and materials for which Americans have gained a deservedly high reputation, and if by their use the profits and spending powers of the community are increased, the reaction on British trade cannot be otherwise than beneficial. The remedy is not to exclude the American manufacturer by differential treatment which will raise the price upon the consumer, but for the British manufacturer to show that he is still able to hold his own in competition.

The agricultural implement maker, for instance, is much in evidence at every show throughout the Kingdom, and widely advertises the awards and medals he has received, but meanwhile not only makes no headway against his American rival abroad, but is positively allowing him to encroach on his preserves at home. Is it perhaps because he remains a rigid fixture in the rural districts where labour is cheap, instead of removing to the industrial centres where it is dear, and learning, as so many before him have done, that it is the surest road to cheap production?

It does not always happen that comparisons are so favourable, and in colonial possessions and foreign countries alike, where Great Britain and its industrial rivals stand on more equal terms, the latter sometimes make actually, as well as relatively, the greater headway. Changes of this character are bound to become more numerous as time goes on, and no legislation can entirely check them. It is not always the invader who gains : sometimes trade is voluntarily surrendered because it has ceased to be profitable. As far as foreign countries are concerned, Great Britain can exercise no controlling influence in the legislation that regulates such matters, and at best can only ask for conditions as favourable as its competitors. But the lesson apparently has not yet been fully learned, that the trade policy which best assures the prosperity of each component part of the British Empire will prove in the long run best for it as a whole.

APPENDIX.

The reader is again advised to exercise the utmost caution in the use of the following tables, and before drawing conclusions to consult whatever in the text of the book bears upon them. The figures are in all cases official; either reproduced exactly as published, or, as in sections of table C, from calculations based upon them, but distribution of trade according to countries is in some instances notoriously misleading. This is freely admitted by the Board of Trade statisticians, but they cannot remedy it without laying themselves open to charges of manipulation.

Hong-Kong is throughout included among foreign countries and not British possessions, as its trade originates in, or is destined for, the Chinese Empire. A few items in tables D and E are excepted from this treatment where the commodities are evidently meant almost exclusively for the consumption of European residents.

Tables A and B exclude all movements of bullion and specie, which form no part of the actual trade of the United Kingdom. Table C however includes these movements, because where they are of any consequence it is owing to bullion being a product of the possessions. Comparisons between table A and the first section of table C, reversing imports and exports, which under ordinary circumstances should be fairly close, are thus rendered of little value as regards the colonial export and British import.

The other side does fairly correspond, as there is little colonial import of gold.

Table C excludes all internal trade between groups of possessions, except in the case of West Africa, where the small movements recorded consist mainly of transfers of silver coin. But no account is taken of the trade—a good deal of it merely transit—between the different States of Australia, between Cape Colony and Natal, or between the various West India Islands.

Tables D and E do not by any means include all British and Irish exports, but only such as attain to considerable value, or are subject to keen international competition.

TABLE A.

United Kingdom—Merchandise Imports and Exports with Principal British Possessions.

	IMPORTS.				EXPORTS.			
	Average of 5 years, 1891–95.	Average of 5 years, 1896–1900.	1901 only.		Average of 5 years, 1891–95.	Average of 5 years, 1896–1900.	1901 only.	
Canada	£12,881,244	£19,527,710	£19,854,585		£7,290,036	£7,378,965	£9,250,526	
Australia	23,232,297	21,869,250	24,217,669		17,132,690	20,273,482	23,513,662	
New Zealand	8,133,546	9,399,585	10,594,587		3,651,191	4,844,785	6,068,230	
South Africa	5,536,680	5,293,379	5,132,308		9,418,116	13,724,468	18,939,147	
India	28,612,325	26,539,451	27,391,734		29,426,016	30,429,720	35,746,399	
West Indies	2,654,241	2,104,060	2,280,530		3,337,418	2,837,526	2,806,890	
West Africa	1,962,848	2,258,918	1,954,580		1,797,652	2,254,040	2,716,499	
Straits Settlements	4,794,754	4,957,765	6,112,304		2,215,029	2,658,986	3,282,728	
Ceylon	4,198,622	4,962,083	4,476,552		1,000,829	1,347,452	1,594,544	
Mauritius	214,167	142,125	318,311		293,974	333,511	1,028,698[1]	

[1] Inclusive of £581,838 for Cable Materials.

TABLE B.

United Kingdom—Merchandise Imports and Exports with Principal Foreign Countries.

	IMPORTS.			EXPORTS.		
	Average of 5 years, 1891–95.	Average of 5 years, 1896–1900.	1901 only.	Average of 5 years, 1891–95.	Average of 5 years, 1896–1900.	1901 only.
Europe—						
Germany	£26,598,072	£28,722,718	£32,207,214	£29,898,930	£35,170,050	£34,221,080
Holland	28,200,082	29,723,951	32,871,843	14,303,447	13,522,384	13,744,021
Belgium	17,142,757	21,601,221	24,666,081	12,815,594	13,679,782	12,624,691
France	44,575,067	52,293,618	51,213,424	21,109,117	21,768,732	23,700,280
Austria-Hungary	1,387,264	1,265,787	1,191,294	1,748,658	2,422,885	2,838,904
Russia	21,228,632	21,029,288	21,903,574	9,931,418	13,991,630	14,210,953
Sweden and Norway	12,054,114	15,027,898	15,352,063	6,423,821	8,673,850	9,280,287
Denmark	8,851,676	11,786,623	14,440,232	3,043,176	3,965,396	4,240,417
Spain	10,731,251	13,753,427	14,040,184	4,676,383	4,634,628	5,455,523
Portugal	2,730,734	3,026,211	3,305,150	1,995,325	2,251,237	2,093,992
Italy	3,182,799	3,379,450	3,383,858	6,308,066	7,131,249	8,293,484
Roumania	3,668,140	2,304,645	3,993,970	1,388,253	1,202,153	1,096,262
Greece	1,588,643	1,604,398	1,465,985	934,612	1,083,925	1,745,175
Turkey	5,324,950	5,476,906	5,838,556	6,503,614	5,985,038	7,207,054
(Including Turkey in Asia).						

Asia—						
China (Including Hong-Kong).	9,625,524	8,423,327	7,536,525	2,718,960	3,567,046	4,658,508
Japan	8,209,452	7,077,343	3,753,151	1,830,290	1,383,133	1,021,064
Java & Dutch East Indies	2,365,906	2,330,479	2,192,572	319,145	414,096	1,239,841
Philippine Islands	913,878	564,513	694,746	2,701,810	1,447,132	1,994,226
Persia	583,225	369,592	355,036	200,124	173,301	181,880
Africa—						
Egypt	6,418,757	4,885,511	3,621,310	11,905,646	10,261,847	9,767,650
Tripoli, Tunis, & Morocco	1,314,549	946,889	914,762	1,028,479	744,766	899,047
West Africa	1,407,096	1,459,916	1,221,514	685,416	592,428	452,309
Canary Islands	889,984	628,250	462,514	1,110,383	698,967	304,699
America—						
United States	37,651,150	34,164,721	38,607,319	141,015,465	120,864,316	96,107,093
Cuba and Porto Rico	2,024,126	1,404,304	2,206,887	38,070	32,688	147,631
Mexico	1,673,079	1,937,521	1,530,468	263,506	486,866	510,767
Central America	854,465	886,456	1,040,336	911,256	875,635	1,122,452
Colombia, Venezuela, and Ecuador	1,742,797	1,864,594	2,185,023	815,768	759,016	809,453
Brazil	4,440,061	6,185,557	8,072,271	4,957,794	4,459,651	3,990,435
Argentina	6,972,701	6,323,996	5,189,340	12,414,865	9,307,845	5,616,280
Uruguay	1,367,857	1,340,901	1,391,830	474,501	359,251	304,395
Chili and Peru	4,550,480	3,550,657	3,781,328	6,127,600	5,274,225	4,982,364

TABLE C.

Total Oversea Imports and Exports of Principal British Possessions with the British Empire and Foreign Countries.

	IMPORTS.			EXPORTS.		
	Average of 5 years, 1891–96.	Average of 5 years, 1896–1900.	1901 only.	Average of 5 years, 1891–95.	Average of 5 years, 1896–1900.	1901 only.
With United Kingdom—						
India	Rx.63,289,881	Rx.62,770,607	Rx.68,804,204	Rx.37,093,736	Rx.34,981,591	Rx.42,954,618
Canada	£8,070,961	£7,263,399	£8,839,349	£12,684,812	£18,729,241	£21,642,936
Australia	19,476,634	21,781,450	25,237,032	23,793,306	24,599,196	25,194,923
New Zealand	4,312,217	5,457,435	6,885,831	7,322,021	8,732,492	9,295,375
South Africa	11,856,031	16,951,577	20,801,881	13,810,253	19,154,976	11,021,682
West Indies	3,780,007	3,406,228	3,526,293	3,021,573	2,510,235	2,298,277
West Africa	2,027,937	2,683,998	3,494,917	1,572,572	1,760,405	1,452,178
Straits Settlements	2,915,664	2,871,366	3,116,678	3,558,063	3,741,616	5,196,801
Ceylon	1,180,015	1,800,603	2,058,306	2,939,747	3,572,246	3,343,916
With other British Possessions—						
India	Rx.7,160,611	Rx.8,353,465	Rx.11,942,252	Rx.13,639,484	Rx.17,151,708	Rx.19,519,103
Canada	£564,152	£540,004	£787,959	£991,724	£1,145,538	£1,654,973
Australia	2,653,672	3,409,119	4,536,709	2,285,377	4,709,149	11,684,727[1]
New Zealand	1,812,230	1,976,360	2,913,866	1,310,547	1,688,515	2,907,412
South Africa	763,701	1,869,140	6,587,949	53,742	143,011	13,687
West Indies	760,533	579,437	607,322	290,362	219,614	300,697
West Africa	75,144	125,609	178,365	84,531	146,248	156,374
Straits Settlements	3,412,660	5,297,466	5,872,752	1,360,269	1,504,284	1,821,994
Ceylon	3,067,979	4,033,050	4,583,619	662,270	1,014,557	1,248,989

With Germany—						
India	Rx.1,623,392	Rx.2,102,101	Rx.2,603,684	Rx.6,277,524	Rx.7,716,417	Rx.9,219,745
	£980,100	£1,388,457	£1,412,754	£201,301	£311,339	£440,045
Canada . . .	1,183,430	2,009,898	2,799,956	1,445,281	1,902,281	2,552,458
Australia . .	74,153	150,846	198,521	5,691	16,023	10,470
New Zealand .	417,813	990,510	1,118,285	126,995	145,861	234,541
South Africa .	57,565	60,812	68,625	100,436	102,839	108,108
West Indies .	349,145	369,280	475,359	658,009	895,816	1,176,663
West Africa .	306,940	501,974	602,449	504,333	516,782	516,309
Straits Settlements .	26,101	118,848	127,057	120,925	232,849	352,724
Ceylon . .						
With United States—						
India	Rx.1,525,413	Rx.1,551,568	Rx.1,364,344	Rx.4,318,563	Rx.5,923,049	Rx.7,232,283
	£11,207,417	£16,511,515	£22,702,399	£8,266,740	£10,408,648	£14,873,061
Canada . . .	1,624,562	3,756,080	5,854,136	1,341,563	3,552,996	3,373,876
Australia . .	382,315	751,695	1,415,260	427,278	443,426	519,079
New Zealand .	615,036	2,576,578	2,640,193	82,439	42,833	8,449
South Africa .	2,444,522	2,447,343	2,643,485	3,579,659	3,456,611	3,773,813
West Indies .	112,033	103,071	154,599	19,657	16,872	23,158
West Africa .	139,246	102,550	130,435	1,258,030	2,213,166	3,150,494
Straits Settlements .	7,590	21,603	27,558	248,279	412,705	364,203
Ceylon . .						
With other Foreign Countries—						
India	Rx.12,387,278	Rx.16,454,186	Rx.20,756,867	Rx.49,692,416	Rx.48,136,920	Rx.43,065,061
	£2,617,463	£2,547,396	£3,466,221	£955,783	£1,207,692	£1,763,156
Canada . . .	2,401,034	2,749,841	3,968,476	4,767,421	6,291,407	6,950,334
Australia . .	128,369	225,438	404,437	108,040	127,654	149,088
New Zealand .	961,333	1,746,527	2,973,599	400,948	729,381	936,287
South Africa [2] .	813,897	931,859	978,478	940,942	1,030,904	1,143,593
West Indies [3] .	243,495	258,433	327,281	689,675	454,489	451,975
West Africa .	14,185,862	16,485,304	20,022,541	12,101,885	13,531,122	14,859,090
Straits Settlements .	273,439	722,618	711,922	189,416	433,157	684,121
Ceylon [4] .						

[1] Principally gold to India and South Africa.
[2] Includes trade with Delagoa Bay.
[3] Includes transit trade between Trinidad and Venezuela.
[4] Increase due principally to development of the transit and re-export trade of Colombo.

TABLE **D.**

British and Irish Exports in which British Possessions predominate.

	TO BRITISH POSSESSIONS.		TO FOREIGN COUNTRIES.	
	Five years' average, 1896 to 1900 inclusive.	1901.	Five years' average, 1896 to 1900 inclusive.	1901.
Beer and Ale	£1,167,550	£1,261,623	£484,689	£521,275
Spirits	1,523,147	2,006,131	487,348	626,186
Confectionery . . . . . . }	890,360	{ 569,341 / 528,419 }	474,399	{ 180,231 / 272,893 }
Pickles and Sauces	483,136	952,232	260,870	288,975
Salt	273,877	309,594	186,460	199,546
Medicines and Drugs	761,306	914,053	394,203	425,917
Soap	532,356	628,704	311,320	370,820
Candles	176,879	236,392	188,956	196,322
Cutlery	331,800	391,578	267,728	245,200
Glass and Glassware	548,870	665,139	370,893	392,016
Furniture	361,998	408,115	248,406	225,758
Plate and Plated Wares	240,517	337,030	181,881	163,992
Musical Instruments	140,567	165,182	49,355	60,203
Wearing Apparel	4,224,419	4,825,338	741,213	745,921
Haberdashery and Millinery . . .	1,254,857	1,235,183	260,790	225,133
Boots and Shoes	1,284,198	1,465,990	271,240	187,200
Hats and Caps	676,958	818,564	429,479	418,464
Cotton Hosiery	267,981	333,522	105,910	86,460
Woollen ,, ...	594,198	697,429	261,518	195,906
Flannels, Blankets, Shawls, Rugs, Covers, etc.	857,616	907,159	454,422	273,265
Umbrellas	409,123	384,881	74,301	61,293

Iron—				
Bar, Sheet, Plate, and Hoop	767,502	1,027,103	976,628	945,365
Galvanised Sheets	1,187,859	1,166,540	2,004,991	1,802,896
Railroad	1,569,699	1,554,846	2,064,854	1,794,989
Tubes and Pipes	430,997	568,722	573,878	498,552
Nails, Screws, Rivets, etc.	142,700	156,690	249,172	235,089
Wrought, and Manufactures of	808,246	856,407	1,256,109	1,277,694
Machinery—				
Locomotives	691,949	604,059	1,219,391	702,300
Mining	153,501	146,802	355,748	638,411
Carriages—				
Railway Passenger	184,520	213,475	454,623	357,472
„ Waggons, etc.	642,105	397,559	1,324,554	748,683
Cycles	203,484	542,963	373,928	544,949
Unenumerated	138,485	89,225	205,184	186,474
Electric Lighting Apparatus	180,271	228,630	372,506	251,913
Telegraph Wire and Material	1,068,770	812,793	2,079,215	596,885
Paper, all kinds	558,077	542,599	1,101,873	989,227
Stationery	588,894	466,169	638,125	530,078
Books	587,219	527,659	965,553	850,307
Toys and Games	95,555	...	272,863	...
Saddlery and Harness	155,764	163,951	429,586	312,262
Cement	187,642	305,300	396,332	334,885
Sailcloth	122,090	118,023	132,122	114,629

TABLE E.

British and Irish Exports in which Foreign Countries predominate.

	TO *FOREIGN COUNTRIES*.		TO *BRITISH POSSESSIONS*.	
	Five years' average, 1896 to 1900 inclusive.	1901.	Five years' average, 1896 to 1900 inclusive.	1901.
Coal, Coke, and Fuel .	£20,609,059	£28,023,984	£1,722,916	£2,310,764
Coal Products (Tar, etc.) .	1,546,101	1,073,714	130,223	77,539
Pig-Iron .	3,600,933	2,414,092	180,491	216,435
Chemicals and Dyestuffs .	4,455,110	3,903,052	1,049,462	1,315,357
Textile Yarns—				
Cotton .	7,040,319	6,133,577	1,899,223	1,843,455
,, Lace and Net, principally for Embroidery	1,774,166	2,006,847	555,397	659,972
Woollen, Worsted, and Alpaca .	6,515,878	5,134,954	105,599	103,698
Linen .	939,176	812,239	9,940	12,442
Jute .	456,970	506,220	6,920	8,383
Silk .	220,755	212,468	29,453	81,843
Textile Fabrics—				
Cotton Piece Goods .	27,649,287	29,769,105	21,977,202	26,731,622
,, Unenumerated .	1,428,143	1,438,946	885,551	1,090,162
Woollen Stuffs .	4,415,489	3,875,162	1,132,539	1,323,912
Worsted ,, .	5,098,355	3,757,474	1,760,008	2,088,522
Carpets and Furniture Coverings .	522,521	444,613	352,960	420,715
Linen Piece Goods .	2,839,282	2,872,686	559,755	610,176
,, Unenumerated .	818,887	781,788	217,193	274,518
Jute Piece Goods .	1,703,523	1,808,260	285,656	335,470
Bags and Sacks .	421,022	456,063	49,245	44,801
Silk Fabrics .	978,656	959,294	508,815	470,087

Sewing Thread, etc—				
Cotton	3,086,549	3,108,389	430,068	482,600
Linen	155,520	144,344	75,093	82,775
Woollen Smallwares	135,043	142,706	82,291	99,340
Rubber Manufactures	1,053,267	932,071	273,371	330,344
Cordage and Twine	241,763	270,163	204,487	264,293
Oilcloth	681,172	777,143	413,605	520,864
Leather	1,219,680	1,097,940	183,955	223,886
Earthenware and China	1,263,607	1,168,444	671,805	824,353
Painters' Colours and Materials	1,001,761	1,072,309	754,525	935,674
Iron				
Tin Plates	2,518,143	2,820,979	674,671	883,109
Wire	437,089	501,795	429,856	466,048
Cast, and Manufactures of	603,507	572,531	513,982	548,664
Steel Bars, Sheets, and Plates	2,793,711	2,129,988	643,115	771,281
,, Manufactures	593,616	657,976	410,466	486,909
Brass	310,714	319,151	219,092	273,850
Copper Manufactures	798,075	812,646	621,631	724,763
Hardware	851,129	737,959	637,949	699,867
Implements and Tools—				
Agricultural	232,736	237,481	170,456	156,296
All other	607,050	623,179	392,544	475,028
Instruments—Scientific Surgical, etc.	206,880	258,584	183,025	244,207
Machinery—				
Agricultural (Steam)	592,531	562,214	61,398	58,754
Other (,,)	1,061,185	928,258	560,104	797,369
Agricultural (not Steam)	685,865	644,481	112,928	88,407
Sewing	1,103,778	1,468,454	65,477	83,527
Textile	5,283,952	3,747,735	1,134,869	978,143
All other	3,956,756	3,765,160	1,821,901	2,278,193

INDEX